THE CODE IN THE HANDS OF THE LAITY

THE CODE
IN THE HANDS OF THE LAITY

Canon Law for Everyone

REV. LAURENCE J. SPITERI, PhD, JCL

Introduction by Archbishop Justin Rigali of St. Louis

ALBA·HOUSE   NEW·YORK

SOCIETY OF ST. PAUL, 2187 VICTORY BLVD., STATEN ISLAND, NEW YORK 10314

ST PAULS

Library of Congress Cataloging-in-Publication Data

Spiteri, Laurence John, 1950-
    The code in the hands of the laity: canon law for everyone / Laurence
    J. Spiteri; introduction by Archbishop Justin Rigali of St. Louis.
        p.   cm.
    Includes bibliographical references.
    ISBN 0-8189-0763-0
    1. Canon law — Popular works.   2. Marriage (Canon law) — Popular
    works.   I. Title.
    LAW
    262'.9'4 — dc21   97-1376
                                                            CIP

Nihil Obstat:
Monsignor Craig A. Cox, JCD
Censor Deputatus
1 May 1996

Imprimatur:
Cardinal Roger Mahony
Archbishop of Los Angeles
1 May 1996

The *Nihil Obstat* and *Imprimatur* are official declarations that
the work contains nothing contrary to Faith and Morals. It is not implied
thereby that those granting the *Nihil Obstat* and *Imprimatur* agree
with the contents, statements or opinions expressed.

Produced and designed in the United States of America by the
Fathers and Brothers of the Society of St. Paul,
2187 Victory Boulevard, Staten Island, New York 10314,
as part of their communications apostolate.

ISBN: 0-8189-0763-0

Printing Information:

Current Printing - first digit	1	2	3	4	5	6	7	8	9	10

Year of Current Printing - first year shown

1997	1998	1999	2000	2001	2002	2003	2004	2005

Table of Contents

Abbreviations

AA	*Apostolicam Actuositatem**
AG	*Ad gentes**
AS	*Apostolica sollicitudo*
CCC	*Catechism of the Catholic Church*
CD	*Christus Dominus**
CLSA: Commentary	*The Code of Canon Law: A Text and Commentary*
DH	*Dignitatis humanae**
DV	*Dei Verbum**
EN	*Evangelii nuntiandi*
ES	*Ecclesiae sanctae*
ES I	*Ecclesiae sanctae* section I
ES III	*Ecclesiae sanctae* section III
GE	*Gravissimum educationis**
GS	*Gaudium et spes**
J	*The Jurist*
LG	*Lumen Gentium**
Navarre	*Code of Canon Law Annotated*
PB	*Pastor Bonus*
PC	*Perfectae Caritatis**
PO	*Presbyterorum Ordinis**
REU	*Regimini Ecclesiae Universae*
SC	*Sacrosanctum Concilium**
SCa	*Studia Canonica*

Documents marked with an asterisk (*) are from Vatican Council II.

Foreword

Father Laurence Spiteri has worked with diligence and zeal in order to present to the laity a quick reference tool for a better understanding of the Code of Canon Law and the many canonical-pastoral issues which it deals with in the contemporary Church.

In his work, *The Code in the Hands of the Laity*, Father Spiteri has been inspired by the teaching of the Second Vatican Council on the dignity of the laity and on their calling to share actively in the life of Christ's Church. He has shown how this spirit of Vatican II has indeed been captured by the Code of Canon Law and this needs to be increasingly understood and lived by the laity.

A guiding principle in the present work is that the laity have been personally commissioned to the apostolate of the Church by the Lord Himself. Because of this, the Code of Canon Law, which regulates the pastoral activity of the Church, is extremely relevant for their Christian lives.

Following the Code, Father Spiteri tries to shed light on the Church's life, on her institutions and on her sacraments. His own personal zeal as a priest is seen in his desire to make the Church better known. Nowhere does Father Spiteri make a bigger effort to introduce his readers to the Church's pastoral reality than in his treatment of matters affecting marriage. His pastoral sensitivity, gained from personal experience in assisting many persons involved in marriage cases, is an expression of the Church's larger pastoral concern to proclaim the rights and duties of all Christ's faithful and to help them live joyfully and effectively their discipleship of Jesus.

It is my hope that this work will indeed attain its aim, leading the laity to a better understanding of many of the canonical-pastoral realities of Christ's Church, in which we all find salvation and life.

†Justin Rigali
Archbishop of St. Louis
Solemnity of the Assumption of
the Blessed Virgin Mary, 1996

Preface

The aim of this book is to give a handy reference to the lay person for a better understanding of the canonical-pastoral issues in the contemporary Church. Each chapter is brief, supplied with references to the 1983 Code of Canon Law for the Latin Rite Catholics, conciliar and post-conciliar documents, the recently issued *Catechism of the Catholic Church*, as well as other literature on the subject matter. Some topics are presented in a number of chapters, with cross references. The reason for this approach is to enable the reader to acquaint himself or herself with the topic in a few minutes and be able to go back to it without much trouble. I hasten to add that reading this book does not make one a canon lawyer! The reader will find many references to commentaries, books and articles for the purpose of having a deeper look at a specific topic. These references are restricted to the ones written in the English language and which are reasonably accessible. There are numerous works on each subject matter written in many other languages by prominent canonists and theologians, especially in French, German, Italian, Latin, Spanish, Polish and Portuguese.

LJS
Feast of St. Joseph the Worker, 1996

THE CODE IN THE HANDS OF THE LAITY

1. The Laity

Code and the Laity — Introduction

Some people are under the impression that the Catholic Church is exclusively composed of the Pope, the bishops and their clergy. This is incorrect because it is the People of God, that is clergy and laity, who form the Church.[1] It is clear that the laity comprise the great majority in the Church.

Believers do not exist and function in a vacuum. They relate to one another and belong to a larger community. Furthermore, each community within the People of God relates to all the other communities for all belong to the one Body of Christ.[2] It is due to this interrelationship that each Church member complements another in the ministry of proclaiming the Gospel and celebrating the presence of the Risen Lord in our midst.[3]

The Code of Canon Law, officially revised in 1983, is one of the ways in which the legal or canonical relationship between the different members of the People of God is presented.[4] Therefore, the Code must be rooted in Church doctrine and theology.

The subject matter of the Code and the Laity will be discussed

---

[1] See *AG* 2, 7; *LG* 9, 17; *CCC* 777.

[2] See 1 Corinthians 10:17; 12:12, 26; Romans 12:5; Colossians 3:15; *LG* 7; *CCC* 790-791.

[3] See Romans 12:3-8; Ephesians 4:7-16; 1 Corinthians 12:12-31. See also *LG* 7; *CCC* 791; Pope John Paul II's apostolic constitution, *Sacrae Disciplinae Leges*, through which the 1983 Code of Canon Law was promulgated, that is made into law.

[4] See *Sacrae Disciplinae Leges*. The 1983 Code of Canon Law is essentially for the Latin Rite Roman Catholics. Catholics who belong to the Eastern Churches are bound by their own Code of Canon Law. See *Navarre*, 81, n. 1.

in the following few chapters. First there are some comments on the
Holy Father's decree promulgating the 1983 Code of Canon Law.
Comments on pertinent statements of Vatican II will follow. Then there
will be a very brief presentation of *ministry* and *apostolate* in the
Church as found in the Code. Finally, since a person usually joins a
group to carry out a ministry or an apostolate, there will be a presentation of the pertinent canons in the 1983 Code and what ramifications
they have on the different kinds of lay associations of the Christian
faithful. An independent section is dedicated to the issue of associations of the Christian faithful.

Code and Laity — 1

Pope John Paul II promulgated the 1983 Code of Canon Law through
his apostolic constitution, *Sacrae Disciplinae Leges*, on January 25,
1983.[5] He states in it that there is a new way of thinking in the newly
revised Church law.[6] It reflects the mind of Vatican II.[7] Its purpose is
that of service. Its principles of interpretation show how one should
apply the law to ministry in the Church. This mindset renders canon
law pastoral because it presents and supports the agenda for the
Church's way to relate to contemporary life in meeting the needs of
the People of God.

Preceding Vatican II, ministry and apostolate was too often identified with the clergy, that is with bishops, priests and deacons. While
ministry was restricted exclusively to the clergy, the laity were allowed
to assist in an apostolate only by invitation. They had to be commissioned and were subordinate to the hierarchy. At the time, the right to
form an association of the Christian faithful for apostolic purposes was

---

[5] It was Pope John XXIII who, on January 25, 1959, announced that he intended to
convoke the Second Vatican Council as well as establish a Pontifical Commission to
revise the 1917 Code of Canon Law.

[6] See John Paul II, "Code and Council," *J* 43 (1983) 267-272. See also L. Orsy, "The
Meaning of *Novus Habitus Mentis*: The Search for New Horizons," *J* 48 (1988) 427-
447.

[7] See Pope John Paul II, *Sacrae Disciplinae Leges*.

unusual. There was a pronounced inequality between clergy and laity.[8] This reality was reflected in the older 1917 Code of Canon Law. Vatican II brought a radical change to this mindset.

Vatican II teaches that within the diversity of the Church's members there is a fundamental equality rooted in the Sacrament of Baptism.[9] In fully recovering the ancient notion of the priesthood of the faithful,[10] though different in nature from the ordained priesthood, clergy and laity are called to assist one another in the Church's mission.[11] Their diverse functions in the Church are interrelated.

The sharpened clarification that the baptized and confirmed lay person is commissioned to the apostolate by the Lord himself gave a new understanding of the role of the laity in the life of the Church. This is clearly reflected in the 1983 Code of Canon Law. For example, canon 204, 1 defines a Christian as one who has been incorporated in the Church through baptism and who, for that reason, shares in Christ's priestly, prophetic and royal office in his or her own way and has an important role to play in the Church's mission to the world;[12] canon 208 upholds the basic distinction between the ordained and the laity, but presents the two roles as complementary and supportive of one another since all Christians are called to participate in Christ's redemptive work.[13] The 1983 Code, however, limits the use of the word *ministry* to the ordained and to those laity installed in a specific ministry, while reserving the word *apostolate* to the non-ordained.[14] Occasion-

---

[8] See *CLSA: Commentary*, 8-10. The right of the faithful to form associations for different apostolic ends was stated by *AA* 19. See also *Navarre*, 197-198, n. 225.

[9] See *LG* 32; *CCC* 872. See *Navarre*, 186, n. 204; 190-191, n. 208.

[10] See *LG* 10; *CCC* 1546-1547, 1592.

[11] See *AA* 2, 23; *CCC* 872-873.

[12] C. 204, 1 is based on *LG* 9-17, 31, 33-36; and *AA* 2, 3, 6, 7, 9, and 10. See also *CCC* 871, 1213; *Navarre*, 186, n. 204.

[13] C. 208 is based on *LG* 32. See also *CCC* 872; *Navarre*, 190-191, n. 208.

[14] See c. 759. Suggested readings: Cardinal Joseph Bernardin, "In Service of One Another," *Origins* 18/11 (August 18, 1988) 132-138; W. Borders, "You Are a Royal Priesthood," ibid., 165, 167-180; J. Huels, *The Faithful of Christ: The New Canon Law for the Laity*; J. Komonchak, "Church and Ministry," *J* 43 (1983) 273-288; R. McBrien, *Ministry: A Theological, Pastoral Handbook*; *Navarre*, 190-202; K. Osborne, *Ministry: Lay Ministry in the Roman Catholic Church, its History and Theology*; W. Rademacher, *Lay Ministry: A Theological, Spiritual, and Pastoral Handbook*.

ally you will find the terms being inapppropriately interchanged.

It is within the context of cooperation that article 24 of the conciliar decree *Apostolicam Actuositatem* speaks of a gradation in the collaboration between the laity and the hierarchy in the Church. It begins with the most remote and moves up to a very close collaboration. The basic level with the least interaction between the two takes place on the level of the temporal order. The highest, in which the hierarchy entrusts and commissions the laity with roles directly related to specific pastoral duties where the laity's apostolate is under the full direction of the hierarchy, is the most intimate.

Code and Laity — 2

The 1983 Code does not provide a technical definition of *ministry*. Nevertheless, it discusses ministers and their ministerial functions.

Ministers do not act in their own name but on behalf of the Lord who entrusted to the Church the threefold duty to teach, sanctify and govern.[15] All ministry and apostolate are rooted in one's relationship to the community, whether a person is ordained or not. Thus, a person's ministry or apostolate does not stand on its own for the very structure of the Church is based on those relationships which form *Communio*. This *Communio* is the unifying relationship between the Pope and all the bishops of the world, between the See of Rome and all dioceses, between the bishops and all their dioceses throughout the world, between every bishop and the priests in his diocese, between every bishop and the fold entrusted to his care, between the priests within a diocese and throughout the world, between each pastor and his parishioners, and between every parishioner in each parish.[16] *Communio* is all encompassing for it embraces every member in the Church. It is through *ministry* and the *apostolate* that the Church fulfills Christ's mandate

---

[15] Suggested readings: R. Broderick, "Ministries," *The Catholic Encyclopedia*, 388-391; J. Lynch, "The Limits of *Communio* in the Pre-Constantinian Church," *J* 36 (1976) 159-190. See also suggested readings listed in n. 14.

[16] See *LG* 8, 12, 13, 23, 26, 42, 51; *CCC* 811, 814, 826, 830-836, 870, 949, 951, 953, 959.

to make disciples of all nations and to carry out the mission which He entrusted to the Church.[17] It is Christ himself, therefore, who is the ultimate source of all ministry and apostolate in the Church.[18]

The 1983 Code contains a very narrow meaning of *ministry*.[19] The canonical understanding of *ministry* is the directing in an authoritative capacity (i.e., *in the name of the Church*) of a part of the threefold responsibility of the Church to teach, sanctify and govern in the name of Christ. It is called "official ministry."

There are a number of ways through which official ministry is canonical. Some persons are commissioned to act in a specific role in the name of the Church through the granting of an office[20] or by being delegated[21] or through other designations, such as a mandate.[22] The commissioning itself identifies those who speak and act in the name of the Church.

Code and Laity — 3

Americans are very familiar with the Bill of Rights, just as the British are familiar with the Magna Carta. These are legal documents which guarantee certain rights to the citizens of each country. Canons 208-223 of the 1983 Code contain a similar guarantee for all the members of the Catholic Church. These canons list not only the rights but also the duties of the Christian faithful, acknowledging that charisms are given to the Church for the sake of ministry.[23] The canons are rooted in the Council's teachings and list a number of these rights.

The right to a fundamental equality in fact, dignity and action

---

[17] See Romans 1:1. See also *LG* 18, 24, 27; *CCC* 874, 876, 879, 895, 1551.

[18] See *LG* 18, 21, 24; *CCC* 874, 1549-1551.

[19] See chapter entitled, Code and Laity — 1.

[20] For example, the office of a judge in a tribunal.

[21] For instance, a visiting priest in a parish is delegated to witness a marriage.

[22] For example, a religious community is entrusted with the running of a Catholic hospital.

[23] Suggested readings: see n. 14.

by virtue of baptism is affirmed in canon 208. Every member of the faithful has a right and freedom to cooperate in building up the Church.[24]

The right of Catholics to evangelize is stated in canon 211.[25]

The right to make known to one's pastor one's needs and hopes, and to supply him with advice in Church matters is affirmed in canon 212, 2-3. Catholics also have the right to participate in shaping public opinion and to make their opinions known to other members of the faithful.[26]

The right to receive the sacraments, to religious and spiritual instruction, to worship, and to Christian education is upheld in canons 213-214 and 217.[27]

The right to found and direct associations with charitable or pious purposes as an expression of Christian calling is stated in canon 215. It asserts the right to assembly.[28]

The right of Catholics to apostolic activity is affirmed in canon 216.[29]

The right to academic freedom, to freely choose one's status in life, to a good name and reputation, to privacy, to vindicate and defend oneself in Church court, to be judged justly is stated in canons 218-221.[30]

The 1983 Code, responding to the Council's directives, also provides a list of the Catholic's duties. Thus, canons 209 and 212 charge Catholics with the duty to subsist in union with the Church and obey its teachers and proper superiors.[31] Canon 210 charges Catholics with

---

[24] C. 208 is based on *LG* 32; *GS* 49, 61. See also *CCC* 872, 1632, 1642, 2234, 2362; *Navarre*, 190-191.

[25] C. 211 is based on *LG* 17; *AG* 1, 2, 5, 35-37. See also *CCC* 51, 53, 65, 142, 776, 1103, 1270, 2032, 2587.

[26] C. 212 is based on *LG* 25, 27; *AA* 6; *PO* 9; *GS* 92. See also *CCC* 907.

[27] The canons are based on *LG* 37; *SC* 19; *PO* 8, 9; *GE* 68. See also *CCC* 1269, 1568; *Navarre*, 192-193, nn. 213, 214; 194, n. 217.

[28] C. 215 is based on *AA* 18-21; *PO* 8; *GS* 68. See also *CCC* 1568.

[29] C. 216 is based on *LG* 37; *AA* 24, 25; *PO* 9. See also *CCC* 1269.

[30] These canons are based on *GE* 10; *GS* 26, 27, 29, 52, 62. See also *CCC* 94, 1657, 1906-1908, 1912, 1931, 1935, 1936, 2206, 2322; *Navarre* 194-196, nn. 218, 219, 220, 221.

[31] These canons are based on *LG* 11-13, 23, 25, 30, 32, 37; *AA* 9, 10; *GS* 1, 92; *PO* 9. See also *CCC* 907.

the duty to lead a holy life and promote sanctity.[32] Canon 222 charges Catholics with the duty to promote the Church's teachings on social justice, to help the needy, and to support the Church and its ministers in their ministry.[33] Canon 225 affirms the right and duty of Catholics to work as individuals or in associations to spread the Gospel.[34]

In conclusion, all of the aforementioned rights and duties function within the framework of the common good under the leadership of proper Church authority.[35]

Personality in the 1983 Code

There are a number of definitions which describe a person. For example, there is a physical or natural person, a fictitious person, a corporate person, and so forth. One of the notions contained in the 1983 Code is that of the *juridic person*. It is a very important and exclusive concept in Church law.

The Code does not provide a definition of a juridic person, though it contains a very intricate notion of it. Thus, a juridic person is an artificial person in the eyes of the law,[36] distinct from natural or physical persons who constitute it or administer it or for whose benefit it exists; is established by the competent Church authority for an apostolic purpose;[37] possesses the capacity of a continuous existence, even when specific members die; acquires rights and obligations under the law;[38] and is solely accountable to canon law and its creator, that is Church authority.[39]

---

[32] C. 210 is based on *LG* 39-42; *AA* 6. See also *CCC* 851, 905, 2044.

[33] C. 222 is based on *AA* 8, 21; *AG* 36; *PO*, 20, 21; *DH* 1, 6, 14; *GS* 26, 29, 42, 65, 68, 69, 72, 75, 88. See also *CCC* 2043.

[34] C. 225 is based on *LG* 31, 33; *AA* 2-4, 7, 17; *AG* 21, 36; *GS* 43. See also *Navarre*, 197-198, n. 225.

[35] C. 223.

[36] It is similar but *not* equivalent to a corporation in civil law.

[37] Such as for the purpose of education.

[38] For example, one can own property or enter into a contract.

[39] See A. Gauthier, "Juridic Persons in the Code of Canon Law," *SCa* 25 (1991) 77-92; *Navarre*, 134-135, n. 114; 136-137, n. 116-117; 258.

There are two kinds of juridic persons in Church law: public and private. A *public juridic person* is created either by the law itself[40] or by a decree issued by the competent Church authority. On the other hand, a *private juridic person* is always created by a decree issued by the competent Church authority which possesses executive power of governance.

The distinction between public and private juridic persons is a brand new one in Church law. It is rooted in conciliar documents, particularly in *Apostolicam Actuositatem*.[41] The conciliar teaching is reflected in canons 298-329. The notion is based on the right of every Catholic to form and join an association of Christian faithful.

The distinction between a public and a private juridic person is of extreme importance. In the pre-Vatican II Church the apostolate was too often identified with bishops, priests, and deacons. The laity could assist only by invitation and had to be commissioned and subordinate to the hierarchy. At the time there was no such thing as a right to form an association of the Christian faithful for apostolic purposes. Vatican II, however, recovered an earlier notion that all the faithful, by virtue of baptism and confirmation, are commissioned to build up the Body of Christ. In recovering the notion of the priesthood of the faithful and retaining the expression *apostolate of the laity* as one of the two expressions of the Church's apostolate, each group (ordained and non-ordained) is called to assist the other.[42] The clarification that the laity are commissioned to apostolate by the Lord himself opened the door for the right to form associations of the faithful and empowered the laity to do so without necessarily waiting for an invitation from the hierarchy.

The Council laid the foundation for a mutual relationship between the two apostolates in article 24 of *Apostolicam Actuositatem* where it traces five levels of collaboration, beginning with a remote

---

[40] An example of this is a diocese (c. 373) or a parish (c. 515, 3). The law *itself* gives the entity its canonical status.

[41] See *AA* 18, 19, and 24.

[42] See *AA* 2; *CCC* 872-873. See also chapter entitled, Code and Laity — 1.

kind of collaboration to a more increased involvement of the laity who become, thereby, more dependent on the hierarchy. The conciliar document provides the theological foundation for the distinction between a public and a private juridic person as formulated in the Code. This teaching finds a succinct expression in canons 215-216.

Associations of the Laity — 1

The 1983 Code presents three kinds of associations of the Christian faithful: public, private, and *de facto*. A public association of the Christian faithful is a public juridic person[43] for it is established, that is erected, and given a mission by the competent Church authority who approved its statutes. This is executed through an official decree.[44] On the other hand, a private association of the Christian faithful[45] can be a private juridic person.[46] The members seek recognition from the competent Church authority, who reviews its statutes and grants it private juridic personality through a decree. This kind of association is not necessarily given a mission or mandate. However, a simple recognition of an association by the Church does not mean that the association has been granted a juridic personality. Finally, the third kind of an association of Christian faithful is *de facto*. These *de facto* associations are not officially recognized by Church authority. It should be noted that where an association of Christian faithful lacks civil incorporation, each individual in that association remains liable under civil law.

It is usually the case that associations of Christian faithful begin at the *de facto* level and in time may seek to acquire private and, eventually, even public juridic personality. The Code states that an "official ministry" in the Church can be erected into a public association

---

[43] See chapter entitled, Personality in the 1983 Code.
[44] CC. 312-314. See *Navarre*, 252-257.
[45] See c. 299. See also *Navarre*, 258-261.
[46] See c. 312 and c. 322. See also *Navarre*, 253-254, n. 312; 259, n. 322.

of the Christian faithful[47] when a decree is issued by a competent Church authority,[48] who gives it a mission or a mandate.[49] Canon 312 specifies who is the competent Church authority to do so: for a diocese it is the diocesan bishop, for the nation it is done by the appropriate conference of bishops, and for the world it is done by the Apostolic See.[50] Canon 313 states that the decree by which the public association of the Christian faithful is established grants it public juridic personality.[51] According to canon 314, the statutes or by-laws or internal governing laws of the association must be approved by the same competent Church authority.[52]

Thus, when one looks at who has the competent authority to grant juridic personality to a certain kind of an association of the Christian faithful, one finds that the Holy See is the competent authority to grant juridic personality to an association whose members live all over the world. The association can be termed as *international* because its members live in many countries and not because it aims and/or assists in projects promoted or being implemented all over the world. The pertinent national conference of bishops is the competent authority when the members of the association are found throughout that nation, that is, in at least some of its dioceses. The diocesan bishop is the competent authority for those associations which are local and/or whose members reside only within his diocese. In other words, it is the residence of an association's members rather than its mission or goal which dictates who is the competent Church authority to which it should have recourse for requesting juridic personality.[53]

---

[47] Suggested readings: J. Amos, "A Legal History of Associations of the Christian Faithful," *SCa* 21 (1987) 271-297; *Navarre*, 245-248; R. Page, "Associations of the Faithful in the Church," *J* 47 (1987) 165-203.

[48] See c. 301, 1.

[49] See c. 313. See also *Navarre*, 254, n. 313-314.

[50] See *Navarre*, 252-254, n. 312.

[51] C. 313 reflects *AA* 20, and Pope Paul VI, *Ecclesiae sanctae* I, 35. The latter papal document contained provisional norms that were to be used until the promulgation of the revised Code of Canon Law, which took place in 1983. *Public juridic personality* is discussed in the chapter entitled, Personality in the 1983 Code.

[52] Thus, an auxiliary bishop cannot issue such a decree *unless* by a special mandate.

[53] See n. 50.

Associations of the Laity — 2

It might be asked: how does an organization of the Christian faithful move from a lower to a higher kind of an association according to the Code? A simple recognition of an association of Christian faithful by the Church does not automatically mean that it has been granted any kind of juridic personality. In fact, each member can remain liable to both civil and canon laws.

The Code provides a specified means by which a *de facto* association of Christian faithful can become a private association of Christian faithful with the status of a private juridic person in the Church.[54] A request for a change in status should be made after the members have undergone a reasonable period of honest prayerful discernment and consulted with competent Church leaders, canonists, and organizations. The erection of a *de facto* association of Christian faithful to a private association of Christian faithful takes place when the competent Church authority reviews its statutes and issues a decree which grants the association juridic personality. Private associations of Christian faithful usually do not have a ministry unless they are given a mandate which makes their ministry an ecclesiastical one.[55]

A private association of Christian faithful can seek to become a public association of Christian faithful by asking the competent Church authority to approve its statutes and to issue a decree which bestows on it public juridic personality. Once again prayerful discernment and consultation should be made by the members before submitting the request to the competent Church authority.

Public associations of Christian faithful have an official ministry because the competent Church authority has granted them a canonical mission which is stated in the decree of erection. All juridic persons, be they public or private, are subject and accountable to different levels of ecclesiastical authority. One advantage of the 1983 Code is that it is no longer necessary for every apostolic endeavor of the faithful to be under the *complete* supervision of Church authority.

---

[54] See chapter entitled, Code and Laity — 3.
[55] Ibid.

Associations of the Laity — 3

The status of an association of the Christian faithful as being either a public or a private juridic person has the following ramifications:

1. Public associations of the Christian faithful are always established by the competent Church authority. By this very fact, it is a public association of the Christian faithful.[56] Private associations of the Christian faithful are established by the faithful themselves.[57]

2. Public associations of the Christian faithful have their own statutes *approved* by the competent Church authority.[58] Private associations of the Christian faithful have their statutes *reviewed* by the competent Church authority.

3. Public associations of the Christian faithful are closely governed by Church authority.[59] Private associations of the Christian faithful are governed primarily by their own statutes and less governed by Church authority.

4. Public associations of the Christian faithful receive a mission to act *in the name of the Church*.[60] Private associations of the Christian faithful can receive a mission, though it is not necessary for them to do so.

5. Public associations of the Christian faithful are always public juridic persons,[61] that is the very establishment of the association makes them so. Hence, all of their goods are ecclesiastical goods and are governed by the norms of Book V of the Code. On the other hand, private associations of the Christian faithful can always be erected into private juridic persons, though they need not be so.[62] Furthermore, their goods and

---

[56] See c. 301, 1, and c. 314; *Navarre*, 247-248, n. 301; Page, 174-175, 184-185.

[57] Such associations can include the clergy. See c. 299, 1-2; Page, 172-173.

[58] See c. 314; Page, 167-169.

[59] See c. 315 and cc. 317-319; *Navarre*, 254-257, nn. 315, 317-319. Page, 185, 187-189.

[60] See c. 313; Page, 184.

[61] Ibid.

[62] See c. 322, 1-2; Page, 192.

possessions are not considered ecclesiastical goods and their management is governed by their own statutes.[63]

The above five points are an attempt by Church law to codify and specify the ramifications of the Council's teaching on the different levels of relationships between the laity and the hierarchy. In essence, the difference between public and private associations of the Christian faithful is rooted in the degree of their relationship to Church authority. Finally, it should be noted that civil law does not recognize juridic personality for this is a strictly canonical notion. This is the reason why such associations are usually civilly incorporated. A civil incorporation of a juridic person, however, does not alter the status of the juridic person in canon law.[64]

Parents and Catholic Education — 1

The 1983 Code has twenty-nine canons specifically dedicated to Catholic education.[65] The Code asserts the right of parents in the educational process of their children.[66] This approach is a faithful reflection of conciliar and post conciliar teachings. Vatican Council II teaches that parents, in the process of educating their children, play a very important role in the teaching mission of the Church.[67]

---

[63] See c. 1257, 2.

[64] See Gauthier, 85; D. Hermann, "The Code of Canon Law Provisions on Labor Relations," *J* 44 (1984) 174-176.

[65] CC. 793-821.

[66] The Code asserts in diverse canons scattered throughout it the right and duty of parents to be active participants in the Christian education of their children.

[67] See for example *LG* 11, 35; *GS* 47-52; *AA* 11; *GE* 3, 6, 7. Suggested readings: Congregation for Catholic Education, "The Religious Dimension of Education in a Catholic School," *Origins* 18/14 (5 September 1988) 213, 215-228; H. Buetow, *The Catholic School: Its Roots, Identity, and Future*; Cardinal R. Castillo Lara, "Some General Reflections on the Rights and Duties of the Christian Faithful," *SCa* 20 (1986) 7-32; *CLSA: Commentary*, 564-567; M.A. Hayes, "As Stars for All Eternity: A Reflection on Canons 793-795," *SCa* 23 (1989) 409-427; F. Morrisey, "The Rights of Parents in the Education of their Children (Canons 796-806)," *SCa* 23 (1989) 429-444; Pope John Paul II, *Familiaris consortio*. See also *CCC* 1653, 1656, 2221-2231.

Marital life is a special vocation in the Church.[68] Inherent in this vocation is the duty of building up the People of God through the couple's witness of the union which exists between Christ and his Church, as well as through their fulfillment of the obligation to develop a Christian family which is perceived as the domestic church.[69]

Parents belong to the laity, with some occasional exceptions such as married permanent deacons with children. As such, they are charged with the general obligation to carry out the mission of the Church that is a responsibility of all Christians, each responding to his or her state in life.[70] Thus, through their way of living, parents are charged to teach their children through concrete examples and in their witness as a married couple how to transform the world by adhering to the message of Christ and his Church.

Canon 226 speaks about marriage and family life.[71] It is within the framework of marriage and family life that the Church consistently upholds and insists upon the right and duty of parents to educate their children as members of the Church and citizens of their country. The backdrop of this insistence is the fact that in many countries, civil governments constantly attempt to control schools and monopolize the students' education. Confronting this reality, the Church insists that parents are the primary educators of their children and have the right and duty to determine how that education should be carried out. This right and duty can be exercised by sending their children to private or parochial schools as well as by taking advantage of the educational opportunities provided by the government. Though the right and duty are not absolute, they are fundamental. Consequently, following the teachings of the conciliar and post conciliar documents, the Code establishes a solid parental role in the education of children.

The Church teaches that by its very nature marriage is ordained

---

[68] See *LG* 11.

[69] See *LG* 35; *GS* 48, 49, 52.

[70] See c. 225. The canon is based on *LG* 31, 33; *AA* 2-4, 7, 17; *AG* 21, 36; *GS* 43. *Navarre*, 197-198, n. 225; and all the chapters dedicated to Code and Laity.

[71] C. 226 is based on *LG* 11, 35; *AA* 11; *GS* 47-52; *GE* 3. See also *CCC* 1652, 2221, 2225-2226, 2228-2229, 2249, 2253; *Navarre*, 198-199, n. 226.

for the procreation and education of children.[72] This Church teaching is reflected in canons 1055 and 1136. The procreation and education of children are essentially linked. Thus, parents have the solemn duty and consequent right to provide for their children's physical, social, cultural, moral and religious formation. The religious formation of their children is of primary importance.[73]

Parents and Catholic Education — 2

Parents do not stand on their own in meeting the duties and asserting their rights in matters regarding the Catholic education of their children. While parents are charged with the obligation of forming their children in the Catholic faith and in its practice,[74] they also have the right to receive the necessary support from their pastors and other spiritual leaders who are involved in religious education.[75]

Canon 793[76] affirms the right and duty of parents to choose the most appropriate way of educating their children in the Catholic faith and asserts that both Church and state have an interest and responsibility in providing whatever support is needed to carry out this obligation. Thus, the school system should be such that there is a freedom of choice for parents in selecting the appropriate school[77] and that there is mutual cooperation between school administration, teachers, and parents to allow this to come about.[78]

The Code distinguishes between schools which provide a Catho-

---

[72] *GS* 48.

[73] See *LG* 11; *GE* 3, 6; *GS* 48; *DH* 5.

[74] C. 774, 2. The canon is based on *LG* 11, 35; *GE* 3, 6-8; *AA* 11, 30; *GS* 48; *EN* 71. See also *CCC* 906, 2225-2226.

[75] C. 776. The canon is based on *LG* 28, 29; *CD* 30, 35; *PC* 8; *AA* 3, 10; *PO* 4-9; *EN* 68-71. See also *CCC* 900; *Navarre*, 509, n. 776.

[76] C. 793 is based on *GE* 3, 6-7. See *Navarre*, 518-519, n. 793.

[77] C. 797. The canon is based on *GE* 6. See *Navarre*, 520-521, n. 797.

[78] C. 796. The canon is based on *GE* 5, 7. See *Navarre*, 520, n. 796.

lic education[79] and Catholic schools.[80] Those schools which are established by a civil corporation or are private schools are not Catholic schools in the strict and canonical sense, even though they may provide an excellent Catholic education. On the other hand, a Catholic school is one which is under the complete control of the proper Church authority, religious institute or other public juridic person[81] acknowledged as *Catholic* through a document issued by the competent Church authority. Parents are encouraged, not bound, to send their children to Catholic schools. Whether this is done or not, parents have the obligation to ensure that their children receive a Catholic education.[82]

The Code puts great emphasis on the parents' duty and right to provide their children with proper preparation for the sacraments. This is a role of the parents in the sanctifying mission of the Church.[83] Thus, parents are obliged to have their child baptized soon after birth.[84] Parents also have the primary responsibility to see that their child receives proper preparation for the sacraments of First Penance,[85] Holy Communion,[86] and confirmation.[87] Finally, through the manifestation of their own marital life, parents are to provide a living example and

---

[79] C. 798. The canon is based on *LG* 33; *GE* 8; *AA* 30. Though in some countries, such a directive creates a tension between the Church and non-Catholic schools, parents and Church leaders are still bound to provide supplementary ways of providing the proper education of children as Catholics. See also *CCC* 902; *Navarre*, 521, n. 798.

[80] C. 803. See *Navarre*, 523, n. 803.

[81] See chapter entitled, Juridic Personality in the 1983 Code.

[82] See n. 79.

[83] C. 835, 4. The canon is based on *SC* 26-31; *LG* 41; *GS* 48. The subject matter was developed more fully by Pope John Paul II in his apostolic exhortation, *Familiaris consortio*, particularly in paragraph 56. See also *Navarre*, 547-548, n. 835.

[84] C. 867, 1. It is no longer imperative that a child be baptized as soon as possible. The canon allows for some flexibility in time. See *CCC* 1250; *Navarre*, 567, n. 867. See also chapter entitled, Code and Sacraments of Initiation — 1.

[85] C. 914. The canon is based on *Eucharisticum mysterium* 14, 28, 35. See also *CCC* 1457; *Navarre*, 587-588, n. 914; and chapters dedicated to Penance and Reconciliation.

[86] C. 914. See also chapter entitled, Sacraments of Initiation — 3 and chapters dedicated to the Eucharist.

[87] C. 890. See *CCC* 1306 and chapter entitled, Sacraments of Initiation — 2.

ongoing instruction to their children on the meaning of a true Christian marriage.[88]

Lay Preaching — 1

It is becoming more common that, due to a dearth of priests in a diocese or region, diocesan bishops are entrusting parishes to the pastoral care of persons who are not ordained. Among the responsibilities which such pastoral care entails is the responsibility of preaching the Word of God at liturgical celebrations.[89] There are many places where parishioners are not able to have the Eucharist celebrated every Sunday in their parish church. It falls to the pastoral lay person to preach at the liturgical celebrations when there is no Mass. However, when a priest is able to celebrate Mass at that parish church, it might happen that the pastoral lay person rather than the priest speaks at Mass. It stands to reason that since the pastoral lay minister knows the parishioners and their human condition better than the priest, the lay minister may have a better understanding of how the Word of God may be applied to the daily life of the faithful in that particular place. The fact that a lay person is speaking at the celebration of the Eucharist does not mean that the individual is the homilist at that celebration. By definition, ordained ministers[90] alone may be homilists at the celebration of the Eucharist. On the other hand, lay persons may preach at other liturgical celebrations.[91] Nevertheless, lay preaching is never considered to be a homily.

---

[88] CC. 1063 and 1136. C. 1063 is based on *LG* 41; *GS* 47, 52; *SC* 19, 59, 77. C. 1136 is rooted in *LG* 11; *GS* 48; *GE* 3, 6. See also *Familiaris consortio* 66; *Navarre*, 664, n. 1063-1065; 716-717, n. 1134-1136.

[89] Suggested readings: F. Henderson, "The Minister of Liturgical Preaching," *Worship* 56 (1982) 214-230; P. Norris, "Lay Preaching and Canon Law: Who May Give a Homily?" *SCa* 24 (1990) 443-454; J. Provost, "Brought Together by the Word of the Living God (Canons 762-772)," *SCa* 23 (1989) 345-371; J. Renken, "Canonical Issues in the Pastoral Care of Parishes Without Priests," *J* 47 (1987) 506-521; *Navarre*, 500-506. See also *SC* 35, 52; *LG* 23, 44; *DV* 21, 24; *CD* 12-14; *PO* 4; *CCC* 2033, 2049.

[90] C. 767, 1. The canon is based on *SC* 52. See *Navarre*, 504, n. 767.

[91] C. 766. The canon should be understood within the context of what is stated in *PO* 5. See also *Navarre*, 504, n. 766.

Lay Preaching — 2

Canons 756 through 761[92] serve as an introduction to the canons which address "The Ministry of the Divine Word."[93] These canons discuss the responsibilities with their rationale that each member of the Church has toward the ministry of the Word: the Pope, the College of Bishops, all bishops, priests, deacons, religious and laity.

Canon 756, 1 states that the Pope, by virtue of his universal primacy, has the *unrestricted right* to preach at any time and anywhere in the world.[94] Moreover, as the universal Pastor of the Catholic Church, the Holy Father is responsible to see that the first duty of the entire Church[95] is being fulfilled. This primary responsibility is held jointly with the College of Bishops.[96]

Canon 357, 2 upholds the personal exemption of Cardinals from the jurisdiction of diocesan bishops everywhere. By virtue of this exemption they may preach anywhere without restriction.[97]

Canon 763[98] states that bishops, by virtue of the episcopal ordination, have a *right* to preach anywhere in the Church. It is the act of episcopal ordination which confers upon a bishop the function of teaching. He becomes a member of the College of Bishops through his episcopal ordination.[99] Thus, this canon is an application of the principle which was stated in canon 756, 1 namely that the College of Bishops have a primary responsibility to proclaim the Good News in the universal Church. Preaching is an integral part of the episcopal office.[100]

---

[92] CC. 756-761 are based on *DV* 24. See *Navarre*, "The Ministry of the Divine Word," 500-502.

[93] The subject matter is covered in cc. 756 through 780.

[94] C. 756, 1 is based on *LG* 23, 25; *CD* 3, 4; and *AG* 29. See also *Navarre*, 500-501, n. 756.

[95] The first duty of the Church is the proclamation of the Good News.

[96] See *LG* 23.

[97] See *Navarre*, 282, n. 357.

[98] See *Navarre*, 503, n. 763.

[99] C. 375, 2. The canon also states that the function of teaching is validly exercised in hierarchical communion, that is in union with the Pope and the College of Bishops. C. 375, 2 is based on *LG* 21; *CD* 11. See also *Navarre*, 297-298, n. 375.

[100] See *LG* 25.

Priests and deacons do not have a right to preach anywhere in the universal Church. Rather, they are given the *faculty* to do so.[101] This faculty is given to them by virtue of their canonical status due to their sacramental ordination. However, it may be either restricted or revoked by a competent Church authority under certain conditions, as stated in canons 764 and 765.

Lay Preaching — 3

Council Vatican II states that all the baptized must be concerned with the proclamation of the Gospel.[102] Lay persons, according to canon 766, may be given *permission* to preach by way of exception. This statement should not be taken at face value. Rather, one has to appreciate what the Code means by *preaching*. Preaching in a place which is not sacred is, technically speaking, not preaching.[103] Furthermore, even when a lay person provides catechetical instructions in a church or oratory, the person is not preaching. The reasoning behind this is that preaching, in the strict sense, is closely related to the celebration of the Eucharist.[104] Thus, only the ordinary ministers of the Eucharist have the exclusive right or faculty to preach.[105]

The preaching which takes place within a liturgical celebration is called the *homily*, which is considered as being a part of the liturgy itself.[106] The homily is essentially a liturgical act. The canon states that the homily is the preeminent form of preaching and its nature is that of proclamation, explanation, and instruction in the mysteries of faith and the norms of Christian living. This liturgical act is not restricted to the Eucharistic liturgy, but applies also to other celebrations of the

---

[101] C. 764. See *Navarre*, 503, n. 764.

[102] See, for example, *LG* 12, 31, 33 and *AA* 3, 6, 10.

[103] See *Navarre*, 504, n. 766.

[104] See *PO* 5.

[105] See cc. 762-765.

[106] C. 767, 1. The canon is based on *SC* 35, 52; *DV* 24; *PO* 4. See also *Navarre*, 504, n. 767.

Word which normally precede the administration of a sacrament or other liturgical events. The latter two do not have to take place within the Eucharistic liturgy. It is also noteworthy that the Code clearly states that the homily during a Eucharistic liturgy is restricted to those in sacred orders. Thus, according to the norm of law, lay persons are excluded from delivering a homily. This is a constitutive law which cannot be dispensed by any bishop or priest.[107]

The issue of lay preaching becomes crystallized in those parishes which, though entrusted to a priest, are, in fact, administered by lay persons. Such parishes regularly have no priest to celebrate the Eucharist and also lack a deacon. Such circumstances dictate that Eucharistic services take place on priestless Sundays, holy days, and weekdays.

What should happen on those days when a priest or a deacon is not available to deliver a homily? Should the faithful be left without this vital aspect of Christian instruction? It seems that this is a grave reason and, under such circumstances, the provisions for the exception mentioned in canon 766 should be invoked. The canon states that the competent conference of bishops may issue norms for their territory which specify under what conditions designated lay persons may be granted permission to preach in the capacity of *extraordinary ministers of preaching*.[108] By the same token, it is evident that lay persons are otherwise prohibited from delivering a homily. On the other hand, it should be remembered that when it is necessary that a lay person, due to his or her expertise,[109] should speak at the Eucharistic liturgy or other liturgical celebration, the person is not delivering a homily.

---

[107] See c. 86.

[108] See *CLSA: Commentary*, 552-553.

[109] For example, in the case of a Eucharistic liturgy for small children.

2. Religious

Consecrated Life — 1

There have always been Christians who, from the early times of the Church, dedicated themselves to following the Lord by practicing the evangelical counsels.[1] As time went on, such people began to band themselves together into small groups so as to give some kind of uniformity to their lifestyle.

Today, many people are under the impression that religious life is the only form of consecrated life in the Church.[2] There are, however, a number of forms of consecrated life, three of which are better known.[3] The 1983 Code regulates these three models. They are the

[1] See *PC* 1; *CCC* 918.

[2] C. 573 describes what is meant by *consecrated life* in the Church. See also *LG* 42-45; *CD* 33; *PC* 1, 5; *AG* 18. Suggested readings: M. Azevedo, *Vocation for Mission: The Challenge of Religious Life Today*; R. Daly, ed., *Religious Life in the U.S. Church*; L. Felknor, *The Crisis in Religious Vocations*; G. Ghirlanda, "Consecrated Life in the Life of the Church," *Consecrated Life* 10 (1986) 190-204; J. Hamer, "Is Religious Life Still Possible?" *Origins* 15 (1985) 189-191; S. Holland, "The Code and Essential Elements," *J* 44 (1984) 304-338; idem., "Religious Life," *Chicago Studies* 23 (1984) 77-96; L. Jarrell, "The Legal and Historical Context of Religious Life for Women," *J* 45 (1985) 419-434; J. Lozano, *Life As Parable: Reinterpreting the Religious Life*; R. McDermott, "Consecrated Life and Its Role in the Church and in the World: The Lineamenta for the 1994 Synod of Bishops," *J* 53 (1993) 239-262; E. McDonough, *Religious in the 1983 Code: New Approaches to the New Law*; Navarre, 410, n. 573; D. O'Connor, *Witness and Service: Questions About Religious Life Today*; K. Popko, "Contemplating Religious Life's Future," *Origins* 21 (1991) 219-225; S. Sammon, "The Transformation of Religious Life," *Origins* 21 (1991) 187-191.

[3] There are also two less known lifestyles of consecrated life in the Church: hermits (c. 603, 1) and consecrated virgins (c. 604, 2). Hermits do not have to take vows. See *LG* 43; *PC* 1; *AG* 18, 40; *CCC* 920. Consecrated virgins live in the world. See *AA* 2; *CCC* 922-924. See also H. MacDonald, "Hermits: The Juridical Implications of Canon 603," *SCa* 26 (1992) 163-190; Navarre, 423-424, n. 603-604.

Religious Institutes,[4] *Secular Institutes*,[5] and *Societies of Apostolic Life*.[6] Although these are three distinctly diverse forms of consecrated life in the Church, they do have some elements in common. Thus, all three forms have their own statutes or constitutions,[7] their own authority structure,[8] their own autonomy in electing their superiors and running their own Community.[9] All of them must relate to the competent diocesan bishop in that he is to exercise vigilance over their apostolate within his diocese.[10] The institute or society can be either of pontifical[11] or diocesan[12] right, clerical[13] or lay.[14]

---

[4] C. 607 describes religious life and religious institute. The members of such institutes are usually called "sisters" or "brothers" or "monks" or "friars," etc. Some of the men members are called "father" because they are also priests. Examples of these institutes are Benedictine monks and nuns, Franciscan friars and sisters, Jesuit priests and brothers. See *LG* 42-47; *CD* 33; *PC* 1, 5, 12, 15, 25; *AG* 18; *CCC* 925-927; Broderick, "Nun," 426; idem., "Religious Life," 520; idem., "Sisters," 555; Lozano, *Life As Parable*; J. Hamer, "Is Religious Life Still Possible?"; S. Holland, "The Code and Essential Elements"; idem., "Religious Life"; *Navarre*, 425-426, n. 607; D. O'Connor, "Two Forms of Consecrated Life: Religious and Secular Institutes," *Review for Religious* 45 (1986) 205-219.

[5] C. 710 provides a definition of a secular institute. See *LG* 31, 33, 36, 42-45; *CD* 33; *PC* 1, 5, 11-14, *AA* 2; *AG* 18; *EN* 70; *CCC* 928-929; Broderick, "Institutes, Secular," 295; *Navarre*, 479-480; B.M. Ottinger and A.S. Fischer, eds., *Secular Institutes in the Code: A New Vocation in the Church*; D. O'Connor, 205-219.

[6] C. 731 describes societies of apostolic life. See also *PC* 1, 12-14; *CCC* 930; M. Linscott, "The Consecrated Lives of Apostolic Religious Today," *Review for Religious* 47 (1988) 3-23; *Navarre*, 487-489.

[7] See c. 586, 1 and c. 587, 1. See also *LG* 45; *CD* 35, 3-4; *ES* II, 12. A Community's constitutions and other laws pertinent to that Community are called *proper law*. Suggested readings: J. Gallen, *Canon Law for Religious*; M. Dortel-Claudot, "The Task of Revising the Constitutions of the Institutes of Consecrated Life as Called for by Vatican II," *Vatican II: Assessment and Perspectives — Twenty-five Years After* (1962-1987), R. Latourelle, ed., 90-130; M. Linscott, "The Service of Religious Authority: Reflections on Government in the Revision of Constitutions," *Review for Religious* 42 (1983) 197-217; *Navarre*, 414-416, nn. 586, 587.

[8] That is, their own governmental body. See c. 587; *LG* 45; *PC* 3, 4; *ES* II: 4d, 8, 11, 12b, 13, 14. See R. Hill, "Autonomy of Life" *Review for Religious* 46 (1987) 137-141; M. Linscott, "Basic Governance Structures in Religious Institutes," *Review for Religious* 49 (1990) 928-932; *Navarre*, 415-416, n. 587.

[9] See c. 586, 1 and cc. 617-640, particularly c. 625, 1. Community with a capital letter is used to distinguish it from the local communities which form it. See R. Hill, "Autonomy of Life"; *Navarre*, 430-439.

[10] See c. 591. See also *LG* 45; *CD* 35, 3. If there is an important change in the apostolate of a community, that community must do so with the consent of the diocesan bishop (c. 612). Suggested readings: J. Beyer, "Religious in the New Code and Their Place in the

Consecrated Life — 2

There is a consistent structure among Communities or Institutes of consecrated life which deal with procedures in joining and leaving a Community. These regulations are found in each Community's *statutes* or *constitutions*. Religious Institutes, understandably, have more detailed statutes or constitutions. The other two kinds of consecrated life, however, follow the same pattern. The following are the elements common to these three kinds of consecrated life:

1. An individual freely petitions to try out the Community.
2. The competent superiors in the Community decide whether to accept or reject the individual's application.
3. A *probation* period follows when an individual is accepted.[15]
4. During the probation period an individual is free to leave at any time. The Community also has the option to ask the individual to leave.[16]

Local Church," *SCa* 17 (1983) 171-183; G. Ghirlanda, "Relations Between Religious Institutes and Diocesan Bishops," *Consecrated Life* 14 (1989) 37-71; S. Holland, "The New Code and Religious" *J* 44 (1984) 67-80; H. Hubbard, "The Collaboration Needed by Bishops and Religious," *Origins* 19 (1989) 332-336; E. McDonough, "Canonical Considerations of Autonomy and Hierarchical Structure," *Review for Religious* 45 (1986) 669-690.

[11] The decree erecting this canonical kind of a Community is issued by the Holy See. This is always the case with Religious Orders. See c. 586, 2; c. 589; and c. 593. See also *LG* 45; *CD* 35, 2.

[12] The decree erecting this canonical kind of a Community is issued by a diocesan bishop (c. 579 and c. 594).

[13] This is when the majority of the members are ordained. This applies only to Communities of men religious since men alone can be ordained. See c. 588, 2.

[14] This is when the majority of the members are not ordained. Some of the men religious Communities and all Communities of women religious are not clerical. See c. 588, 3. See also *PC* 10.

[15] C. 597, 2 prescribes that Communities must give a prospective candidate suitable preparation before being admitted into the Community. The Code does not spell out any specific form of preparation. The Community is responsible to specify the preparation program in its proper law. Many Communities have a limited "try-out" or observation period before an individual begins the Novitiate. The Novitiate usually lasts from one to two years, depending on the Community's statutes and/or the discretion of the competent superiors. C. 648, 3 specifies that the Novitiate may not extend beyond two years.

[16] C. 653, 1.

5. An individual makes temporary[17] profession of vows or bonds at the end of the probation period,[18] and becomes a member. The vows or bonds are taken in accordance with their interpretation in the Community's constitutions.[19] This stage of consecrated life is called the *formation* period.[20] During this period, the member and/or the Community can ask for departure at any time.[21]

6. A member takes perpetual vows.[22] Members of secular institutes and societies of apostolic life make a definitive determination rather than perpetual vows.

7. If a member wishes to leave the Community or the Community decides to dismiss the member after perpetual vows or definite determination have been taken, the procedure must strictly follow special rules.[23]

Usually the Community is free to decide whether to allow the person to continue or not during the probation and formation period. There is, however, an exception to this rule. The Community cannot dismiss an individual when that person becomes mentally or physi-

---

[17] That is, for a specific amount of time.

[18] Some Communities take temporary vows for three years; these vows can be renewed yearly after that up to six years. Other Communities take temporary vows for one year, renewable each year up to six years (c. 655). The competent superior may extend the probation period up to nine years (c. 657, 2).

[19] C. 655.

[20] CC. 659-661. See also *CD* 16; *PC* 18; *PO* 19; *ES* II, 19, 33-35, 36, 38; *REU* 73, 2; 77.

[21] Usually this takes place when the individual member is up for evaluation by the competent superiors for the renewal of temporary vows or bonds. If there is to be no renewal of temporary vows or bonds, they are allowed to expire. However, there may be some unusual instances when departure or dismissal takes place prior to the expiration of temporary vows or bonds (c. 657, 1).

[22] See c. 657, 1. See also chapter entitled, Consecrated Life — 3.

[23] See c. 688, 2, c. 691, 2, c. 693, c. 694, c. 696, c. 699, 2, c. 700; and c. 701. See also c. 1395, 2, c. 1397, and c. 1398. There is also dismissal by Church law (c. 694). There are special rules to be followed if a member transfers from one Community to another (cc. 684-685). Departure or dismissal might involve the intervention of the Holy See. Suggested readings: E. McDonough, "Exclaustration: Canonical Categories and Current Practice," *J* 49 (1989) 568-606; R. Ombres, "Dismissal from a Religious Institute," *Clergy Review* 71 (1986) 97-99; idem., "Separation from a Religious Institute," *Clergy Review* 70 (1985) 414-416.

cally ill and the infirmity occurred due to the Community's negligence or because of the Community's apostolate.[24]

Consecrated Life — 3

The first kind of consecrated life in the Church is the centuries old *Religious Institutes*. They are superabundantly rich in their heritage. They are formed of nuns, monks, friars, brothers and sisters. Their role in the Church is to build up the Body of Christ in a special way[25] and enrich it with a deeper holiness[26] through the Community's charism which it has for the sake of the Church.[27] The Code speaks of this form of consecrated life.

An Institute can be either a Religious Order[28] or a Religious Congregation.[29] Each Order and Congregation responds to a specific charism in the Church.[30] Either Community of men religious may have ordained and non-ordained members,[31] though very few communities of them are exclusively comprised of non-ordained members.[32]

All members of religious Communities make a public profession of vows.[33] There is, however, a very important distinction between

---

[24] See c. 689. For dismissal from a Community see chapter entitled, Consecrated Life — 5, and n. 23 in this chapter. See also *Navarre*, 469, n. 689.

[25] See c. 573. See also *LG* 42-45; *CD* 33; *PC* 1, 5; *AG* 18; *CCC* 914-919, 925-927, 933, 944-945, 1973-1974, 2103, 2684, 2687. For suggested readings see chapter entitled, Consecrated Life — 1, nn. 2 and 4; *Navarre*, 410, n. 573; 411, n. 574-575.

[26] See c. 574, 1. See also *LG* 44.

[27] See c. 574, 2. See also *LG* 43; *PC* 2.

[28] Examples of Religious Orders are the Benedictines, Cistercians, Trappists, Carmelites, Franciscans, Dominicans, Augustinians, and so forth. The Orders aforementioned are for men and women.

[29] These Congregations are usually those of men and women who form a religious community of the Third Order such as Carmelite Sisters of the Sacred Heart of Los Angeles, Benedictine Sisters of Bavaria, and Dominican Sisters of San Rafael.

[30] C. 577. See also *LG* 36, 46; *PC* 8a, 11; *Navarre*, 412, n. 577.

[31] For example Benedictine monks have priests and brothers as members. See c. 588, 2; *Navarre*, 416, n. 588.

[32] For example, the Christian Brothers, also known as the De La Salle Brothers.

[33] C. 654. See *LG* 44 and 45.

the kinds of vows which members of an Order and a Congregation take. Members of an Order, men and women alike, take perpetual vows.[34] The women religious in such Orders are called *nuns*, while men religious can be monks[35] or friars[36] or brothers.[37] On the other hand, members of a Congregation[38] take either perpetual or renewable vows. The women religious in such Congregations are usually called *sisters*, while men religious can be either priests or brothers.

Each member of an Order or Congregation takes the three basic evangelical vows of chastity,[39] poverty,[40] and obedience.[41] There are some Orders and Congregations whose members take a fourth vow as well.[42]

Members of Orders and Congregations share some characteristics in common. All members take vows in accordance with their constitutions. They make a public profession of vows. They live a life style in accordance with the charism of the Community and which clearly indicates separation from the world. They also live a life in common.

Consecrated Life — 4

Secular institutes have been rather recently formally recognized in the life of the Church.[43] Members of secular institutes are consecrated and

---

[34] Some Communities referred to these perpetual vows as being solemn vows. The 1983 Code has dropped the distinction between solemn and perpetual vows. See *Navarre*, 449-451, n. 654-658.

[35] A monk can be either ordained or non-ordained.

[36] A friar can be either ordained or non-ordained.

[37] Brothers are always non-ordained.

[38] The greater majority of Congregations are those of women religious.

[39] C. 599. See *LG* 42; *PC* 12; *PO* 16; *Navarre*, 422, n. 599.

[40] C. 600. See *LG* 42; *PC* 13; *PO* 17; *ES* II: 23, 24; *Navarre*, 469-469, n. 688.

[41] C. 601. See *LG* 42; *PC* 14; *PO* 15.

[42] For example, Benedictine monks take the fourth vow of stability, that is, to remain in the same abbey.

[43] Although the concept of secular institutes dates back to the sixteenth century, it was not until 1947 that they were formally recognized as secular institutes which provide a state of perfection in the Church. Pope Pius XII established this recognition in his apostolic

secular. They live in the world[44] to serve as leaven[45] for its conversion through their apostolic activity.[46] They take sacred bonds of the evangelical counsels.[47] They can live either alone or with their family or in community, depending on what is required by their institute's constitutions.[48] Diocesan priests, having informed their diocesan bishop,[49] also can belong to a secular institute.

When a lay person joins a secular institute, that person does not become a religious but remains in his or her lay state.[50] By analogy, when a secular priest joins a secular institute, he does not become a religious. However, because the Holy See formally recognizes secular institutes as a type of consecrated life, each secular institute must follow the provisions of Church law regarding consecrated life in general.[51] Furthermore, secular institutes are also bound to some norms that are found in the Code's section on religious life. The Code specifies this when applicable. Three examples of this are norms pertaining to the departure of clerics incardinated in the secular institute,[52] to dismissal from the secular institute,[53] and to the transfer to another secular institute.[54]

The Code regulates that a member of a secular institute is bound by the constitutions of that institute.[55] On the other hand, the Code

---

constitution, *Provida Mater Ecclesiae*, of February 2, 1947. See *CCC* 901, 928-929.See also *CLSA: Commentary*, 525; *Navarre*, 479-487. For further readings see chapter entitled, Consecrated Life — 1, nn. 2 and 5.

[44] C. 710. See *PC* 11; *CCC* 928; *Navarre*, 480, n. 710.

[45] C. 713, 1. See *CCC* 929.

[46] C. 710 and c. 713, 2. See *LG* 31, 33, 36; *PC* 11; *AA* 2; *AG* 40; *EN* 70; *CCC* 928-929.

[47] C. 712. See *PC* 11; *REU* 74.

[48] C. 714. See *PC* 11.

[49] C. 715, 1.

[50] C. 711. See *LG* 36; *AA* 2. See J. Beyer, "Religious Life or Secular Institutes," *Way* 7 (June 1969) 112-132; *Navarre*, 480, n. 711.

[51] CC. 573-606.

[52] C. 727, 2. The provisions of c. 693 are to be observed. See *Navarre*, 486-487, n. 726-730.

[53] C. 729. The canon contains references to c. 694, c. 695, and cc. 697-701.

[54] C. 730. The canon contains references to c. 684, 1, 2, and 4 and c. 685.

[55] C. 716, 1.

identifies some very basic communal and spiritual activities that should be common to all secular institutes.[56]

The Code specifies that a candidate must spend at least two years of probation before taking temporary sacred bonds.[57] These temporary sacred bonds must be taken for a minimum of five years.[58] One's profession of the sacred bonds makes the individual a member of the secular institute. This juridical act is known as incorporation. The formation period begins upon a member's incorporation.[59] Following the conclusion of temporary incorporation, a member, by mutual agreement of the individual and the secular institute, is to take perpetual or definitive sacred bonds.[60]

Consecrated Life — 5

Societies of Apostolic Life are another kind of institutes of consecrated life.[61] They were known by a number of titles in the past, such as missionary societies or societies whose members live in community without vows. These societies have a very rich tradition.[62] Some of them can trace their origins back to the thirteenth century.[63] Originally these communities consisted of lay persons who lived in common and followed the rule of a Religious Community without taking any vows. After the Council of Trent, similar societies emerged with some of their members becoming priests.[64]

---

[56] C. 716, 2 and c. 719. See *PC* 2e, 5, 6, 11, 13; *CD* 33.

[57] C. 722, 3.

[58] C. 723, 2. See *Navarre*, 484-485, n. 723.

[59] C. 724. See *PC* 18; *ES* II, 33 and 35.

[60] C. 723, 3.

[61] For suggested readings see chapter entitled, Consecrated Life — 1, nn. 2 and 6. See also *CCC* 930; *Navarre*, 487-490.

[62] There are many contemporary societies of apostolic life which have a rich history. For example, the White Fathers, Oratorians, and Columbans. In the United States, one of the most famous of these communities founded in the country is that of Maryknoll.

[63] For example, the Beguines. See Broderick, "Beguines and Beghards," 70.

[64] For example, St. Philip Neri founded the Institute of the Oratorians (1575); St. Charles Borromeo founded the Oblates of St. Ambrose (1578). About fifty years later, St.

Canon 731, 1 describes societies of apostolic life.[65] Members of such societies are not necessarily separated from the world. They are established for an apostolic purpose in the Church. Though the members live in community, they have optional profession of sacred bonds, depending on what is regulated by their constitutions.[66]

Canon 735 states that procedures of admission, probation, incorporation, and training within a society are to be determined by the society's constitutions.[67] When the society admits candidates to the priesthood, their training should follow the same norms set for the training of secular priests, unless other provisions are specified in the society's constitutions.[68]

As in the case of a person joining a secular institute,[69] when a person joins a society of apostolic life, he or she does not become a religious. Furthermore, since a society of apostolic life is recognized as a type of consecrated life, each society must follow the provisions of the Code which speak of consecrated life in general.[70] The Code's section on religious life also contains norms which are applicable to societies of apostolic life. The Code specifies such instances.

A society of apostolic life might have priests as members. When this is the case, the priest is incardinated in the society itself, unless the society's constitutions make other provisions.[71]

Vincent de Paul founded the Vincentians, and with St. Louise de Marillac also founded the Daughters of Charity (1625).

[65] See also *CCC* 914-916, 930.
[66] C. 731, 2. The canon is based on *PC* 1, 12-14.
[67] See also *PC* 18; *ES* I, 33-36.
[68] C. 736, 1.
[69] See chapter entitled, Consecrated Life — 4.
[70] CC. 573-606.
[71] C. 736, 1.

3. Consultation: Parish and Diocesan

Code and Consultation — Introduction

The Church is not simply composed of bishops and their clergy. The Pope, all the bishops, the clergy, the religious, and the laity form the Church.[1] The hierarchy is a very important and essential element in the Church but it remains a part of the People of God. The entire People of God is bound together through *Communio.*[2] There is always a basic unity from the highest to the most basic levels in the Church. This basic unity is forged in a bond of common faith, binding charity, and shared fraternity. Moreover, every member of the Church shares in the responsibility of building up the Body of Christ.[3] Hence, it is proper that a diocesan bishop[4] and the pastor of a parish consult with diverse people so as to enhance the Christian service rendered to the Church in the name of Christ.[5] This active relationship is being presented in the next few chapters. The theme of *consultation* is being discussed

---

[1] See *AA* 2, 7; *LG* 9, 17; *CCC* 777, 790-791.

[2] See *Communio* in the chapter entitled, Code and Laity — 3. See also Ephesians 4:3; 1 Corinthians 12:26-27; *LG* 8, 12, 13, 23, 26, 42, 51; *CCC* 811, 814, 826, 830-836, 870, 949, 951, 953, 959.

[3] See *AA* 2; *CCC* 872-873.

[4] Every diocese has only *one* diocesan bishop. A diocese or an archdiocese, as in the case of Los Angeles, may also have a number of bishops appointed by the Holy See to help the diocesan bishop guide and minister to the fold entrusted to him. These assisting bishops are usually referred to as *Auxiliary Bishops.* See *LG* 23, 27; *CD* 4, 36, 37; *AG* 5, 6, 38; *CCC* 873, 879, 894, 895, 1560.

[5] An excellent article which deals with the decision process in a diocese, and which can also be applied to a parish level, is that of R. Kennedy, "Shared Responsibility in Ecclesial Decision-Making," *SCa* 14 (1980) 5-24. Although the article predates the 1983 Code, it is very future oriented. See also *LG* 10, 18, 21, 24, 27, 33; *CCC* 874, 896, 900, 1547, 1551, 1567.

31

in two phases: the first group of chapters deal with the Code and Parish Consultation, while the second group deals with the Code and Diocesan Consultation.

Consultation is a sound method to be used in matters which affect people's lives. A pastor is entrusted with the spiritual welfare of a number of parishioners.[6] His decisions can affect many of these people's prayer life, personal life and dreams. Consequently, he should consult others before he makes important decisions affecting his parishioners. On the other hand, a diocesan bishop deals with many matters which affect the lives of that portion of the People of God entrusted to him.[7] Consequently, Church law requires that every bishop in charge of a diocese is to consult others before he reaches decisions on very important issues in his diocese. Examples of these are the drawing up of the diocesan statutes, a diocesan pastoral plan, the appointment of a new pastor, the erection or changes in boundaries of a parish.

The act of *consultation* in the 1983 Code has a broader meaning than simply calling for a consultative vote from some persons. It refers to the different types of involvement in helping the competent Church authority fulfill the mission of the Lord. This consultative process can take place through a number of ways in a given parish or diocese.[8]

Code and Parish Consultation — 1

A pastor or a parish administrator needs to consult diverse members of his parish before decisions are made about major parochial policies and projects. The consultation process, for a number of reasons, is of great help to the pastor or administrator. He may have at his dis-

---

[6] C. 519. See *Navarre*, 382, n. 519.

[7] C. 381. See *Navarre*, 302, n. 381.

[8] The Code also speaks about the ways through which the Pope can carry out his consultation. See the chapters entitled, Synod of Bishops.

posal a variety of ways to seek advice. The Code provides two consultative bodies for the administration of a parish.[9]

Canon 536 is dedicated to the first consultative body in a parish: the *Parish Council*. The root of this canon is the conciliar document *Christus Dominus* 27, and the post-conciliar document *Ecclesiae sanctae* I, 16. However, Vatican II promotes the notion of the parish council in other documents as well.[10]

The inception of parish councils in a diocese is the result of consultation undertaken by the diocesan bishop with his presbyteral council.[11] The establishment of a parish council is not demanded by the Code. Its establishment in a parish remains optional.[12] When there is such a council, the pastor or the (priest) parish administrator should consult it on a regular basis. This is to be expected since the spiritual leader in the parish should consult his parishioners about matters which pertain to the life in his parish. On the other hand, parishioners have a right to make known to the pastor their spiritual needs.[13] Thus, the pastor or parish administrator is provided with the possibility of a formidable consultative body. The pastor or, in the absence of a pastor, the (priest) parish administrator[14] is the president of the parish council. The members to be included in the parish council are the paro-

---

[9] Suggested readings for understanding the 1983 Code's concept of *parish*: R. Carlston, "The Parish According to the Revised Law," *SCa* 19 (1985) 5-16; J. Huels, "Parish Life and the New Code," *Concilium* 185 (1986) 64-72. The Code's definition of what constitutes a parish is found in c. 515, 1. See also *CCC* 2179; *Navarre*, 378-379, n. 515.

[10] See, for example, *AA* 27. This notion also appears in *CCC* 911. See also Broderick, "Parish Council," 451-452; *CLSA: Commentary*, 430-433; W. Dalton, "Parish Councils or Parish Pastoral Councils," *SCa* 22 (1988) 169-185; *Navarre*, 394, n. 536; J. Renken, "Pastoral Councils: Pastoral Planning and Dialogue Among the People of God," *J* 53 (1993) 132-154.

[11] Presbyteral Councils are discussed in the chapter entitled, Code and Diocesan Consultation — 1.

[12] See *CLSA: Commentary*, 430-433; Dalton, 169-185.

[13] In fact, c. 212 states that every member of the faithful has a right to do so. See E. Pfnausch, ed., *Code, Community, Ministry*, 62-64. See also *LG* 25, 37; *AA* 6; *PO* 9; *GS* 92; *CCC* 90, 851, 888, 891-892, 905, 907, 1269, 2034-2035, 2044.

[14] When there are a pastor and a parish administrator in the same parish, the pastor is still the ultimate person responsible for his parish. There are also instances when there is a parish administrator between the departure of the outgoing pastor and the appointment of a new one.

chial vicar/s,[15] parochial assistants, the parish lay administrator, the school principal, other parish personnel,[16] and representatives of the parish at large. There is a variety of ways which may be used for electing parish representatives to the council, keeping in mind that the council should reflect the diversity of interests and charisms among the parishioners. Every member of the council should be a Catholic parishioner in good standing.[17] Strictly speaking, a non-Catholic is not a parishioner.[18]

The setup of the parish council is left to particular law, that is the law which is established by the diocesan bishop.[19] Analogous to the cessation of the diocesan pastoral council when the diocese becomes vacant,[20] the parish council also ceases when the parish becomes vacant, that is when the pastor resigns or is transferred or retires or dies.

Code and Parish Consultation — 2

Canons 537 and 1280 of the Code *require* every parish to have a *Parish Finance Council*. This norm is parallel to that found in canons 492-493 which state that every diocese must have a diocesan finance council.[21] The existence of a parish finance council does not depend on the decision of either the pastor or the (priest) parish administrator for it is demanded by Church law. The Code does not specify how this council is to be constituted. Its role is determined by particular legislation.[22]

---

[15] Parochial vicars are usually referred to as *associate pastors*.

[16] Examples of this are those in charge of religious education, ministers to the youth, and R.C.I.A. directors.

[17] This is analogous to the membership on the Diocesan Pastoral Council (c. 512, 3). See chapter entitled, Code and Diocesan Consultation — 5.

[18] For a brief explanation of who belongs to the Catholic Church read *LG* 14, and *CCC* 837.

[19] See c. 139 and c. 391. See also *LG* 2; *CD* 27; *CCC* 894-896.

[20] See chapter entitled, Code and Diocesan Consultation — 5.

[21] See chapter entitled, Code and Diocesan Consultation — 4. See also *CCC* 911; *Navarre*, 395, n. 537; 793, n. 1280.

[22] C. 537. Particular law in this instance means the legislation within a specific diocese.

Therefore, one has to look at the statutes of the diocese to discover what is the responsibility of the parish finance council, how often it should meet, and when the pastor or (priest) parish administrator must consult his finance council for the *validity* of some financial transactions.[23] A quick call to the diocesan pastoral office or its equivalent should provide such information.

Canon 532 clearly states that the pastor is the *direct* administrator of the temporal goods of the parish. He, and not the parish finance council or anyone else, is ultimately responsible for parish finances and the administration of parish Church goods.

One might think that the diocesan bishop has the final word on *all* the financial activities in a parish. This is not the case because the diocesan bishop is not directly responsible for parish finances. Canon 1276, 1 speaks of the supervisory role of the diocesan bishop in overseeing the direct administrators of some of the Church goods.[24] Canon 1279, 1[25] states that the administration of Church goods is the responsibility of the one who immediately governs the public juridic person to whom the goods belong.[26] This means that in the case of a parish it is the pastor and not the diocesan bishop who is the immediate administrator of the parish's Church goods. In any case, the diocesan statutes should clearly spell out when the pastor must seek the permission from his bishop in specified matters which deal with the administration of the parish's Church goods.[27]

When all is said and done, the pastor has two solid consultative sources to assist him in administering the Church goods of his parish: the parish finance council and the diocesan statutes. The latter usually addresses parish finance policies in general terms. On the other hand, the pastor can receive great assistance and insight from the members of his parish finance council in the administration of the parish's

---

[23] See *CLSA: Commentary*, 433; Pfnausch, 112-113.

[24] See *Navarre*, 790-791, n. 1276.

[25] See *Navarre*, 792, n. 1279.

[26] C. 515, 3 states that the law itself gives public juridic personality to a parish. See also *PO* 17.

[27] See c. 1292, 1. See also *Navarre*, 801-803, n. 1292.

finances since the members of the parish finance council are very familiar with their parish's financial situation.

Code and Diocesan Consultation — 1

The *Presbyteral Council* is known by a number of titles. For instance, some dioceses call it the *Council of Priests* while others call it the *Priests' Senate*. This council is one of the means of the consultation process in a diocese. It is a juridic institute restored as a result of the teachings of Vatican II[28] and the post-conciliar document *Ecclesiae sanctae*.[29] Canon 495 has established it as current law. The Code demands that each diocese has a presbyteral council.[30] There are instances in the Code when the validity of a decision rendered by the diocesan bishop rests partly on his consultation with his presbyteral council.[31]

A presbyteral council is, from its name, a consultative body of priests with their diocesan bishop as its head. It is composed in such a way that the diverse ministries undertaken by both secular and regular (religious) clergy in the diocese are reflected in its members.[32] A key norm for its composition is that about half of its members should

---

[28] The restoration of the *presbyteral council* is advocated by Vatican II in *LG* 28; *CD* 27, 28; and *PO* 7, 8. See also *CCC* 1548, 1554, 1562, 1564, 1566-1568, 1582.

[29] *ES* I, 15, 1.

[30] C. 495 is based on *LG* 28; *CD* 27, 28; *PO* 7, 8; *ES* I, 15, 1. See also *CCC* 1548, 1554, 1562, 1564, 1566-1568, 1582; Broderick, "Priests' Councils," 492-493; *Navarre*, 364-368; United States Conference of Bishops, *United in Service: Reflections on the Presbyteral Council*. The term *presbyter* is originally a Hellenistic Judaic term meaning "elder of the community." St. Cyprian, writing in the middle of the third century, refers to the *presbyterium* around the bishop. The term stood for the council of priests who provided the bishop with its advice in the weightier matters concerning the government of his diocese. Hence, the *presbyteral council* is a limited reintroduction of this notion. See J. Lynch, "Co-Responsibility in the First Five Centuries: Presbyteral Colleges and the Election of Bishops," *J* 31 (1971) 14-53.

[31] The Code establishes when a diocesan bishop is required to listen to (*consult*) his presbyteral council and when required to follow the advice (get the *consent*) of the said council. For example, for *validity* of action, the diocesan bishop must *consult*, among other bodies, his presbyteral council to legislate a diocesan tax (c. 1263). Also for *validity*, the diocesan bishop must seek the *consent* of his presbyteral council when it deals with alienating a part of the diocesan patrimony (c. 1292, 1).

[32] C. 498.

be elected, while the rest are members *ex officio* and those named by the diocesan bishop.[33] There is no reason why all those who are not members of the presbyteral council *ex officio* should not be elected by the presbyterate of the diocese.

Canon 501, 1 dictates that some part of this council's membership[34] be renewed over a period of five years. In emphasizing further the importance of the presbyteral council the Code dictates that each diocese must have a presbyteral council within one year of either its suppression by the diocesan bishop[35] or the taking of office by a new diocesan bishop.[36] Lastly, the existence of a presbyteral council is somewhat dependent on the diocesan bishop in that the council ceases to exist when the diocese becomes vacant.[37]

Code and Diocesan Consultation — 2

The *College of Consultors* is another consultative body for the diocesan bishop.[38] There is an affinity between the presbyteral council and the college of consultors. Both councils are always formed of priests, unless there are also auxiliary bishops in the diocese. Furthermore, the diocesan bishop is in charge of both bodies.

Canon 502, 1 states that the diocesan bishop is to select the consultors from his presbyteral council, though its functions are indepen-

---

[33] C. 497. See *Navarre*, 365-367, n. 497-499.

[34] The common opinion among canonists is that at least one third of the presbyteral council should be renewed every five years. The terms of renewal are indefinite. See *CLSA: Commentary*, 405-406. The canon is based on *ES* I, 15, 4.

[35] Before a diocesan bishop dissolves his presbyteral council he must consult the metropolitan archbishop of the area. If the diocesan bishop is the metropolitan archbishop, he must consult the senior suffragan bishop by promotion (c. 501, 3).

[36] C. 501, 2. The canon follows the directives of *ES* I, 15, 4.

[37] Ibid.

[38] C. 502, 1. Although this canon is based on *CD* 27, it does not reflect fully the reorganization of the *college of consultors* which was called for by Vatican II. A good analysis of the college of consultors may be found in J. Hannon's summary of his doctoral dissertation in Canon Law in, "Diocesan Consultors," *SCa* 20 (1986) 147-179. See also *Navarre*, 369-370, n. 502.

dent of the latter. The college of consultors is distinct from and not part of the presbyteral council, even though its members may have initially belonged to it. The Code provides for a minimum of six and a maximum of twelve members in the college of consultors, with each member having a five year term.[39] Although the diocesan bishop appoints every consultor and presides over this consultative body, he cannot dissolve it. When there are auxiliary bishops in a diocese they, too, should be members of the college.[40]

The college of consultors plays a very special role in diocesan affairs. The diocesan bishop should listen to its *advice* especially in matters which pertain to the governance of the entire diocese. On the other hand, there are instances when the diocesan bishop is required to procure the *consent* of the college of consultors. The Code is specific as to when the diocesan bishop is required to consult or to procure the consent of the college in order that his actions may be valid. For example, the bishop must seek the advice[41] of the college before hiring or firing the diocesan fiscal officer.[42] But, the diocesan bishop is bound to seek the consent of the college for alienating certain Church property[43] or risks of worsening the diocesan patrimony[44] or in matters of extraordinary administration.[45] Thus, the deliberations of this college carry lots of weight.

Canon 413, 2[46] states that the college of consultors elects a diocesan administrator when the diocese is impeded.[47] In the event that

---

[39] Ibid.

[40] See c. 407.

[41] The bishop is not bound to follow the advice of the college of consultors in this matter. He simply seeks the consultors' opinion.

[42] C. 494.

[43] C. 1292, 1. The reasoning behind this canon is that such monumental decisions should not rest with one person.

[44] C. 1295.

[45] See c. 127 which speaks about the instances when the indispensable requirement of consultation or consent of groups of persons or of individuals before a superior reaches a certain type of decision. A diocesan bishop is perceived as being one of these superiors. See *Navarre*, 143, n. 127.

[46] C. 413, 2 follows the directives of *CD* 27.

[47] This happens when the diocesan bishop, for some serious reason, is unable to function as the head of his diocese. See *Navarre*, 320, n. 412.

the diocese becomes vacant, the presbyteral council ceases and its functions are taken over by the college of consultors.[48] Canon 419 dictates that in this instance, the college of consultors remains in office to govern the diocese. It is also charged, under certain conditions,[49] with electing a diocesan administrator.[50] This must take place within eight days.[51]

Code and Diocesan Consultation — 3

Another means through which a diocesan bishop carries out the process of consultation in his diocese is through the *Diocesan Synod*.[52] This type of Synod, which is radically different in kind and purpose than the *Synod of Bishops*,[53] is primarily concerned with the legislative government of a diocese. The history of diocesan synods goes back to the fourth century. It has undergone a healthy development with the passage of time. Originally a diocesan synod was comprised solely of clergy. Nowadays, the talents and wisdom of the laity are a welcomed addition to a synodal gathering.

The contemporary understanding of a diocesan synod is that of being a consultative body which is called by the diocesan bishop after he has consulted his presbyteral council.[54] The 1983 Code presents the

---

[48] C. 501, 2. This canon is based on *ES* I, 15, 4.

[49] See chapter entitled, Succession in the Diocese.

[50] The responsibilities of the diocesan administrator and his college of consultors are listed in cc. 272; 413, 2; 419; 422; 485; and 501, 2. These canons are based on *CD* 26, 27; *ES* I, 13, 3, and 15, 4. See *Navarre*, 324-326, nn. 419-420, 421, 423-425.

[51] C. 421, 1.

[52] A good study of the pre-1983 Code understanding of a diocesan synod can be found in the brief article of P. Collins, "The Diocesan Synod — An Assembly of the People of God," *J* 33 (1973) 399-411. See also F. Donnelly, "The New Diocesan Synod," *J* 34 (1974) 68-93. Some of the studies on diocesan synods after the promulgation of the 1983 Code are those of L. Jennings, "A Renewed Understanding of the Diocesan Synod," *SCa* 20 (1987) 319-354; *Navarre*, 346-350; and D. Ross, "The Diocesan Synod: A Comparative Analysis of the 1917 and 1983 Codes of Canon Law," *Monitor Ecclesiasticus* 114 (1989) 560-572.

[53] See chapters dedicated to the Synod of Bishops.

[54] C. 461, 1.

notion of a diocesan synod and all it entails, that is its convocation, who participates, its celebration, the legislation which is drawn up, the communication of the synodal decrees, and the synod's termination. Canon 460 presents the synod as a mixed vehicle which offers a variety of assistance to the diocesan bishop for the good of the People of God entrusted to him.[55] The scope of a diocesan synod goes beyond its legislative orientation. It can be convoked to meet concerns of a diocese or to reorganize a diocese or to offer guidelines for future diocesan agencies and the like.[56]

While an Ecumenical Council and a Synod of Bishops, two other types of consultative bodies in the universal Church, are completely dependent on the Pope, the diocesan synod is completely dependent on the diocesan bishop from its inception to its conclusion. Canon 462 states that the diocesan bishop alone can call a synod, although he can designate other persons to chair its meetings. Canon 468 states that he alone can suspend or dissolve such a synod. Furthermore, if he becomes impeded or vacates his diocese due to his transfer to another diocese or retirement or resignation, the diocesan synod is automatically suspended. This applies also on the demise of the diocesan bishop.

The make-up of a diocesan synod is very diverse, ranging from *ex officio* clerics, to other clerics, to lay religious, to the laity, and to experts in diverse fields.[57] Ecumenical observers can also be invited.[58] Canon 465 states that the synodal members may discuss all the proposed issues on the agenda. The diocesan synod also provides the faithful with the opportunity to express their minds to the diocesan bishop about current important issues in the diocese.[59]

---

[55] C. 460 is based on *CD* 28, 36, and *ES* III, 20.

[56] See c. 461.

[57] C. 463. See also *CCC* 911.

[58] Ibid.

[59] See c. 212, 2. See *CCC* 907. See also chapter entitled, Code and Laity — 2.

Code and Diocesan Consultation — 4

The administration of a diocese needs financial resources and has inherent troubles with expenditures and acquisitions. Church law ascertains that the financial fate of a diocese does not rest solely in the hands of one person, namely the diocesan bishop. Church law makes it mandatory for a diocese to have a *Finance Council*.[60] According to canon 492 the finance council is to be composed of at least three members, lay or clergy or both, with expertise in either financial or legal matters. Each member has a five year term, renewable indefinitely. The diocesan bishop, in consultation with the finance council, is to determine what constitutes ordinary and extraordinary acts of administration in his diocese.[61] However, the limit of expenditure and acquisition in any given diocese is to be set by the competent conference of bishops.[62] It should be noted that this law applies not only to expenditures but also to acquisitions. Furthermore, the Apostolic See regulates when a diocesan bishop must not only have the consent of his finance council, presbyteral council, and the conference of bishops, but must also seek the consent of the Apostolic See if the expenditures or acquisitions go beyond the limit which the latter has set as requiring its prior approval.[63] Each of these consents is required for the *validity* of the bishop's actions.

The finance council works hand in hand with the college of consultors[64] and the presbyteral council.[65] Canon 494, 1-2, requires that

---

[60] C. 423, c. 494, c. 1263, c. 1277, c. 1281, c. 1287, c. 1292, c. 1305 and c. 1310 present the activities of the finance council. A good presentation of the description and responsibilities of the diocesan finance council is that of A. Farrelly: "The Diocesan Finance Council: Functions and Duties According to the *Code of Canon Law*," *SCa*, 23 (1989) 149-166. See also *Navarre*, 361-363; 791-792, n. 1277; 798, n. 1287.

[61] C. 1281, 2. C. 1277 is also related to this topic. See F. Morrisey, "Ordinary and Extraordinary Administration: Canon 1277," *J* 48 (1988) 709-726. See also *CCC* 911.

[62] C. 1292, 1. The current limit in the United States is $3,000,000.00.

[63] See *Navarre*, 1419, n. 18.

[64] The role of the college of consultors is discussed in the chapter entitled, Code and Diocesan Consultation — 2.

[65] The role of the presbyteral council is discussed in the chapter entitled, Code and Diocesan Consultation — 1.

the diocesan bishop is bound to seek the advice of the finance council and the college of consultors before hiring or terminating the fiscal officer. The finance council must also determine the budget of the diocese and be given a yearly account of it.[66] The diocesan bishop is required to have the consent of the finance council for the validity of extraordinary acts of administration as determined according to canon 1277.[67] Its consent is also required for validity in matters which deal with alienation of Church goods between the minimum and maximum limits set by the conference of bishops.[68] Finally, along with the presbyteral council, the finance council must be consulted in matters involving the imposition of a diocesan tax.[69]

Code and Diocesan Consultation — 5

The conciliar documents *Christus Dominus,*[70] *Presbyterorum Ordinis,*[71] and the post-conciliar document *Ecclesiae sanctae*[72] are the basis for the *Diocesan Pastoral Council.* It is another consultative body in a diocese. It is a new set-up (*institute*) in the 1983 Code.[73] The Code does not dictate the establishment of such a council, but strongly encourages it.[74] This council falls entirely under the authority of the diocesan bishop, who alone may convoke it. It is a strictly diocesan structure and serves as a vehicle for pastoral study, evaluation process, and

---

[66] C. 494, 30-40. See *Navarre,* 362-363, n. 494.

[67] See n. 61.

[68] C. 1292, 1. See *Navarre,* 801-803, n. 1292.

[69] C. 1263. For example, the diocesan bishop may not tax members of his diocese without proper consultation. See *Navarre,* 780-781, n. 1263.

[70] *CD* 27.

[71] *PO* 7.

[72] *ES* I, 16, and III, 20.

[73] The canons which deal with the diocesan pastoral council are cc. 511 through 514. The canons are based on *CD* 27; *AG* 30; *PO* 7; *ES* I, 16, 1-3. The 1971 Synod of Bishops, too, discussed the purpose for this council.

[74] See Broderick, "Diocesan Pastoral Council," 163-165; *CLSA: Commentary,* 410-411; Renken, "Pastoral Councils."

proposals to improve the pastoral ministry in parishes.[75] It is evident from the Code that the diocesan pastoral council is a *strictly* consultative body.[76] This means that although the prudent diocesan bishop seeks its advice, he is not bound to follow it.

The membership in the diocesan pastoral council should reflect the overall spectrum of the people living within that diocese. Thus, members should come from every walk of life in the diocese: clergy, religious, and laity.[77] Since the members of this council come from a rich variety of backgrounds, each member's contribution can enlighten the bishop in his understanding of the gifts within the diocese as well as its needs.[78] Although membership is restricted to Catholics,[79] ecumenical concerns can also be put forward, evaluated, and addressed. The diocesan bishop alone is the one who makes the ultimate decision as to what should be done with the findings, insights and recommendations of the council.[80] The diocesan pastoral council goes out of existence when the diocese becomes vacant.[81]

Code and Diocesan Consultation — 6

Another consultative body for a diocesan bishop is the *Episcopal Council* as presented in canon 473, 4.[82] This council is optional. When established, it serves as a cabinet for the diocesan bishop to assist him to coordinate the broad pastoral activities in his diocese. This cabinet is usually made up of auxiliary bishops (when a diocese has them), vicars general, episcopal vicars, and heads of major pastoral depart-

---

[75] C. 511. The canon is based on *CD* 27; *AG* 30; *PO* 7; *ES* I, 16, 1. See also *CCC* 911.

[76] C. 514, 1. The canon is based on *CD* 27; *ES* I, 16, 2.

[77] C. 512. The canon is based on *CD* 27; *ES* I, 16, 3. See also *CCC* 911.

[78] In fact, c. 212 states that every member of the faithful has a right to do so. See chapter entitled, Code and Laity — 2. See also Pfnausch, 62-64; *CCC* 907.

[79] C. 512, 3.

[80] C. 514, 1.

[81] C. 513, 2.

[82] See *Navarre*, 351-352, n. 473-474.

ments in the local Church.[83] The episcopal council usually meets with the diocesan bishop on a regular basis. Major policies which affect the running of the diocese and the diocesan administration are normal subjects for discussion during such meetings. Although a wise bishop listens carefully to his cabinet, he is not bound to follow its advice. As in the case of other consultative bodies in a diocese, the episcopal council is totally dependent on the diocesan bishop for its existence and function. Thus, it ceases to exist when the diocesan bishop dissolves it, or when he is transferred or resigns or retires or dies.[84]

---

[83] For example, the head of the Catholic Charities or Education Department in a diocese.

[84] The fate of the episcopal council is similar to the presbyteral council and the diocesan pastoral council. See chapters pertinent to these two topics.

4. Dioceses

Vicar General — 1

A diocesan bishop cannot possibly be in all places in his diocese at one time. This is especially true in the States where most dioceses tend to be very large in either population or territory. Through its long history, Church leadership has recognized that there should be other bishops and priests who could serve as the *alter ego* for the diocesan bishop or represent him in a special way. They are called *Vicars*. The role of these representatives differ according to the responsibility entrusted to each vicar.

The *Vicar General* is the most important office in the diocesan curia. He serves as a stand-in for the diocesan bishop. The office evolved in the Church in the last nine centuries. Originally the office-holder was allowed to exercise his authority only when the diocesan bishop was outside the diocese or when the diocese became vacant. Eventually, he was given the power to exercise the authority of his office whether the diocesan bishop was present or absent from his diocese. Consequently, the vicar general became the *alter ego* of the diocesan bishop. He has executive and administrative powers almost to the same extent that the diocesan bishop does with the exception made by canon law in canon 134, 3, to which the diocesan bishop can also reserve some powers to himself. Since he is the *alter ego* of the diocesan bishop, his office ceases when the bishop is no longer in charge of the diocese.

The Code has a number of canons dedicated to the office and responsibilities of the vicar general. Canon 475 determines that every diocese must have a vicar general and that, for administrative or pastoral reasons, a diocese could have more than one vicar general.[1] Canon 477[2] states that the appointment and removal of a vicar general is totally dependent on the diocesan bishop's discretion. The decree of appointment must state the term of office. These two provisions do not apply in the case when the vicar is an auxiliary bishop of the diocese. Canon 478, 1[3] speaks about the qualifications of a vicar general. These qualifications are straightforward: he must be at least a priest, thirty years of age, degreed or very knowledgeable in the Church sciences,[4] and possess those personal qualities which the exercise of the office requires.

Vicar General — 2

Canon 479, 1 and 3,[5] speaks of the authority of the vicar general.[6] The authority of the vicar general is ordinary since it is attached by canon law to this ecclesiastical position.[7] However, it is vicarious since he is exercising this power on behalf of the diocesan bishop. The vicar general has executive power and has authority to deal with all the administrative acts in the diocese, except for the provisions of canon 134, 3 and for the ones which the diocesan bishop may decide to reserve to himself. On the other hand, he does not have the authority to pass laws[8] and should follow the norms listed in canons 136 to 144 when he ex-

---

[1] C. 475 is based on *CD* 27 and *ES* I, 14, 1. See *Navarre*, 353-356.

[2] C. 477 is based on *ES* I, 14, 2 and 5. See also *Navarre*, 354, n. 477.

[3] C. 478, 1 is based on *ES* I, 14, 2.

[4] The Code specifically states that the vicar general should have a doctorate or licentiate in either canon law or theology. However, c. 478, 1 also states that a mastery of either would suffice for those who are not degreed.

[5] C. 479, 2 deals with the episcopal vicar and not with the vicar general. See also *Navarre*, 355-356, n. 479.

[6] C. 479 is based on *ES* I, 14, 2.

[7] C. 131, 1.

[8] See cc. 7-22 which speak about the general principles of law, and c. 30 which speaks about the limits on one who possesses executive power. In this instance, these apply to the vicar general. See *Navarre*, "Ecclesiastical Laws," 84-85; 98, n. 30.

ercises his ordinary executive power. The Code is very precise in stating when certain acts which are based on ordinary power rest solely in the authority of the diocesan bishop. In this case, the vicar general does not have the power to perform such acts. Hence, when a law uses the phrase *diocesan bishop*, it applies *only* to diocesan bishops. But when the phrase *ordinary of the place* is used, it includes the vicar general.[9] Moreover, a vicar general may receive all habitual faculties conceded to the diocesan bishop with the exception of the ones expressly designated to the diocesan bishop in the document of consignment from the Holy See.

Canon 480 stands to reason.[10] It states that the vicar general, in his capacity as the *alter ego* of the diocesan bishop, may never act contrary to the latter's mind, will or decisions.

Canon 481[11] deals with the cessation of the authority of the vicar general. This may be brought about in a number of ways: the expiration of the term of office,[12] or resignation,[13] or termination, or when the diocese becomes vacant. However, there is the exception when the vicar general is also an auxiliary bishop in that diocese. If the auxiliary bishop is removed from the office of vicar general, he must be appointed as an episcopal vicar. In the case when the diocese has become vacant, the auxiliary bishop loses his office but retains all the authority attached to that office until a new diocesan bishop takes over the leadership of the diocese. Then, the auxiliary bishop has to be reinstated to the office if he is to continue to exercise its authority.[14]

---

[9] This is in accordance with c. 134, 1.

[10] C. 480 is based on *ES* I, 14, 3.

[11] C. 481 is based on *ES* I, 24, 2 and 5.

[12] The expiration of the term does not take effect until the vicar general is notified in writing by the diocesan bishop. This is in accordance with c. 186.

[13] The resignation takes effect in accordance with c. 187 and c. 189, that is only after the diocesan bishop has been informed. The resignation does not have to be accepted in order to become effective.

[14] See c. 406 and c. 409. The canons are based on *CD* 26; *ES* I, 13, 2 and 3.

Episcopal Vicar

Another *alter ego* for the diocesan bishop is the *Episcopal Vicar*.[15] This notion of this office was introduced at Vatican II and stated in the conciliar document *Christus Dominus*.[16] Pope Paul VI implemented the conciliar imperative in *Ecclesiae sanctae*.[17] The norms of the document are incorporated in the 1983 Code's canons 475 to 481. There can be a number of episcopal vicars in a diocese.[18] The appointment of one or more episcopal vicars is an option for the diocesan bishop.

An episcopal vicar can be a priest or an auxiliary bishop. The requirements for this office are practically the same as those for a vicar general.[19] The authority of the episcopal vicar is also similar to that of the vicar general.[20] However, there are a few differences between the ecclesiastical offices. The vicar general shares with the diocesan bishop in the governance of the entire diocese. He has executive authority to the same extent as the diocesan bishop unless the latter reserves certain powers to himself. On the other hand, the power of governance of the episcopal vicar is limited to a particular region or a specialized kind of ministry or an ethnic group or rite within the diocese. His authority and responsibilities are limited to his mission.[21]

Vicar Forane — Dean

Every diocese is divided into parishes.[22] There are times when the geographical situation of some parishes helps them form a natural clus-

---

[15] Suggested readings: J. Penna, "The Office of Episcopal Vicar," *Proceedings of the Canon Law Society of America* (1990) 107-119; *Navarre*, 353-356; A. Verbrugghe, "The Figure of the Episcopal Vicar for Religious in the New Code of Canon Law," *The New Code of Canon Law*, 2: 705-742.

[16] *CD* 27.

[17] *ES* I, 14.

[18] C. 476. The canon is based on *CD* 23, 27; *ES* I, 14, 1.

[19] See chapter entitled, Vicar General — 1, n. 1.

[20] See the two chapters which deal with the vicar general.

[21] This notion is practically taken literally from *CD* 27.

[22] C. 374.

ter. However, whether the cluster parishes form a natural geographical boundary or not, the diocesan bishop may appoint a priest to assist him in the administration of a group of parishes in a certain district or locality called a *deanery* or *vicariate forane*.[23] There are a number of canons in the Code which deal with the office of dean or vicar forane. The principal canons are 553 to 555.

This office has a very long and rich history in the Church. Canon 553, 1[24] links the title of dean with the ancient title of *archpriest*. The title goes back to the fourth century. It was conferred on a priest who stood in for his bishop in matters which dealt with civil affairs and public worship.[25] The current law still demands that he be a priest since this is an ecclesiastical office which, according to canon 274, 1, has the power of jurisdiction. Furthermore, only the diocesan bishop may appoint a dean.

Canon 554[26] leaves it up to the discretion of the diocesan bishop to set the qualifications for this office. The term of office should be regulated by diocesan law. The diocesan bishop also has the power to remove a dean for a just cause.

Canon 555[27] lists the dean's authority, responsibilities and rights. In other words, this canon provides a job description of the office. Among the dean's responsibilities are those of promoting, coordinating, and supervising the common pastoral activities within his deanery. He also serves as a source of unity and encouragement to his brother priests.

The Code provides instances in which the dean is to be consulted by the diocesan bishop. Canon 524 states that the diocesan bishop should consult the dean in the process of deciding on the suitability of

---

[23] C. 553, 2 states that the appointment of the *dean* or *vicar forane* is made by the diocesan bishop, having consulted the priests ministering in that deanery or vicariate forane. Usually this is done by asking them, by voting, to recommend a priest to this office. The person who gets the most votes generally is appointed by the bishop as the dean of that district. No one but the diocesan bishop can make this appointment. C. 554, 1 explicitly states that the *dean* or *vicar forane* does not have to be a pastor.

[24] C. 553, 1 is based on *ES* I, 19, 1.

[25] See Broderick, "Archpriest," 51-52; *Navarre*, 402-403.

[26] C. 544 is based on *ES* I, 19, 1-2.

[27] C. 555 is based on *CD* 16 and 30; *ES* I, 19, 1. See also *CCC* 1586.

a prospective pastor in that deanery.[28] The diocesan bishop is encouraged to consult the dean of the area in the appointment of an associate pastor within that deanery.[29] These two canons make a lot of sense since the dean should know what are the pastoral and other needs of a given parish within his deanery. It might also be advantageous for the diocesan bishop to consult with the dean while he is conducting an inquiry for the possible removal of a pastor within that deanery.[30]

Finally, the dean may be consulted during a diocesan synod by the fact that he is to be a member of the said synod.[31]

Succession in the Diocese

Canon law provides a specific protocol which must be strictly followed when a diocese becomes vacant. Canon 409, 1 states that if there is a coadjutor bishop in the diocese, he immediately succeeds to the office of diocesan bishop, provided he has legitimately taken possession of the diocese. This occurs before his formal installation. The reason behind this canon is that up to the time when the 1983 Code went into force, a coadjutor bishop did not automatically have the right to succeed the diocesan bishop of the same diocese.[32]

The majority of the dioceses in the world do not have a coadjutor bishop. Hence, there is no automatic succession. It is not unusual to have a lapse of some time between the administration of one diocesan bishop and that of his successor. The Apostolic See requires time for research and discernment in choosing a new diocesan bishop, especially when the death of the diocesan bishop is untimely and sudden.

---

[28] C. 524 is based on *ES* I, 19, 2.

[29] C. 547. The canon is partially based on *ES* I, 19, 2; and 30, 2.

[30] Although c. 1742, 1 does not specify that the diocesan bishop should consult the dean in this procedure, the same canon prescribes that the diocesan bishop consult with two pastors drawn from the list which had been submitted by the presbyteral council.

[31] C. 463, 1, 70.

[32] J. Alesandro offers a good overview of the role of coadjutor bishops and auxiliary bishops in his "Section II: Particular Churches and their Groupings (cc. 368-572)" in *CLSA: Commentary*, 336-341. See also *Navarre*, 318, n. 409; 320-328.

It has already been stated that under certain circumstances, the college of consultors should choose a diocesan administrator within eight days of a vacant diocese.[33] During this time the vacant see has an interim government. Canon 419[34] supplies the normal chain of succession in a vacant diocese where there is no coadjutor bishop. If a diocese has more than one auxiliary bishop, the interim government goes to the senior auxiliary bishop by appointment. If there is only one auxiliary bishop, he takes over. If there is no auxiliary bishop, then the college of consultors govern the diocese up to eight days, that is until they elect a diocesan administrator, unless special provisions had already been provided by the Holy See.[35]

There can be a rare situation where the college of consultors are unable to elect a diocesan administrator within eight days. In this event, the provisions of canon 421, 2 become operative.

The Law of Residence — Introduction

It is very important that a pastor, whether shepherding a diocese or a parish, be accessible to his people not only when it comes to the administration of the sacraments but for other things as well, such as counseling, works of mercy, and so on. This is why the Code of Canon Law speaks about a bishop's, a pastor's and an associate pastor's residence, their vacation time, and their absence for other reasons. The historical background is that, especially in the Middle Ages, there were times when a bishop had more than one diocese under his care, and when a priest was pastor to more than one parish.

Usually these multiple dioceses or parishes assured their holder a substantial income. But it was impossible for such bishops or priests to be always in residence in every diocese or parish entrusted to their care. Needless to say, despite the Church's numerous attempts to limit

---

[33] See chapter entitled, Code and Diocesan Consultation — 2.

[34] C. 419 is based on *CD* 26; and *ES* I, 13, 3.

[35] For example, the Holy See may appoint as diocesan administrator the retiring diocesan bishop until his successor is named and takes possession of the diocese.

and eliminate the practice of being in possession of more than one diocese or parish, such situations were open to much abuse in the past. The law of residency effectively curtails such abuses. Nowadays there are some dioceses where it has become necessary to appoint the same pastor to more than one parish for some serious reason, such as a shortage of priests.

The Law of Residence — Bishops

Canon 395 speaks about the canonical requirements of residence for a diocesan bishop. The rationale behind this is that the bishop should always be solicitous to lead and meet the needs of that section of the People of God entrusted to him.[36] The canon is interrelated to other canons which deal with other clerics. Hence, canon 395 also applies to clerics in general,[37] auxiliary bishops in a diocese,[38] pastors,[39] priests who form a parish team ministry,[40] and parochial vicars.[41] Canon 395 of the 1983 Code is a simplification of the 1917 Code where absence without permission from a higher competent Church authority was allowed up to three months of every year.

The 1983 Code requires the personal presence of the diocesan bishop in his own diocese.[42] He can be absent up to one month,[43] whether continuous or interrupted, for a just cause.[44] This absence does not include the *ad limina Apostolorum*[45] visit and attendance at either

---

[36] See *Navarre*, 310, n. 395.

[37] See c. 283.

[38] See c. 410.

[39] See c. 533.

[40] See c. 543, 2, 1°.

[41] See c. 550. Parochial vicars are also known as associate pastors.

[42] See c. 395, 1.

[43] See c. 395, 2.

[44] The Code does not specify the cause.

[45] The *ad limina Apostolorum* visit has an ancient history. Nowadays it takes place every five years when the diocesan bishop is required to submit to the proper authorities in Rome his five-year report on the status of his diocese. At this time he is also to venerate the tombs of St. Peter and St. Paul and meet personally with the Pope (cc. 399-400). See *CLSA: Commentary*, 335.

councils or synods of bishops or conference of bishops or any other office or ecclesiastical mission entrusted to him. Through a parallel canon,[46] the time the diocesan bishop spends on retreat is not counted as part of his month's vacation.

Canon 395, 3 states that unless there is a serious and urgent reason, the diocesan bishop is to be present in his diocese for Christmas, Holy Week, the Easter Triduum, Pentecost, and Corpus Christi.

Canon 395, 4 reflects a practical aspect of canon law. The 1917 Code had stated that the bishop could be absent from his diocese up to three months. The 1983 Code expanded this absence to six months. Under the current law, however, a real concern is not raised unless the diocesan bishop has an illicit absence for over six months. In this case, he can be disciplined in accordance with canon 1396. The canon deals with penalties for violation of the obligation of residence. The canon applies not only to diocesan bishops but also to coadjutor and auxiliary bishops,[47] pastors,[48] priests who form a parish team ministry,[49] and parochial vicars.[50]

The Code allows a certain discretion in its application of penalties, depending on the gravity of the offence for unjustifiable absences. If the person, however, is obstinate in not returning to his diocese or parish, he could be deprived of his office. In the case of pastors and parochial vicars, the diocesan bishop would take the initiative to impose penalties. In the case of a diocesan bishop, the metropolitan archbishop is to report the problem to the Holy See. It is up to the Holy See to impose penalties on a diocesan bishop.[51] There is nothing stated

---

[46] In this instance this means the application of another canon which has similar provisions under similar circumstances. The canon in question relating to this topic is c. 533, 2.

[47] C. 410 speaks about the residence of coadjutor and auxiliary bishops. See *Navarre*, 319, n. 410.

[48] C. 533, 1 speaks of the obligation of residence of individual pastors. See *CD* 30, 1.

[49] C. 543, 2, 1° speaks of the obligation of residence for priests who form a parish team ministry. This follows the directive of *CD* 30, 1. See also the chapter entitled, The Law of Residence — Priests, n. 56.

[50] C. 550 speaks of the obligation of residence for associate pastors or parochial vicars. It follows the directive of *CD* 30, 1.

[51] See c. 395, 4. See also c. 1396.

explicitly about penalties for the violation of residence by a coadjutor or auxiliary bishop. It is presumed that their diocesan bishop brings the problem to the attention of the Holy See, which alone can take appropriate action.[52]

The Law of Residence — Priests

Canon 533 speaks of the obligation of residence of the pastor of a parish. Canon 533, 1 states that he should reside in the parish house or rectory. However, there is a possibility where the *local ordinary*[53] can permit a pastor to reside elsewhere as long as he is accessible to the faithful entrusted to him. This law is very pertinent to the United States, where it is becoming more frequent that a pastor ministers to more than one parish. In this case the pastor should preferably reside in a house with other priests.

Canon 533, 2 states that a pastor is entitled to a month's vacation. He can also make an annual retreat. This is similar to canon 283, 2[54] which states that a cleric is entitled to make an annual retreat. The analysis of the canons pertaining to residence reveals that the Code is more strict about the absence of a pastor than that of the diocesan and the coadjutor and auxiliary bishops. Thus, if a pastor is to be absent for more than one week from his parish, even if he stays within his diocese, he is to notify the local ordinary. A pastor who seriously violates the obligation of residence falls under the provisions of canon 1396.[55]

According to canon 543, 2, 1°, priests who form a parish team ministry,[56] are bound by the same law of residence as that applying to a pastor.

---

[52] This is one of the *major causes* reserved to the Apostolic See. The latter is the only one which may adjudicate a bishop (c. 1405, 1, 3°).

[53] See chapter entitled, Vicar General — 2.

[54] C. 283, 2 follows the directive of *PO* 20.

[55] See chapter entitled, The Law of Residence — Bishops.

[56] These priests are sometimes, and incorrectly called co-pastors. These priests are in charge of the parish *in solidum*, that is, *as one*. They have the same duties, functions,

Canon 550[57] speaks about the obligation of residence required of parochial vicars. The law requirements are identical to those for a pastor, even when a parochial vicar is ministering to more than one parish.[58]

---

and responsibilities as a pastor (c. 543, 1). A parish can only have one pastor at a given time.

[57] C. 550 is based on *CD* 30, 1.

[58] See c. 533. See also *Navarre*, 398-401, n. 545-552.

5. Conferences and Synods of Bishops

Conferences of Bishops — Introduction

Conferences of bishops are groupings of bishops and are found all over the world. Every Latin Rite diocese in the world belongs to a specific conference of bishops. The grouping of bishops in the United States is called the *National Conference of Catholic Bishops* or the *NCCB*.[1] It is frequently mentioned from pulpits, in Church bulletins, and the news media. The term refers to all the Latin Rite Catholic bishops in the United States as a group.[2] The National Conference of Catholic Bishops is comprised solely of these bishops who, as a unit, exercise pastoral authority for the faithful within the States. Other countries and ecclesiastical regions in the world have their own conference of bishops. They exist in accordance with the dictates of the 1983 Code of Canon Law. The conference of bishops in the United States also has a civil counterpart. It is known as the *United States Catholic Conference or the USCC*.[3] Its membership, unlike the National Conference of Catholic Bishops, is not limited to bishops.

The National Conference of Catholic Bishops meets twice a year. The November meeting always takes place in the nation's capital, Washington, D.C. The other gathering is held in June and can meet anywhere in the United States.

The notion that all the Catholic bishops in a nation or a specific

---

[1] See Broderick, "National Conference of Catholic Bishops," 416-417.

[2] The bishops of the Eastern Catholic Churches in the United States are invited to attend the NCCB meetings in the capacity of guests and not as members of the Conference.

[3] See Broderick, "United States Catholic Conference," 590-591.

territory meet on a regular basis is not new in the history of the Church.[4] While national synods or councils require certain strict legal procedures and involvement of Rome, the informal gatherings of bishops for pastoral planning have a long history of their own. For instance, the archbishops of France gathered on a regular basis from 1561 until the eve of the French Revolution in 1789. They addressed issues which involved Church-State relations, as well as items of common discipline in the Church in France. The bishops of Belgium began meeting since the establishment of the country's independence in 1830. The gathering of the German bishops has been regularized since 1867.[5] The United States archbishops began meeting on a regular basis in 1884. During World War I the archbishops and four delegates of the bishops met as the *National Catholic War Council*. After the war, the U.S. bishops resolved to meet on a regular basis as the *National Catholic Welfare Council*[6] and Rome approved their resolution in 1922.[7] The gatherings of bishops in different parts of the world were left to their own discretion until Vatican II.

The Council made obligatory the meetings of the bishops of a nation or in a region. The obligation is stated in the conciliar document *Christus Dominus*, 37-38. Pope Paul VI added further legal specifications of such meetings in his motu proprio *Ecclesiae sanctae*.[8] Finally, the obligation was incorporated in the new Code which dictates that each conference of bishops must meet at least once a year.[9] The canons which cover the conferences of bishops are essentially canons 447-459.[10]

---

[4] T. Reese's books *Episcopal Conferences: Historical, Canonical, and Theological Studies* (edited), and *A Flock of Shepherds: The National Conference of Catholic Bishops*, give an exhaustive history of these conferences.

[5] See F. Carroll, *The Development of Episcopal Conferences*, 4-64.

[6] See Broderick, "National Catholic Welfare Conference," 416.

[7] See *CLSA: Commentary*, 363-364; P. Huizing, "The Structure of Episcopal Conferences," *J* 28 (1968) 164-165; R. Kutner, *The Development, Structure and Competence of the Episcopal Conference* (1972) 3-37; E. McKeown, "The National Bishops' Conference: An Analysis of Its Origin," *The Catholic Historical Review* 66 (1980) 565-583.

[8] *ES* I, 41.

[9] C. 453.

[10] See *Navarre*, 338-346. Other canons which refer to conferences of bishops are: c. 206, c. 788 and c. 851 (catechumenate); c. 221 (administrative courts); c. 221 and c. 1733

Conferences of Bishops — 1

The Code makes it very clear that a *conference of bishops* is different from any other assembly of bishops, be it local or regional or worldwide. Its power is limited. No decision can be made by the conference which would bind a diocesan bishop who does not agree with it.[11]

A quick review of the canons indicates the following:

(a) Only the Apostolic See or an Ecumenical Council[12] can erect or suppress or change or modify conferences of bishops. Once established, a conference of bishops enjoys automatic public juridic personality[13] so that it continues to exist even when the bishops forming that conference are not meeting as a body.[14]

(conciliation procedures); c. 284 (clerical attire rules); c. 278, c. 298, c. 299 and c. 312 (approval of associations of Christian faithful); c. 312 (establishment of associations of Christian faithful); c. 305 and c. 323 (supervision of associations of Christian faithful); c. 320 and c. 326 (suppression of associations of Christian faithful); c. 337 (college of bishops); c. 360 and c. 775 (catechesis); c. 377 (diocesan bishops); c. 433 and c. 435 (ecclesiastical regions); c. 439 and c. 441 (councils); c. 502 (college of consultors); c. 523 (appointment of pastors); c. 755 and c. 844 (ecumenical responsibility); c. 809, c. 810, c. 812 and c. 818 (colleges and universities); c. 830 (censorship); c. 852, c. 854 and c. 867 (baptism); c. 891 (age of confirmation); c. 902 and c. 905 (concelebration); c. 964 (location for confessions); c. 1000 (ritual for anointing of the sick); c. 1253 (days of penance); and c. 1274 (clerical support).

[11] See H. Muller, "The Relationship between the Episcopal Conference and the Diocesan Bishop," *J* 48 (1988) 111-129.

[12] According to the teachings of Vatican II and their faithful reflection in the Code, the Apostolic See and the College of Bishops assembled in an Ecumenical Council are the two subjects of Supreme Authority in the Church. According to c. 361 the "Apostolic See" includes the Pope himself and those Roman Curia offices which assist him in his ministry of primacy in the Universal Church. For the presentation and discussion of the meaning of "Supreme Authority in the Church," see *LG*, "Explanatory Note." See also *CLSA: Commentary*, 259, 261-263, 265-266, 268, 277; *Navarre*, "Bishops' Conference," 338-339; K. Rahner, "The Hierarchical Structure of the Church, with Special Reference to the Episcopate," *Commentary on the Documents of Vatican II*, I:186-216; idem., "On the Relationship between the Pope and the College of Bishops," *Theological Investigations* 10, 50-70; J. Ratzinger, "Announcements and Prefatory Note of Explanation," *Commentary on the Documents of Vatican II*, I: 297-305.

[13] C. 114 states how juridic persons are established in the Church. C. 115 presents the types of juridic persons in the Church. C. 116 states what constitutes public and private juridic persons in the Church. See also chapter entitled, Personality in the 1983 Code.

[14] C. 449. The canon is based on *CD* 38, 5.

(b) The Code is very elastic about the territory which can be covered by a specific conference. Hence, conferences may be either national or international in character.[15]

(c) Bishops who exercise a pastoral responsibility or have a particular function within the territory, and those equivalent to them in law as stated in canon 368,[16] are the only members of a conference of bishops.[17] Consequently, bishops lose their membership upon retirement. However, a particular conference of bishops can make other provisions.

The review of the pertinent canons to this subject continues in the next chapter.

Conferences of Bishops — 2

The following are further regulations provided by the Code in regard to conferences of bishops:

(d) Every conference is a public juridic person. As such, each conference must have its own statutes[18] which define its purpose, constitution, government, and operation.[19] Although each conference writes its own statutes, they must be approved by the Holy See.[20] Among the issues which the statutes should determine are who and what kind of voting power each bishop possesses, though diocesan bishops and those equiva-

---

[15] C. 448. This canon is based on *CD* 38, 1 and 5.

[16] C. 368 is based on *LG* 13, 23, 26; *CD* 11; *AG* 19. See also *CCC* 761, 804, 814, 831, 833-836, 882, 886, 887, 893, 938, 1202, 1312, 1462, 1548, 1569, 1561.

[17] See c. 447 and c. 450. These two canons are based on *LG* 23; *CD* 3, 37, 38. See also *CCC* 833, 835, 882, 886, 887, 938, 1202, 1560.

[18] See c. 117.

[19] See c. 94, 1. This is in accordance with *CD* 38, 3, and *ES* I, 41, 1-2.

[20] C. 451. The canon is based on *CD* 38, 3; and *ES* I, 41, 1 and 2.

lent to them and coadjutor bishops[21] must always have a deliberative vote.[22]

(e) Each conference must have officers,[23] a permanent council,[24] and meet at least once a year.[25]

(f) A conference may issue pastoral decrees.[26] It has the authority to do so for the faithful living within its territory[27] as long as they have been approved by two-thirds of the bishops who have a deliberative vote.[28] The content of such a decree becomes binding after it has been reviewed by the Holy See and properly promulgated.[29]

(g) A copy of the minutes and acts of each conference are forwarded to the Congregation for Bishops in Rome.

(h) A conference of bishops has the responsibility to convoke a plenary or national council, to choose the location for the gathering, to select its president,[30] and to determine its agenda.[31]

(i) A conference is to determine the number of major superiors of religious institutes of men and women who are to attend and participate in the national councils.[32]

---

[21] The 1983 Code states that coadjutor bishops have the right to succession and will automatically succeed to the see when it becomes vacant (c. 403, 3, and c. 409, 1). Auxiliary bishops and titular bishops and archbishops do not possess this right.

[22] C. 450 and c. 454. Both canons are based on *CD* 38, 2.

[23] See c. 452 which speaks about the president, vice-president, and the other officers of each conference.

[24] C. 451 and c. 457. These canons are based on *CD* 38, 3; and *ES* I, 41, 1 and 2.

[25] C. 453.

[26] C. 455. The canon is based on *LG* 27 and *CD* 38, 4. See also *CCC* 894-896.

[27] This is in accordance with c. 29. These general decrees, upon proper approval, become particular law.

[28] The 2/3 majority of those who have a deliberative vote is needed whether such persons are present for the vote or not. Hence, there are instances when voting has to be done by mail.

[29] The conference itself determines how such decrees are promulgated. Unless otherwise stated they go into effect one month after promulgation (c. 8, 2, and c. 455, 3).

[30] The president of every conference of bishops must be a diocesan bishop and have received approval from Rome.

[31] C. 441.

[32] C. 443, 3, 2°.

(j) Conferences elect and send their own representatives to the World Synod of Bishops.[33]

(k) Each conference determines the maximum amount of money which a diocesan bishop may use in administering Church possessions and spending without having recourse to the conference and of a higher amount for similar purposes without seeking permission from the Apostolic See.[34]

Code, Conferences of Bishops, Missions — 1

The purpose of the next three chapters is to present how the 1983 Code of Canon Law, in the spirit of Vatican II and the papal document *Ecclesiae sanctae*,[35] contains norms relating to the missionary activity of the Church. The specific norms which deal with this subject matter are canons 781-792. The canons clearly indicate that current Church law is rooted not only in past Church laws but also in Church teachings and theology, particularly those of Vatican II and recent papal teachings.

Canon 781 speaks about the fundamental missionary activity of the Church. The proclamation of the Good News is the responsibility of every Church member since every Catholic is entrusted with a missionary role at the time of baptism. This is reinforced at confirmation. The canon is rooted in the conciliar document *Ad gentes* 2, 35, 39,[36] as well as other conciliar and post-conciliar documents.[37]

Canon 782 explicitly states that it is the responsibility of the bishops to stimulate and supervise official missionary activity.[38] References

---

[33] C. 346, 1.

[34] C. 1279 and c. 1281. See also chapter entitled, Code and Diocesan Consultation — 4, nn. 61 and 62; *Navarre*, 792, n. 1279; 793-794, n. 1281.

[35] The motu proprio *Ecclesiae sanctae* was issued by Pope Paul VI on 6 August 1966.

[36] See also *CCC* 248, 257, 294, 767, 850, 868.

[37] For example, the conciliar documents *DH* 13, and *LG* 23, and the post-conciliar document *EN* 9-15, 50-56. See also *CCC* 833, 835, 843, 882, 886, 887, 938, 1202, 1560.

[38] See *Navarre*, 512-513, n. 782.

to this may be found in the conciliar documents *Ad gentes* 6, 29, 38, *Christus Dominus* 6, and *Lumen Gentium* 23 and 24.[39] The canon, however, does not mention any role for the conferences of bishops, although *Ad gentes* 31 and 39, and *Ecclesiae sanctae* III, 3-11, assign them special roles.[40]

Canon 783 speaks about the serious obligation for members of institutes of consecrated life (women and men religious) to share in the missionary activity of the Church. This canon is rooted in the conciliar documents *Lumen Gentium* 44, *Ad gentes* 15, 18, 23, 27, and *Perfectae Caritatis* 20; as well as Pope Paul VI's *Ecclesiae sanctae* III, 10-12.[41]

Canon 784 supplies the canonical definition of what it means to be a missionary: a believer in Christ who is sent to the missions by a legitimate ecclesiastical superior. Although this definition is rooted in *Ad gentes* 23, it is not as rich in its meaning as the conciliar definition which includes such elements as a calling by the Lord and one being a minister of the Gospel.[42]

Canon 785, 1 describes lay catechists, their formation process, their type of lifestyle, and their mission. The basic source of this canon is *Ad gentes* 17, 26 and 35.[43] This directive can also be applicable to those persons involved in the R.C.I.A. program as well as those who teach religion. Canon 785, 2 presents a more detailed form of what was stated in canon 785, 1.[44]

Canon 786 provides the definition of missionary activity and states when the Church in a particular region or country ceases to be a strict missionary territory in the usual sense one understands mission lands to be. This canon is rooted in *Lumen Gentium* 17 and *Ad gentes*

---

[39] This is also reiterated in the apostolic constitution *REU* 82. See also *CCC* 767, 830, 833, 835, 854, 882, 886, 887, 938, 1560, 1202, 1551, 1560, 2068.

[40] Though c. 782 does not refer to the special role of the conferences of bishops, the directives remain in effect. See *CLSA: Commentary*, 560.

[41] The obligation is also mentioned in *EN* 69. See also *CCC* 854, 905, 914, 933, 1270; *Navarre*, 513, n. 783-783.

[42] See also *CCC* 849, 853-854, 1270.

[43] See also *CCC* 6-10, 906, 1697, 2688; *Navarre*, 513-514, n. 785.

[44] The directive was implemented by *ES* III, 18, 24. See also *CCC* 854.

6 with its following paragraphs.[45] The descriptive terms in the canon are borrowed from *Ad gentes* 6.

The entire canon 787 delineates further the activity and mission of a missionary person. The canon addresses those missionaries who live in what Christians perceive to be pagan territories. Canon 787, 1 speaks about the local Church's dialogue with non-believers. The exchange should take place at the latter's level of cultural relevance and understanding so that it may lead to the eventual understanding of the Gospel message.[46] The missionary should never attempt to westernize such cultures and peoples as a prelude to conversion to the Catholic Faith. Consequently, there is a great need for the missionary to understand the local culture and to speak the local language or dialect. This directive is rooted in *Ad gentes* 11 and 12.[47] Canon 787, 2 addresses the issue of the instruction in the faith of those who are judged ready to accept Christianity. It reflects the conciliar teaching in *Dignitatis humanae* 2 and 3, and *Ad gentes* 13.[48]

Code, Conferences of Bishops, Missions — 2

Once the seed of Christianity has been sown through missionary activity and prayer, there arrives a time when it grows within a person so that he or she may be received into the Catholic fold. Due to this, the role of the *catechumenate* and what follows[49] play a major role in the life of the Church. The 1983 Code, in its fidelity to Vatican II and the teachings of recent Popes, reflects this journey of faith.

The catechumenate was restored as a result of the teaching of Vatican II.[50] Canon 788[51] deals with the process of the catechumenate

---

[45] See also *CCC* 776, 830, 845, 1270, 1540, 2032; *Navarre*, 514-515, n. 786.

[46] See also *CCC* 854, 856, 2472; *Navarre*, 515, n. 787.

[47] The directive is reiterated in *EN* 51-53.

[48] See also *CCC* 1738, 1782, 2104, 2106.

[49] The period after the Rite of Initiation is called the *Mystagogia*. See also *CCC* 1075.

[50] See *SC* 64-65. See also *CCC* 1229, 1230, 1232, 1249, 1258-1260.

[51] C. 788 is based on *AG* 13 and 14. The establishment of the catechumenate was implemented by *ES* III, 18. See also *CCC* 1233, 1248, 1249.

which must be faithfully implemented. Canon 788, 3 empowers the conferences of bishops to issue regulations on the rights and duties of catechumens. *Ad gentes* and the papal document *Ecclesiae sanctae*, however, do not make any reference to this responsibility of the conferences of bishops. Hence, the canon's directive goes beyond that of the conciliar and papal documents.

Canon 789 speaks of the *Mystagogia* — the period of instruction which follows baptism.[52] The canon is rooted in *Ad gentes* 15. Upon analysis this canon lacks the richness of the conciliar document and also fails to include the latter's encouragement in fostering an ecumenical spirit in the neophyte.[53]

Canon 790, 1, divided into two sub-sections, speaks of the responsibility of the diocesan bishop living in mission lands.[54] The diocesan bishop is the guide and uniting force of the apostolate within his diocese. He is directed to coordinate the missionary life within his own diocese. Thus, he is to supervise all missionary activity and make formal contracts with those missionary communities working within his diocese so as to ensure and advance the welfare of both missions and missionaries. This directive reflects a sound practical approach in the relationship between the diocesan bishop and missionaries. Verbal or vague agreements may prove to be inadequate. Rather, binding contracts between the two subjects would ensure a smooth and just relationship. The canon, unfortunately, falls short of stating what *Ad gentes* 30 proposes: the bishop's relationship with missionaries in his diocese should evoke spontaneous zeal. Canon 790, 2 forcefully reminds all missionaries, including religious, of their responsibility to adhere to the diocesan bishop's directives within his diocese. This norm was stated by the Council in *Ad gentes* 30.[55]

---

[52] See n. 49.

[53] A neophyte is a convert from unbelief or a non-Christian religion to the Catholic faith.

[54] The directive is based on *AG* 30 and 32. It was implemented by *ES* III, 17.

[55] See *Navarre*, 516-517, n. 790.

Code, Conferences of Bishops, Missions — 3

The Code, in canon 791, shifts its attention from the diocesan bishops in missionary lands to the worldwide episcopate. The canon reflects the universal responsibility of the entire Church toward mission lands. The canon specifies some means through which every diocesan bishop should foster missionary cooperation. The rationale behind the canon is that a bishop is not ordained solely for his diocese but for the entire world and that the dioceses are united in *Communio*, that is in a bond of common faith, binding charity, and shared fraternity.[56] The canon is divided into four sections. It is based on *Ad gentes* 29, 38, 39, and *Ecclesiae sanctae* III, 3, 4, 5, 6, 8, 23, among other conciliar and post-conciliar documents. Section 1 of the canon charges the diocesan bishop to promote within his diocese missionary vocations to the clerical, religious and lay states in life. Bishops are encouraged to send overseas some of their better priests who volunteer for the missions, in accordance with the wishes of the Council.[57] Section 2 of the canon directs each diocesan bishop to appoint one of his priests in the capacity of diocesan director for the missions.[58] Section 3 of the canon calls for an annual Mission Day for the specific purpose of prayer, to heighten awareness of the missions, and to take up a collection for the missions.[59] The Church in the United States wholeheartedly meets this directive by being abundantly generous in offering financial support to the missions. Section 4 of the canon calls for a further annual monetary donation to be forwarded to the Holy See specifically for the support of missions.[60]

Canon 792 is solicitous for priests who come to a diocese from mission lands. It directs every conference of bishops to initiate and

---

[56] See the chapters entitled, Code and Laity — 3, and Code and Consultation — Introduction.

[57] See *AG* 30 and *ES* III, 5 and 6. See also *CCC* 849, 858-859.

[58] The directive is in accordance with *AG* 29 and *ES* III, 4.

[59] The directive is in accordance with *ES* III, 3.

[60] This directive is in accordance with *ES* III, 8.

foster means of providing hospitality and assistance to such priests who either study or do pastoral work within a conference's territory.[61]

Finally it should be noted that the 1983 Code speaks about the responsibility of the conferences of bishops in regard to the missions in two instances only: the regulation of the catechumenate as found in canon 788, 3 and canon 792. The other functions of the conferences of bishops listed in *Ad gentes* 38 and *Ecclesiae sanctae* III, especially the episcopal commission for missionary lands,[62] are missing from the Code.

Conferences of Bishops and the Missions — 1

There are many responsibilities which conferences of bishops have in the life of the Church. The relationship between these conferences and missionary activity is very important because the Church is missionary by nature in that Christ commissioned his disciples to "go and teach all nations."[63] The Council Fathers of Vatican II had this mission in mind when they spoke about conferences of bishops in the conciliar document *Ad gentes*.[64]

The terms *conferences of bishops* or *episcopal conferences* or wording to their equivalent appear in fourteen places in the aforementioned conciliar decree on the Church's missionary activity. These four chapters will enumerate and present a concise review of these references in this decree and how the directives came to be implemented in the postconciliar era.

One of the most effective means of expanding missionary ac-

---

[61] The canon is based on *AG* 38 and *ES* III, 23, which present the directive in the context of a diocesan bishop's responsibility instead of a conference of bishops per se. See also *CCC* 1560.

[62] *ES* III, 9.

[63] Mark 16:15.

[64] The conciliar document, known in English as the *Decree on the Church's Missionary Activity*, was published on December 7, 1965. The laws contained in the decree were to become effective on June 29th of the same year. See W. Abbott, *The Documents of Vatican II*, 630, note.

tivity was the reestablishment of the *Permanent Diaconate*. The diaconate is the first degree of the sacrament of Holy Orders. For many centuries in the first Christian millennium, men were ordained solely for the purpose of being *permanent* deacons.[65] Eventually ordination to the diaconate became perceived as the final step before ordination to the priesthood. Hence, the permanent diaconate fell into disuse. Vatican II, however, wanted to restore the ordained ministry of permanent diaconate. Thus, *Ad gentes* 16 directs the conferences of bishops to restore the sacramental Order of Permanent Diaconate where it is deemed opportune. The Council suggests that men who are either catechists or properly designated leaders of Christian communities, especially in mission lands, be evaluated as possible candidates for the permanent diaconate.[66]

Ad gentes 18 encourages the cultivation of various forms of religious life in the young mission churches.[67] It advises conferences of bishops to ensure that there be no needless multiplication of religious congregations which possess the same charism, lest religious life and the apostolate be adversely affected.

Ad gentes 20 directs conferences of bishops to provide priests, religious and lay religious leaders in mission lands with proper theological, spiritual and pastoral programs aimed at refreshing and updating such persons on a regular and permanent basis. The said conferences should also provide the clergy preparing for foreign missions with programs which equip them to carry out their mission in a specific culture. Hence, programs should entail the study of the local culture, religions, languages, customs, etc.[68] Furthermore, the conferences should form a common plan to meet and dialogue with groups of qualified ministers in mission lands.

---

[65] See Broderick, "Deacon," 153-154.
[66] See idem., "Permanent Deacon," 471-472. See also *CCC* 1536, 1543, 1569-1571, 1588, 1593, 1596, 1630.
[67] See also *CCC* 931.
[68] See also *CCC* 854.

Conferences of Bishops and the Missions — 2

Ad gentes 22 speaks about a coordinated effort. Thus, the Council Fathers direct those conferences of bishops which exist within the same socio-cultural milieu to coordinate among themselves a common effort to adapt the Christian message to the indigenous cultures.

Ad gentes 26 expresses the desire of the Council Fathers for regional conferences of bishops in mission lands to have an abundance of highly qualified personnel. The areas of expertise should be in the sacred and social sciences, as well as in indigenous languages, history, and customs. Experts in these areas should be utilized with eagerness. This directive is a logical follow-up of what is said in paragraph 20.

Ad gentes 29 states that all missions and missionary activities fall solely under the competence of the Congregation for the Propagation of the Faith. It calls for the reform of the said Congregation.[69] Thus, there is to be a consultation process with the worldwide episcopate for this purpose. The reform is to take into account the proposals of the worldwide conferences of bishops and their representatives. There are to be meetings, under the authority of the Pope, called at fixed intervals for consultation.

Ad gentes 31 charges all conferences of bishops to coordinate jointly their efforts to direct, promote, and pool together their resources for worldwide missionary activities.

Ad gentes 32 speaks about the expiration of the commission for missionary activity given to religious communities in a particular region or country. It calls for dialogue between the pertinent conference of bishops and the religious communities. They should jointly deliberate and draw up new norms governing the relations between the di-

---

[69] The projected reform in organization and function of the Congregation *Propaganda Fidei* took form in two stages. The first one was brought about through Pope Paul VI's apostolic constitution, *Regimini Ecclesia universae* of August 15, 1967. At the time the name of the Congregation was slightly changed to that of the Sacred Congregation for the Evangelization of People. The second stage of reform was enacted through Pope John Paul II's apostolic constitution, *Pastor Bonus* of June 28, 1988.

ocesan bishop and such communities. These norms are to be based on the outline of general principles drawn up by the Holy See.

Ad gentes 33 also calls for active communication. It directs the conferences of bishops and the conferences of men and women religious of the same region or country to enter into a close dialogue. They are to discern and implement the best combined efforts in setting up programs which prepare and equip missionaries as well as promote missionary activity.

Finally, the Council Fathers, in *Ad gentes* 38, encourage bishops in non-missionary countries to send some of their diocesan priests as missionaries. The conferences of bishops are to jointly coordinate the training of these future missionaries. Likewise, they should give a fraternal welcome and due pastoral care to those priests who come to their region from missionary lands to either study or perform pastoral ministry.

So, through these directives, Vatican Council II promotes unity, dialogue, and coordination among conferences of bishops in meeting the Lord's commission to his disciples: "Go forth and teach all nations."[70]

Conferences of Bishops and the Missions — 3

Pope Paul VI responded with great fervor to the directives on missionary activity expressed by the Council Fathers of Vatican II in the decree *Ad gentes*. He issued an apostolic letter called, *Ecclesiae sanctae*.[71] Section III of this papal document speaks about the implementation of the Council's said decree in regard to conferences of bishops. Thus, the next two chapters contain references to both documents in order to show how the directives of Vatican II were put into practice through papal mandate.

---

[70] See also *CCC* 849, 858-859.

[71] The apostolic letter *Ecclesiae sanctae*, issued on August 6, 1966, contained provisional laws which were to be observed for the fulfillment of the decrees of Vatican Council II until the promulgation of the revised Code of Canon Law. The new Code was promulgated in 1983.

The terms *conferences of bishops* or *episcopal conferences* or wording to their equivalent appear eight times in *Ecclesiae sanctae*, section III. Each reference is being examined.

Pope Paul VI, in *Ecclesiae sanctae* III, 2, invites all of the worldwide conferences of bishops to immediately forward to the Holy See general questions related to missionary activity so that they would be considered at the then upcoming first Synod of Bishops.[72] This indicates that, in accordance with *Ad gentes* 29, every conference of bishops should have a worldwide missionary concern. Every diocesan bishop should be concerned not only with what is happening in his own diocese but also extend his concern to the entire People of God.[73] Every member of the Catholic Church should have a similar worldwide missionary concern.

Ecclesiae sanctae III, 3, directs each conference of bishops to include various invocations for the missions in the newly established rite of the Prayer of the Faithful at Mass.[74] This is another instance where every Catholic is reminded to have a worldwide missionary concern as had been indicated in *Ad gentes* 36.

Pope Paul VI, in *Ecclesiae sanctae* III, 9, directs each conference of bishops to set up a commission for the missions. Its aim is to foster missionary activity and awareness, as well as coordinate these efforts among the dioceses which form each conference of bishops. Furthermore, these commissions are to be in contact with one another and distribute missionary aid according to needs. The background of this directive is *Ad gentes* 27. The document underscores the importance of open and continuous communication between the worldwide conferences of bishops.

---

[72] See chapter entitled, Synod of Bishops — Introduction.

[73] See chapters dedicated to Code, Conferences of Bishops, Missions.

[74] *SC* 53 called for the restoration of this ancient rite.

Conferences of Bishops and the Missions — 4

Pope Paul VI, in his attempt to implement the directives of the conciliar document *Ad gentes*, states in *Ecclesiae sanctae* III, 15, that every conference of bishops was to propose representatives to take part in the then upcoming projected reform of the Congregation for the Propagation of the Faith.[75] The main purpose of the Congregation was to care for the administration and expansion of all the missions. The representatives were to have a deliberative vote. This papal directive is in compliance with *Ad gentes* 29.

Ecclesiae sanctae III, 17, directs the Congregation for the Propagation of the Faith to consult, among other Church bodies, the conferences of bishops. Afterwards the Congregation is to outline general principles to serve as instructions for agreements between diocesan bishops and missionary religious communities in their mutual negotiations. This is of singular importance when contracts regarding missionary activities are about to expire or have to be renegotiated. This directive is in compliance with *Ad gentes* 32.

Ecclesiae sanctae III, 18, directs conferences of bishops in missionary lands to unite into an organic group according to their sociocultural heritage. This reflects *Ad gentes* 22 and 29. Such conferences are to coordinate their efforts with the Congregation for the Propagation of the Faith in the areas of (1) acculturation of missionaries as stated in *Ad gentes* 10, 11, 22;[76] (2) proper adaptation of the Christian faith, Church teachings and liturgy to the indigenous people as directed by *Ad gentes* 11, 13, 14;[77] (3) improved methods of evangelization and catechesis as found in *Ad gentes* 19; (4) proper understanding of one's commitment to the religious life as stated in *Ad gentes* 18; (5) a constant theological and sociological updating for those involved in mission work as taught in *Ad gentes* 16;[78] (6) distribution of missionaries according to the local needs.

---

[75] See chapter entitled, Conferences of Bishops and The Missions — 2, n. 69. Suggested reading: J. Provost, "Local Church and Catholicity in the Constitution *Pastor Bonus*," *J* 52 (1992) 299-334.

[76] See also *CCC* 856, 2472.

[77] Ibid.

[78] See also *CCC* 1570-1571.

In conclusion, it is evident from the papal document that the conferences of bishops have a worldwide responsibility in meeting the Lord's command: "Go forth and teach all nations."

Synod of Bishops — Introduction

Since the early times of the Church, its bishops — known by a variety of titles — have gathered together in specific places and for specific reasons, mainly to refute heresies, discuss doctrine, set Church policies, and establish or restore discipline which affected either the entire Church or specified Christian communities. The gatherings of bishops in the form of Ecumenical Councils and the other kind of gatherings of bishops of a specific region or country or countries can all be referred to as *Synods*.

The first Synod ever called in Church history is known as the Council of Jerusalem or the Apostolic Council, held around the year 51 A.D. It is mentioned in the Acts of the Apostles 15. It was convoked by the Apostles, under the leadership of Peter. This Synod set a number of policies which had both temporary as well as far-reaching consequences. For instance, a decision which had a limited and immediate effect was that Christians did not have to follow the Jewish dietary laws. On the other hand, the most far-reaching consequential decision was that no Gentile was required to become a member of the Jewish faith before embracing Christianity.

An *Ecumenical Council* is a *Synod*. Thus, Vatican Council II can be referred to as the Vatican II Synod. An Ecumenical Council is usually[79] convoked by the Pope[80] who formally gathers together the bishops of the world, presides over the gathering in person or through his legates, and gives papal confirmation to its decrees which bind all Catholics. The first Ecumenical Council was that of Nicaea in 325 A.D. and the last to date was Vatican Council II (1963-65). There have been

---

[79] The earlier Ecumenical Councils were not convoked by the Pope but their decrees were eventually confirmed by him, making them binding on all Catholics.

[80] The proper title for the Pope in the Code of Canon Law is *Roman Pontiff*.

22 such Councils or Synods. However, it was not until 1123 that the first Ecumenical Council[81] held in the West was directly convoked by the Pope (Callistus II), who personally presided over it.[82]

Another kind of Synod is the gathering of bishops of a specific region or country. The Synods of Baltimore are examples of such gatherings. They consisted of seven provincial and three plenary councils between 1829 and 1884. The last plenary council produced the famous *Baltimore Catechism* which influenced the American Catholic believer until the convocation of Vatican Council II.[83] A recent example of a Synod for a number of countries is the Synod of Africa. The third through the seventh centuries witnessed a number of historic local Synods assembled in Northern Africa.[84]

A new kind of Synod emerged as a result of the wish expressed by the Council Fathers of Vatican II.[85] These gatherings are referred to as a *Synod of Bishops*. Pope Paul VI established the Synod of Bishops through the apostolic letter motu proprio *Apostolica sollicitudo* of September 15, 1965. This kind of Synod met for the first time in 1967. Such Synods are convoked by the Pope, usually presided over by three delegates personally chosen by him, meet in Rome, and involve bishops and other representatives from all over the world.

Synod of Bishops — 1

The 1983 Code of Canon Law, in canons 334 and 342-348, legislates on the Synod of Bishops. As indicated in the introductory chapter, the institute of this particular kind of Synod is new in the Church. Pope Paul VI established it in 1965. The notion arose from Vatican II's deliberations and eventual decision that some means were to be es-

---

[81] This Council is known as Lateran I. It was held in March and April, 1123.

[82] See Abbott, 740; Broderick, "Ecumenical Councils," 181. See also L. Pivonka, "The Revised Code of Canon Law: Ecumenical Implications," *J* 45 (1985) 533-534.

[83] See Broderick, "Synods of Baltimore," 63-64.

[84] See Broderick, "African Councils," 27; ibid., "Carthage, Councils of," 95.

[85] See *CD* 5.

tablished to ensure the continuation of communication between the Pope and the worldwide episcopate once the Council was over. According to *Apostolica sollicitudo* I, the *Synod of Bishops* was to be a[86] central Church organism in Rome, representative of the entire Catholic episcopate,[87] permanent in character, consultative in nature, and subject directly and immediately to the Pope.[88] Its nature is to give counsel to the Pope, on whom it has complete dependence.[89] The Synod of Bishops could be comprised of a General Assembly,[90] or an Extraordinary Assembly,[91] or a Special Assembly.[92] These characteristics are now included in the canons of the 1983 Code. However, the Code omits some of the elements enumerated in the papal document, *Apostolica sollicitudo*.

The Code states that the Synod of Bishops, in some measure, is representative of the entire episcopate. Consequently, when the Extraordinary Synod of Bishops meets it is also, to a certain extent, an elected body.

Canon 334 addresses the issue of the Synod of Bishops' assistance to the Pope in exercising his primacy.[93] The Synod serves as a principal means to do so. The canon makes subtle distinctions among the means which are used by the Pope to assist him in exercising his primacy. It indicates that the other institutes mentioned in it, such as the College of Cardinals and the Roman institutes,[94] assist the Pope

---

[86] The Synod of Bishops is *one* organism or institute among other institutes in Rome. However, the nature of the Synod of Bishops is quite different than most, if not all, of the other institutes in Rome. See G. Fransen, "New Code — New Perspective," *J* 45 (1985) 370-371; *Navarre*, 266-267, n. 334; 270-275; J. Schotte, "The Synod of Bishops: A Permanent yet Adaptable Church Institution," *SCa* 26 (1992) 289-306.

[87] Representation at the Synod of Bishops is not limited to the Roman Rite but includes the Oriental Churches.

[88] See *AS* I:1-4.

[89] See *AS* II, 1.

[90] See *AS* II, 5.

[91] See *AS* II, 6.

[92] See *AS* II, 7.

[93] C. 334 is based on *CD* 10. See also *REU* 1; *CCC* 834, 877, 879, 882, 886, 891, 937-939, 2051.

[94] The Roman Curia, Papal Legates and the Congregations are Roman institutes.

on a different level. Moreover, the nature of the Synod of Bishops has a different function than that of the Roman Curia.[95]

Canons 342-348 are a simplified version of *Apostolica sollicitudo*, from which they are derived. Canon 342 describes the Synod as a means to foster a closer unity between the Pope and the worldwide College of Bishops. The former, as a consultative body, is to assist the Pope in his governance of the Church, and as a body it is to address certain issues concerning the Church in the contemporary world. Although the canon is based on *Apostolica sollicitudo* I-II, it omits the latter's reference to "mutual assistance" between the Pope and the bishops as pertaining to the inner life of the Church. The canon also omits the representative function of the Synod for the universal Church, rather than for the Latin Rite Church only. *Apostolica sollicitudo* states this function and, as to date, these directives have been followed at every Synod of Bishops.

Canon 343 will be discussed in a subsequent chapter.[96]

Canon 344[97] refers to the direct authority of the Pope and the nature of the Synod of Bishops in six articles: 1. the Pope convokes the Synod; 2. he ratifies the elections of its members and appoints other members;[98] 3. he determines the topic for discussion; 4. he sets the agenda; 5. he presides over the Synod in person or through his representatives; and 6. he determines the fate of the Synod once it is assembled. The first five specifications in this canon follow rather carefully the provisions of *Apostolica sollicitudo*, but omit some details.[99]

Each delegate, though representing the viewpoint of his episcopal conference, speaks from his own pastoral and personal experience regarding a given issue on the agenda. Provision 6 in the canon is an addition to those found in *Apostolica sollicitudo*.

---

[95] See *CD* 9; *CLSA: Commentary*, 274. See also T. Rausch, "The Synod of Bishops: Improving the Synod Process," *J* 49 (1989) 245-257.

[96] See chapter entitled, Synod of Bishops — 3.

[97] C. 344 follows the directives of *AS* III.

[98] The Roman Pontiff may appoint up to 15% of the total assembly. See *AS* II, 10.

[99] For example, the canon omits the proportionality of representation by the episcopal conferences as stated in *AS* II, 8.

Synod of Bishops — 2

One of the foremost questions about the Synod of Bishops is: to what extent does the Synod represent all of the bishops in the Catholic Church when the Pope calls it to meet in Rome? Current Church law supplies the major part of the answer to the question.

Canon 345 states that there can be three types of Synod: Ordinary, Extraordinary, and Special. This canon is derived from the papal document motu proprio *Apostolica sollicitudo.*[100]

The issue of representation is perhaps best described in canon 346 which deals with membership. Canon 346, 1 states that when the Synod meets as a General Assembly, representation consists of the presidents and (proportionate) representatives of each of the episcopal conferences in the world, the heads of the departments of the Roman Curia, the Eastern Patriarchs, papal appointees,[101] and ten men religious elected by the unions of supreme moderators[102] of the clerical religious institutes.[103] Canon 346, 2 concerns the Extraordinary Session. Such a meeting is held when special attention and a speedy resolution are needed for a very important issue in the universal Church. Its membership is basically comprised of the presidents of various episcopal conferences, papal appointees, and three men (clerical) religious supreme moderators.[104] Canon 346, 3 addresses the issue of Special Synods. It states that membership selection for a Special Session is to be made from those areas for which the Special Synod has been convoked, i.e. to deal with the special problems in that particular region.[105]

---

[100] See *AS* II, 4. Note that what *AS* calls an "Assembly," the Code calls a "Session." Moreover, the Code calls "Ordinary Session" what *AS* calls "General Assembly."

[101] Papal appointees usually include women religious and lay persons.

[102] C. 346, 1 follows the provisions of *AS* V, VII, X, XII.

[103] There are religious institutes of men which are not clerical. See chapter entitled, Consecrated Life — 1, nn. 13, 14.

[104] C. 346, 2 follows the directives of *AS* VI. See also *CLSA: Commentary*, 284-285; *Navarre*, 273-274, n. 346.

[105] For example, Pope John Paul II held one of these meetings in 1980 with the Church in Holland to deal with specific issues affecting the Church in that country. C. 346, 3 follows what is stated in *AS* VII.

The Code presents different levels of representation of the Catholic episcopate.[106] Canon 346 begins with the notion that most of the Synod members in the Ordinary Session represent all of the episcopal conferences in the world. A decrease in representation occurs in the case of the Extraordinary Session since only the presidents of each episcopal conference participate. Finally, representation becomes more limited in the Special Session for such a synodal gathering logically contains more members from the region for which this kind of Synod was called and less representatives from the rest of the worldwide Catholic episcopate.

When all is said and done, it may be stated that the entire Catholic episcopate can bring its concerns by having perennial access to the permanent General Secretariat presided over by the papal appointed General Secretary who resides in Rome.[107] Further appointees by the Pope and elected experts assist the General Secretary in the preparations for the next Synod of Bishops. Canon 348, 1 dictates that the responsibility of these consultors ceases as soon as the next Synod convenes.[108]

Synod of Bishops — 3

There is a prevalent tendency to associate the governing power in the Catholic Church with the Pope and the bishops. Previous chapters presented how the Synod of Bishops is accountable directly to the Pope.[109] and that it represents all the Catholic bishops in the world.[110] But does a Synod have any authority to set policy for the Universal Church?

When establishing the Synod of Bishops, Pope Paul VI made it very clear that its nature was to give counsel to the Pope, on whom it

---

[106] This is in compliance with *AS* V-VIII, X, XII.

[107] This is in compliance with *AS* XII.

[108] This is in compliance with *AS* XII. See *Navarre*, 275, n. 348.

[109] See chapter entitled, Synod of Bishops — 1.

[110] See chapter entitled, Synod of Bishops — 2.

has complete dependence.[111] It is an agency of the papacy, delegated to provide advice to the Pope in his ministry of primacy. *Apostolica sollicitudo* distinguishes between a Synod of Bishops and an Ecumenical Council. Both bodies represent the entire Church. But when a Synod of Bishops issues a decree, it does not do so on its own authority because it is given such authority by the Pope. He needs neither to consult it nor is he bound to follow its counsel. Such a Synod has delegated authority. On the other hand, an Ecumenical Council issues decrees on its own authority which is not delegated by the Pope. These concepts are reflected in the Code.[112]

Canon 334 addresses the role of the Synod's assistance to the Pope in exercising his primacy.[113] The Latin text of the Code clearly identifies the Synod of Bishops as being the *principal* way to assist the Pope. The next sentence speaks of those who assist the Pope on a different level. Thus, for example, while the Cardinals as a body[114] and on an individual basis and other (Roman) institutes act in the name of the Pope, the Synod of Bishops does not. Three things emerge from this canon: the Synod is primarily conceived as a consultative body, it is principal among all the bodies consulted by the Pope, and it is not a legislative body.

Canon 342 reiterates that the Synod is a consultative body to assist the Pope.[115] The canon omits *Apostolica sollicitudo*'s reference to "mutual assistance" between the Pope and the bishops.[116]

Canon 343 speaks of the authority and competence of the Synod. Its resolutions are not decisions but must be sent to the Pope who decides what should be done next.[117] This canon reinforces the Synod's

---

[111] See *AS* II, 1.

[112] C. 341, 2 and c. 343 speak about the delegated authority of a Synod of Bishops. C. 341, 1 speaks about the authority of an Ecumenical Council. The canons follow the teaching in *LG* 22 and *AS* II.

[113] C. 334 is based on *CD* 10. See also *CCC* 877, 879, 2034, 2039; *Navarre*, 266-267, n. 334.

[114] That is, the institute of the College of Cardinals. See c. 349.

[115] The papal document follows the directives of *LG* 23 and *CD* 5. See *Navarre*, 271, n. 342.

[116] See *AS* I-II.

[117] C. 343 follows the directive of *AS* II. See *Navarre*, 271-272, n. 343.

consultative role. Even when a Synod is delegated to have a deliberative role, its decisions still require confirmation by the Pope. Nevertheless, the whole matter of consultation covers a very broad consideration of issues.

Canon 347, 2 reiterates the intimate dependence of a Synod on
the Pope by stating that if the See of Rome becomes vacant after a
Synod has been called, the Synod is suspended until such time that
the new Pope decides whether the Synod should continue, or its agenda
should be changed, or if it should be dissolved.

In summary, the institute of the Synod of Bishops was established
by Pope Paul VI in 1965 in response to Vatican II's request for an
ongoing communication between the Pope and all the bishops in the
Church. It is a papal agency, representative of the Catholic episcopate,
totally dependent on the Pope, and has a consultative vote. Even if the
Pope gives a Synod a deliberative vote, its decrees would become binding only upon their confirmation and promulgation by the Pope.

6. The Liturgy

Code and Liturgy — Introduction

A very clear instance where one can appreciate the diversity in ecclesial practices and unity in Church doctrine is the *Liturgy*. There are at least twenty-four different liturgical Rites in various degrees within the Roman Catholic Church. For example, the Eucharist can be celebrated in the Roman, Ambrosian, Mozarabic, and the twenty-one Eastern Churches' Rites. The contents of the following chapters deal with the 1983 Code and the Liturgy. They apply only to the *Roman Rite*.

Book IV of the 1983 Code of Canon Law is entitled, "The Office of Sanctifying in the Church." It runs from canon 834 to canon 1253.[1] These canons deal with the Church's life of prayer and how it is celebrated. They are *liturgical law* because they address the public exercise of worship, the glory of God, and the salvation of souls.[2] Liturgical laws are not confined to the Code of Canon Law.[3] They are also found in the official Roman[4] liturgical books,[5] rites,[6] and the in-

---

[1] One should keep in mind that these laws are applicable to the Latin Rite of the Church. Roman Catholics who belong to the Eastern Churches have their own liturgical norms.

[2] Suggested readings: *CLSA: Commentary*, 594-595, 596-597; J. Huels, *Disputed Questions in the Liturgy Today*; idem., *One Table, Many Laws*; idem., "The Interpretation of Liturgical Law," *Worship* 57 (1981) 218-236; E. Kilmartin, *Christian Liturgy*; F. McManus, *Thirty Years of Liturgical Renewal: Statements of the Bishops' Committee on the Liturgy*; Navarre, 545-546; R.K. Seasoltz, "The Sacred Liturgy: Development and Directives," *J* 43 (1983) 1-28. See also *CCC* 1084-1090.

[3] See c. 2 which states that liturgical law possesses its own autonomy.

[4] That is, the text has been issued by Rome. Usually the text is in Latin and then it is translated into the vernacular languages. C. 838, 2-3 states that the competent conference of bishops must procure the *recognition* from the Holy See for the translation of such books. In this case the authentic translation of the book belongs to

81

troductions to such documents.[7] Thus, there are codified (inside the Code) and non-codified (outside the Code) liturgical laws. All of the laws listed in these documents are universal liturgical laws. Liturgical laws listed outside the 1983 Code explain the theory behind the liturgical celebration, its implementation, the theological values, and so forth.[8] On the other hand, for the most part, the 1983 Code does not define or determine the rites themselves. Rather, the Code's main concern rests with who is involved, their qualifications and eligibility, the place, the time of celebration, the registration of a sacrament, and the requirements for a licit and valid celebration of the rite.

The Code is not really concerned with how to conduct a rite or the relationship between those who celebrate them. Codified liturgical laws are often concerned with the liturgy from the viewpoint of extrinsic discipline. Nevertheless, the sources of these canons are the liturgical books approved by Rome and the conciliar documents, particularly the constitution on the Sacred Liturgy, *Sacrosanctum Concilium*.

There are also particular liturgical laws. Such laws are found in the corresponding liturgical books of various nations and regions, as well as in decrees and statutes of dioceses and groups of dioceses which follow the Roman Rite.

---

the conference. However, if the competent conference of bishops seeks the approval of the Holy See, the latter becomes more involved and is deemed as the authentic authority which issues the translation. See *Navarre*, 549-551, n. 838.

[5] For example, the Sacramentary of the Mass. The primary focus of the liturgical books is on how to celebrate well a particular sacrament or liturgy. The liturgical books have been undergoing revision for the past few years so that their norms will follow the directives laid down in the 1983 Code. See *CLSA: Commentary*, 595-596.

[6] For example the Rite of Christian Burial. *Rite*, in this context, means either an approved religious function or ceremonies or prayers. See Broderick, "Rite," 527.

[7] The introductions are technically called *praenotanda*. These introductions are very important because they express the mentality of the Supreme Legislator, the Roman Pontiff, regarding the content of the document following the introduction, as well as the kind of, and reasons for, the changes.

[8] The larger part of liturgical law is found in the liturgical documents and not in the 1983 Code of Canon Law.

Code and Liturgy — 1

The Sanctifying Office of the Church in the 1983 Code is twofold: the holiness of the individual and the community, and worship. As can be seen from the many quotes and references to the documents of Vatican II, this part of the Code has been vastly shaped by the conciliar teachings.

Canon 834, 1 provides the definition of *liturgy* in the Church.[9] It is an all-embracing definition because it includes the celebration of the sacraments. Although the sanctifying office of the Church is broader than the Liturgy,[10] the Liturgy serves as the preeminent way of carrying it out.[11]

Canon 834, 2 makes a distinction between public and private worship. Public worship, whether on a community or individual level, is carried out in the name of the Church by an officially deputized person, that is, a baptized Catholic,[12] through acts which the competent Church authority has approved.[13] Liturgical actions are always celebrations of the Church rather than private actions.[14] It goes without saying that certain liturgical worship can be carried out only by the ordained.[15]

---

[9] C. 834, 1 is based on *SC* 7. See also *CCC* 1070, 1088, 1089, 1181, 1373; *Navarre*, 546, n. 834.

[10] The *liturgy* does not exhaust the prayer life of the Church. See c. 839, 1. See also *SC* 12, 13; *LG* 12; *CCC* 92, 93, 761, 785, 798, 801, 804, 814, 823, 831, 834, 836, 889, 951, 1303, 2003.

[11] See *SC* 13. See also *CCC* 1675.

[12] C. 834, 2 is based on *LG* 11; and *SC* 14. See also *CCC* 825, 1119, 1141, 1251, 1270, 1273, 1285, 1303, 1324, 1422, 1440, 1499, 1522, 1535, 1641, 1656, 2204, 2225, 2226.

[13] This means that any rite found in the approved liturgical books is part of *liturgy*, while all the prayers and devotional actions not found in the liturgical books fall outside *liturgy*. See *CLSA: Commentary*, 598; *CCC* 1140, 1145-1162.

[14] See c. 837, 1. The canon is a direct quote from *SC* 26. See also *SC* 27-32. Even when a priest celebrates what some people call a private Mass, the celebration is far from being private because it is a celebration of the Church itself. See also c. 837, 2; and *CCC* 832, 893, 1312, 1462, 1561.

[15] For example, the Liturgy of the Eucharist may be celebrated only by a priest and a bishop (c. 900), while diaconal, priestly and episcopal ordinations may be performed only by bishops (c. 1012).

Canon 835 is divided into four sections, with each section defining particular responsibilities and activities of a specific member or members of the Catholic Church.[16] Canon 835, 1 provides a good definition of the role of the diocesan bishop in the liturgy. He is the moderator of the entire liturgical life within his diocese.[17] Canon 835, 2 furnishes a definition of the role of the priests in the liturgy. They possess a limited share of the full ordained priesthood of the bishops, and participate in the liturgy, although they are dependent on their diocesan bishop to do so.[18] Canon 835, 3 provides a straightforward and limited description of the role of the deacon in the liturgy.[19] The canon states that deacons participate in the liturgy in accordance with the norms set in law. Canon 1169, 3, which also speaks about the role of deacons, reiterates the directive.[20] Thus, in this case, one has to revert to the liturgical books in order to find out what a deacon can do during a liturgy. Canon 835, 4 speaks about the liturgical role of the rest of the Christian faithful who are not ordained.[21]

Code and Liturgy — 2

The conciliar document *Lumen Gentium*, particularly paragraph 11, attempts to clarify the ecclesial aspect of each sacrament and the relationships among them. *Lumen Gentium* 11 shows how the People of God relate to one another through the celebration of each sacrament. The Code contains a limited reflection of this relationship.

Canon 213 affirms the right of every Christian believer to the sacraments and the obligation of the ministers to make the sacraments available to the faithful.[22] The Code puts great emphasis on the im-

---

[16] The conciliar background of this canon is *LG* chapter V. See *Navarre*, 547-548, n. 835.

[17] C. 835, 1 is based on *SC* 41; *LG* 26, 41; and *CD* 11, 15. See also c. 838, 4.

[18] See *LG* 28, 41; *CD* 15; *PO* 5.

[19] C. 835, 3 is based on *LG* 39, 41. See also *CCC* 823, 1251, 1570, 1641, 2045.

[20] C. 1169, 3 is based on *LG* 29. See also *CCC* 1569-1571, 1582, 1588.

[21] C. 835, 4 is based on *SC* 26-31; *LG* 41; and *GS* 48.

[22] See c. 843, 1. See also *SC* 19; *PO* 4; *CCC* 888, 1102, 1122; *Navarre*, 192-193, n. 213; and the chapter entitled, Code and Laity — 2.

portance of preparation for the sacraments[23] and the involvement of the community.[24] All of this takes place within the context and embrace of the community of believers. Thus, the Code speaks about the role of parents in preparing their children for the reception of the sacraments; the role of the community in preparing and participating in the R.C.I.A. parish program; the remote and proximate roles of the community and families to prepare prospective spouses.[25] Upon analysis the approach presented in the Code is based on a rippling effect: it begins with the nuclear family and expands to encompass and reach the community of believers at large. Moreover, this approach is a faithful reflection of the conciliar and post-conciliar teachings of the Church.

Apart from the emphasis on the preparation for the sacraments, the Code comments on the disposition of the individual as well as on the liturgical role of those faithful who are ordained or not ordained.[26] Liturgy is properly deputized through the sacraments of baptism and confirmation,[27] then through the installation into the lay ministries, and ultimately through those which require sacred ordination. Lay men can be liturgically installed into the lay ministries of lectors and acolytes.[28]

Code and Liturgy — 3

The 1983 Code regulates on the sacraments primarily in canons 840 through 1165. The regulation pertaining to each sacrament is very systematic. The canons deal with each sacrament's matter and form,

---

[23] C. 843, 2 states that the Christian faithful have a claim on the minister to prepare them for the reception and celebration of a sacrament. On the other hand, c. 776 sees the pastor as the key person in the parish to foster catechesis. See also *LG* 37; *Navarre*, 554-555, n. 843.

[24] See n. 22 in this chapter.

[25] See c. 226, 2; c. 774; c. 776; c. 793, 1; c. 851, 2; c. 890; c. 914; and c. 1136. See also *CCC* 2223-2226, 2230.

[26] See chapters entitled, Code and Laity, 1 through 3.

[27] See c. 225. See also *LG* 31, 33; *AA* 2-4, 7, 17; *AG* 21, 36; *GS* 43; *CCC* 94, 798, 853, 864, 871, 897-898, 900, 913, 932, 940, 942; *Navarre*, 197-198, n. 225.

[28] C. 230, 1. There can be other lay ministries, such as that of catechist. See *CLSA: Commentary*, 167.

the validity and liceity of the celebration, the minister, the recipient, the sponsors and witnesses when needed, and the registry of the reception of the sacrament. Sacraments have a vertical and a horizontal dimension. They are not only means to go to heaven, but also contain a communitarian aspect. The sacraments are the masterpieces of God.[29]

Canon 840[30] presents the nature of sacrament.[31] Each sacrament focuses on the action of the Lord in the Church and the ecclesial *communio*.[32] Sacraments are basic actions of Christ with salvific effects. The Church grows, matures and perfects its relationship to Christ through the sacraments. Thus, every sacrament always has ecclesial effects. On the other hand, the Church is also concerned about the quality of the minister's celebration of the sacraments and how the celebration reflects the disposition of the minister and the recipients of the sacraments. It is through the sacraments that one especially deepens one's relationship with the Lord.

The Church is further concerned with the *validity* of each sacrament. It is not enough to have words, gestures and celebrations. The Church must ensure that in the case of the celebration of a sacrament, these words, gestures and celebration are the actions of Christ and the Church.[33] Thus, canon 841 speaks about the requirements for the validity of a sacrament. The Supreme Authority in the Church, the Roman Pontiff and an Ecumenical Council, possesses exclusively the ultimate power to determine what constitutes a valid sacrament.[34]

Canon 842, 1 repeats what has been consistently taught down the centuries: baptism is the necessary basis for a Christian believer

---

[29] See *LG* 10-11; *PO* 4; *SC* 59; *CCC* 78, 120, 166, 460, 512-560, 696, 792, 815, 849, 950, 1084, 1105, 1113-1134, 1154, 1201, 1205, 1236, 1257, 1272, 1304, 1327, 1396, 1547, 1582, 2003, 2817.

[30] C. 840 is based on *SC* 6, 7, 14, 26-28, 59; and *LG* 7, 14. See also *CCC* 562, 788, 790, 791, 793, 798, 815, 837, 846, 1070, 1076, 1086, 1088-1089, 1113, 1123, 1140, 1141, 1144, 1181, 1249, 1257, 1373, 1482, 1517; *Navarre*, 552-552, n. 840.

[31] The terminology in c. 840 was especially influenced by the doctrinal statement of *SC* 59. See *CLSA: Commentary*, 607; *CCC* 1123; *Navarre*, 552-553, n. 840.

[32] See chapter entitled, Code and Laity — 3.

[33] See *CCC* 752, 795, 1090, 1136, 1140, 1348.

[34] See *Navarre*, 553-554, n. 841.

to validly receive any of the other six sacraments.[35] There are no exceptions to this.

Canon 842, 2 makes another strong doctrinal statement: the sacraments of baptism, confirmation, and the Eucharist are so interrelated that the three sacraments constitute the full Christian initiation.[36]

Canon 844 is a key canon. It can be referred to as the *ecumenical canon*. It is a very complex canon and raises some very important issues such as: who are we as Catholics? Who are those Christians who are not Catholics?[37] What is our relationship to them? The canon also sets the conditions for sacramental sharing.

The value which underlines canon 844 is the policy stated in the conciliar document, *Decree on Ecumenism* 8. The conciliar text deals with sacramental intersharing. This sharing is dependent on two principles. The first principle is that of the meaning of ecclesial unity in the Catholic Church. According to this principle, there is no place for ecumenical intersharing of sacraments. This is a restricting principle. On the other hand, the second principle is that of sacramental unity in the sharing of grace. This principle allows for ecumenical sharing.[38]

Canon 844, 1 affirms that sacramental sharing normally reflects and symbolizes full ecclesial unity.

Canon 844, 2-3 speaks about the exceptions to the principle. These two norms are intertwined in that they deal with the reciprocity of the sacraments of reconciliation, Eucharist, and anointing of the sick between the Roman Catholic Church and those Churches whose validity of the sacraments is recognized by the Catholic Church.[39] The

---

[35] C. 849 reiterates the doctrinal statement. See *LG* 11, 16, 40; *AG* 14; *PO* 5; *CCC* 761, 879, 841, 843, 844, 847, 1119, 1175, 1181, 1213, 1233, 1348, 1251, 1260, 1270, 1273, 1281, 1285, 1303, 1324, 1392, 1426, 1440, 1499, 1522, 1641, 1656, 2204, 2225, 2226; *Navarre*, 554, n. 842; 560-561, n. 849.

[36] See *CCC* 1213.

[37] The 1983 Code uses the term *Churches* to refer to the Orthodox Churches. This term can also refer to the Old Catholic Church and the National Polish Church. On the other hand, the Code uses the phrase *Ecclesial Community* to refer to those Churches with a Protestant background. See *CCC* 1399, 1401, 1462.

[38] See *Navarre*, 555-557, n. 844.

[39] For example, the Orthodox Churches.

intersharing of these sacraments may be celebrated under certain conditions.

Canon 844, 4 deals with the administrative life of the Church, that is with concrete decisions regarding the administration of sacraments.[40] The Apostolic See allows the conferences of bishops and the diocesan bishops to determine when a Catholic minister can administer the three aforementioned sacraments to Christians who are not Catholics.[41]

Canon 844, 5 is a very practical and sensitive canon. It raises the issue of consultation with non-Catholic Churches and Ecclesial Communities by the diocesan bishop and the pertinent conference of bishops before the two latter bodies pass legislative acts regarding ecumenical sacramental participation.

Finally, the introductory canons to each of the sacraments[42] serve as a tool which provide a job description for the minister of each sacrament.

---

[40] C. 844, 4 is a concrete example of how Christian Unity can be promoted on the local level.

[41] C. 755 speaks about the responsibility of the Apostolic See, the conferences of bishops, and the diocesan bishop in promoting Christian Unity. See also *CCC* 820, 2748.

[42] C. 849 is the introductory canon for baptism; c. 879 is for confirmation; cc. 897-899 are for the Eucharist; c. 959 is for reconciliation; c. 998 is for anointing of the sick; cc. 1008-1009 are for Holy Orders; and c. 1055 is for marriage.

7. The Sacraments of Initiation

Code and Sacraments of Initiation — 1

Canon 842, 2 states that the sacraments of baptism, confirmation, and the Eucharist are so interrelated that the three sacraments constitute the full initiation of a Christian.[1]

    Canons 849 to 878 are devoted to the *sacrament of baptism*.[2] Canon 849, the introductory canon, is a theological statement about the implication of baptism for life within the Christian community.[3] It specifies that the sacrament is conferred *only* by true water and the prescribed form of words. The canon also speaks of its necessity for salvation,[4] the forgiveness of sins,[5] the new life as a child of God,[6] the conferral of an indelible character,[7] and one's incorporation into the

---

[1] See chapter entitled, Code and Liturgy — 3. See also *CCC* 1210-1419.

[2] Suggested readings: The Bishops' Committee on the Liturgy, *Christian Initiation of Adults: A Commentary*; P. Baillargeon, *The Canonical Rights and Duties of Parents in the Education of their Children*; M. Collins, "Order for the Christian Initiation for Children: The Ritual Text," *Catechumenate* 10 (1988) 322-340; B. Daly, "Canonical Requirements of Parents in Cases of Infant Baptism According to the 1983 Code," *SCa* 20 (1986) 409-438; J. Huels, "Preparation for the Sacraments: Faith, Rights, Law," *SCa* 28 (1994) 33-58; F. Morresey, "The Rights of Parents in the Education of their Children," *SCa* 23 (1983) 429-444; M. Quinlan, "Parental Rights and Admission of Children to the Sacraments of Initiation," *SCa* 25 (1991) 385-401; J. Robertson, "Canons 869 and 868 and Baptizing Infants Against the Will of Parents," *J* 45 (1985) 631-638; W. Woestman, *Sacraments: Initiation, Penance, Anointing of the Sick: Commentary on Canons 840-1007*. See also *CCC* 1229-1284.

[3] See *CCC* 1213; *Navarre* 560-561, n. 849.

[4] See *LG* 14, 16; *CCC* 846-847, 1257, 1277.

[5] See *CCC* 977, 1226, 1263, 1279, 1425.

[6] See *CCC* 460, 505, 1265.

[7] See *CCC* 1272, 1274, 1280.

Church.[8] The canon should be related to other canons in the 1983 Code. For example, canon 96 states that a person is incorporated into the Catholic Church through baptism and thereby acquires certain rights and obligations as a member of the Christian faithful. Then canons 204, 223 and 225 state that because of baptism, a person should be involved in the life of the Church, particularly in one's community. Finally, canon 841 reiterates the necessity of baptism while canon 845, 1 affirms that baptism cannot be repeated.

Canon 851 deals with the preparation for baptism.[9] Canon 851, 1° speaks about the importance and necessity of preparation for the baptism of the catechumen.[10] On the other hand, canon 851, 2° focuses on the pastoral responsibility to prepare parents and sponsors for an infant's baptism.

Since baptism is necessary, there is a basic flexibility for its reception which is much more so than any for the other sacraments. The reason why the breadth of provisions for baptism is so vast is because of the salvific necessity of baptism. Thus, there is plenty of flexibility for the time,[11] the place,[12] and the minister of baptism.[13]

A recent issue has arisen in regard to a minister refusing to baptize an infant. Canon 868, 1, 2° states that there should be a *postponement* and not a denial of baptism when there is a solid suspicion to conclude that the infant will not be brought up in the faith. Once the suspicion is removed and the persons involved have received the necessary catechesis, the infant should be baptized.[14]

Canons 872 to 874 speak about sponsors. The infant's parents may not be sponsors. One sponsor suffices.[15] The sponsor must be at

---

[8] See *LG* 10, 11, 13, 37; *AG* 1, 7, 23; *CCC* 782, 784, 790, 804, 871, 1141, 1267-1270.

[9] C. 851 is based on *SC* 64, 67; *LG* 14; *CD* 14; and *AG* 14. See also *CCC* 815, 837, 846, 1232, 1233, 1248, 1255, 1257; *Navarre*, 561-562, n. 851.

[10] Note that according to c. 11 a catechumen is not bound by Church laws for the person is still a non-Christian.

[11] See c. 856.

[12] See c. 857, c. 859 and c. 860.

[13] See c. 861, c. 862, and c. 868, 2. See also *CCC* 1248, 1256.

[14] See *Navarre*, 567-568, n. 868.

[15] It is usual for an infant to have two sponsors: a godfather and a godmother. The Code discourages a multiplication of sponsors. See *CCC* 1255.

least sixteen years of age.[16] The sponsor should be a confirmed and practicing Catholic. A Christian belonging to another faith can serve as a *witness*, along with a Catholic sponsor.[17]

Sacraments of Initiation — 2

The proclamation of the promise to send the Spirit to rest upon the Messiah, God's anointed, dates back to Old Testament times.[18] The promise was fulfilled in the descent of the Spirit upon the Lord Jesus at his baptism.[19] The Spirit, however, was not to remain solely upon the Messiah but, as already alluded to in the Old Testament[20] and promised by Christ himself,[21] the Spirit was to be bestowed upon the members of the People of God. The Lord's promise of the sending of the Spirit was fulfilled on the first Pentecost.[22] Since the time of the early Church, the bestowal of the fullness of the Spirit was signified by having the Christian anointed with a perfumed oil,[23] following the laying on of hands. Eventually, this Christian rite was called the sacrament of confirmation.[24]

Confirmation is the completion of baptism. Canons 879 to 896 are devoted to the *sacrament of confirmation*.[25] The structure of these

---

[16] The diocesan bishop can establish a different age. The minister of baptism can also make an exception on an individual basis.

[17] The ecumenical document *Decree on Ecumenism* 57, states that when there is an Orthodox, that person is a *sponsor* rather than a witness.

[18] See Isaiah 11:2, 61.

[19] See Matthew 3:13-17; John 1:33-34.

[20] See Ezekiel 36:25-27; Joel 3:1-2.

[21] See Luke 12:12; John 3:5-8; 7:37-39; 16:7-15.

[22] See Acts 2:11-18.

[23] The perfumed oil is called *chrism*.

[24] See *LG* 11, 12, 26; *CCC* 1285-1321.

[25] Suggested readings: G. Austin, *The Rite of Confirmation: Anointing with the Spirit*; M. Balhoff, "Age for Confirmation: Canonical Evidence," *J* 45 (1985) 549-487; R. Barrett, "Confirmation: A Discipline Revisited," *J* 52 (1992) 697-714; Woestmann, *Sacraments*; Huels, "Preparation for the Sacraments"; A. Kavanaugh, *Confirmation: Origins and Reform*; F. Quinn, "Confirmation Reconsidered: Rite and Meaning," *Worship* 59 (1985) 354-370; P. Turner, *Confirmation: The Baby in Solomon's Court*.

canons is similar to those dedicated to baptism: an introductory canon[26] is followed by canons on the ceremony,[27] the minister,[28] the recipient of the sacrament,[29] the sponsors,[30] and registration.[31] As in the case with baptism, confirmation has a grounding for the faithful to participate in the threefold duties of the Church.[32] Anointing is required for validity,[33] imposition of hands is required for the integrity of the rite.[34] Bishops are the ordinary ministers of confirmation.[35] A priest can confirm in virtue of the faculty given to him either by law[36] or by delegation from the bishop.[37]

There are fewer canons about confirmation than there are about baptism because the former is not perceived as absolutely necessary for salvation. The affinity between confirmation and the other two sacraments of initiation[38] is clearly seen in the Confirmation Rite through the renewal of the Baptismal Vows and the reception of the Eucharist.[39] Although the presentation of the sequence of the Sacraments of Initiation and the canons pertinent to them give the impression that confirmation should be received before the Eucharist, in practice the Eucharist is received before one is confirmed.

Canon 879, the introductory canon, is a theological statement about the nature of confirmation.[40] The canon relies on the liturgical

---

[26] C. 879. See *Navarre*, 572, n. 879.

[27] C. 800 and c. 801.

[28] CC. 882-888. See *Navarre*, 573-575.

[29] CC. 889-891. See *Navarre*, 575-576.

[30] CC. 892 and 893.

[31] CC. 894-896.

[32] See *CCC* 1316.

[33] See *CCC* 1300, 1320.

[34] See *CCC* 1299 for the prayer during the imposition of hands.

[35] See *CCC* 1290, 1312, 1313.

[36] This is the case when the priest is baptizing an adult convert or when there is danger of death. See *CCC* 1314.

[37] An example of this is when there is a huge amount of persons to be confirmed and the bishop needs assistants in confirming them.

[38] That is the sacraments of baptism and Eucharist.

[39] See *CCC* 1298, 1316, 1321.

[40] See *LG* 11; *AG* 36; *PO* 5; *CCC* 1119, 1251, 1270, 1273, 1275, 1281, 1285, 1303, 1324, 1392, 1440, 1449, 1656, 2204, 2226. It should also be recalled what is stated in c. 845, 1, namely, the sacrament cannot be repeated.

book of the rite of confirmation for its full appreciation and the traditional understanding of the character which the sacrament imparts on
its recipient.[41] The next two canons deal with the celebration of the
rite of confirmation. Canon 800 deals with the rite of confirmation itself. Canon 800, 1 deals with the matter and form of the sacrament:
anointing with chrism on the forehead, imposition of hands, and the
formula prescribed in the liturgical book of the rite of confirmation.[42]
Canon 800, 2 states that the confirming minister, be he a bishop or a
priest, must use the chrism which has been consecrated by a bishop.[43]
This regulation is aimed at reflecting the *communio* between the diocesan bishop and his local church.

Canon 881[44] states that the celebration of confirmation should
preferably take place during the Eucharist.[45] On the other hand, canon
888 supplies the conditions under which the sacrament is conferred
outside the Mass. Furthermore, when a person is receiving the Sacraments of Initiation in one celebration, one should follow the provisions of canons 857 through 860.

Canons 882 to 887 speak about the minister of confirmation and
criteria to confirm.[46] The ordinary minister of the sacrament is the
bishop, while the extraordinary minister is a priest. The diocesan bishop
has the obligation to see to it that confirmation is conferred upon those
faithful within his diocese who are prepared and willing. Canon 889
states the criteria for one to receive confirmation.[47] On the other hand,
canon 890 reflects the responsibility of the different members of the
Christian community in preparing one to be confirmed.[48] Canon 891
speaks about the age for confirmation.[49] Although the law mentions

---

[41] See *CCC* 1293, 1295, 1296, 1304, 1305.

[42] See *CCC* 1293-1301.

[43] The exception to this is when one is in danger of death and is confirmed by a priest.
See c. 833, 3°. See also *CCC* 1290, 1297.

[44] C. 881 is based on *SC* 71. See also *CCC* 1298.

[45] See *CCC* 1297-1301.

[46] See *CCC* 1306-1314.

[47] See *CCC* 1319.

[48] See *CCC* 1309.

[49] Ibid.

that one should be confirmed when one reaches the age of discretion, it also allows the competent conference of bishops to set an earlier or later age for confirmation.[50]

Canons 892 and 893 speaks about the responsibility and qualifications of the sponsors. As in the case with baptism, neither parent of the one being confirmed can be a sponsor.[51] Furthermore, it is no longer required that a sponsor be of the same sex as the one being confirmed. Canon 892 speaks about the sponsor's involvement in the entire process connected with confirmation as well as the spiritual life of the individual following his or her confirmation. Canon 893 states that a sponsor must have the same qualifications as required to be a godparent at baptism.[52] It is recommended that one of the baptismal godparents should be the sponsor for confirmation.[53]

Sacraments of Initiation — 3

The *Eucharist* was instituted by the Lord himself during the Last Supper held on the night before his death.[54] It is the sacrifice of his Body and Blood, a memorial of his death and resurrection.[55] He charged his disciples to celebrate the Eucharist until his return in glory.[56]

The Eucharist is seen as the culmination of the Sacraments of Initiation.[57] The mystery of the Church is fully realized in the celebration of the Eucharist.[58] Moreover, there is a further permanent reality which goes beyond the Eucharistic celebration. Consequently, there

---

[50] The NCCB, in 1983, reaffirmed a 1972 decision to authorize each diocesan bishop to determine the age for confirmation in his diocese. See *CLSA: Commentary*, 639-640; *Navarre*, 1420, n. 891.

[51] See c. 874.

[52] Ibid.

[53] See *CCC* 1311.

[54] See Matthew 26:17-29; Mark 14:12-25; Luke 22:7-20; 1 Corinthians 11:23-36. See also *CCC* 611, 1323, 1337-1340, 1406.

[55] See *CCC* 1323, 1362-1367, 1402.

[56] See *CCC* 1130, 1402.

[57] See *CCC* 1212, 1322.

[58] See *CCC* 1369, 1407.

are provisions for the reverence and veneration of Jesus Christ in the Eucharist.[59]

Canons 897 through 958 are devoted to the *sacrament of the Eucharist*. The primary sources of these canons are the conciliar document, *Constitution on the Sacred Liturgy*, and the *General Introduction to the Roman Missal*. The canons themselves frequently refer to the latter document through the phrase "in accordance with the norm of the liturgical laws."

The canons are divided according to themes on the Eucharist. Canons 897 and 898 are fundamental canons. Canons 899 through 933 deal with the Eucharistic celebration. Canons 934 through 944 address the Veneration and Reservation of the Eucharist. Canons 945 through 958 speak about Mass offerings.

Canons 897[60] and 898[61] are the introductory canons. They are doctrinal canons which present the notion, importance, and one's relationship to the Eucharist.[62] While canon 897 focuses on the notion of the Eucharist and its relationship to the other sacraments, canon 898 states the implications with regards to the Christian faithful. There is

---

[59] There is a vast amount of writing on the Eucharist. The following are a handful of suggested readings: *CLSA: Commentary*, 643-672; Vatican Council II, *Constitution on the Sacred Liturgy*, particularly chapter II; Pope Paul VI, encyclical letter, *Mysterium fidei*; Congregation of Rites, instruction, *Eucharisticum mysterium*; USCC Bishops' Committee on the Liturgy, *Holy Communion: Commentary on the Instruction "Immensae Caritatis"*; idem., *The Body of Christ*, 1977; idem., *Eucharistic Celebration*; Pope John Paul II, apostolic letter, *On the Mystery and Worship of the Holy Eucharist*; idem., apostolic letter, *On Reserving Priestly Ordination to Men Alone*; Sacred Congregation for the Sacraments and Divine Worship, instruction, *On Certain Norms Concerning Worship of the Eucharistic Mystery*; J. Huels, *One Table, Many Laws*; idem., "Preparation for the Sacraments"; idem., "Stipends in the New Code of Canon Law," *Worship* 57 (1983) 513-525; Cardinal Roger Mahony, pastoral letter, *Priestly Ministers: Signs of Life in Christ*; idem., pastoral letter, *The Day on Which We Gather*; K. Osborne, "Eucharistic Theology Today," *Worship* 63 (1989) 98-125; Sacred Congregation for the Sacraments and Divine Worship, instruction, *On Certain Norms Concerning Worship of the Eucharistic Mystery*; Woestman, *Sacraments*. See also *CCC* 737, 1322-1419.

[60] C. 897 is based on *SC* 10; *LG* 3, 11, 17, 26; *CD* 30; *AG* 14; and *PO* 5. See also *CCC* 541, 543, 669, 763, 766, 776, 824, 832, 893, 960, 1074, 1175, 1181, 1233, 1248, 1270, 1324, 1312, 1364, 1392, 1405, 1561, 2032.

[61] C. 898 is based on *SC* 48; and *PO* 5. See also *CCC* 1175, 1181, 1324, 1392; *Navarre*, 578-579, n. 898.

[62] See *CCC* 1328-1332.

a correct stress on the importance of catechesis about the Eucharist, especially the role pertaining to the pastor. These two canons show the intimate relationship between the Eucharistic Christ and his Church. The Eucharist is Church focused by its very nature since the Church is meaningless without the Eucharist.

The underlining theme of canon 899 is the relationship between the different members of the Church in the celebration of the Eucharist.[63] It sets the tone for the next thirty-three canons.[64]

Canons 912 through 923 are a series of canons which deal with the reception of the Eucharist within the larger framework of the faithful's participation in the celebration of the Eucharist (Mass).

Canon 912 is the key canon for interpreting all of the canons on the Eucharist. While canon 213 states that the faithful have a right to the sacraments, canon 912 explicitly affirms this right in terms of the faithful's reception of the Eucharist. The canon also spells out the necessary condition for the reception of the Eucharist: the person must be baptized.[65] This condition has been already stated in canon 842, 1. Furthermore, the norms which specify the restriction of the reception of the Eucharist by baptized non-Catholics in canon 844, 3-4 must be followed.

Canon 913 ensures that children, properly prepared, can receive the Eucharist.[66] On the other hand, canon 914 charges parents and pastors with the responsibility of preparing children for the reception of the sacrament.[67] Once again the Code emphasizes the importance of parents and pastors, among other instructors, as being responsible for proper catechesis of those who are preparing themselves for the reception of a sacrament. This is a good example of the relationship between canons in different parts of the Code. Finally, First Penance should precede First Holy Communion.

Canons 915 and 916 list who is prohibited from receiving Holy

---

[63] C. 988 is based on *SC* 14, 26, 33, 47; and *PO* 5, 13. See also *CCC* 1140-1141, 1175, 1181, 1323-1324, 1392, 1398, 1464, 1466, 1548, 1552.

[64] See chapter entitled, The Eucharist — 1.

[65] See *Navarre*, 586, n. 912.

[66] See *Navarre*, 586-587, n. 913.

[67] See *CCC* 2226.

Communion: those who are excommunicated or interdicted and persons in grave sin. However, canon 916 outlines how these prohibitions can be lifted, that is, through sacramental confession and its accompanying penance.[68]

Canon 917 specifies the conditions under which one can receive Holy Communion twice in one day,[69] including its reception outside Mass.[70]

Canon 919 deals with the Eucharistic fast.[71] It is stated that there should be one hour fasting from food and drink expect for water, medicine, the infirm and in between Masses when a priest celebrates more than one Mass on a given day. The Easter Duty is still upheld.[72]

Canons 921 and 922 address the reception of the Eucharist in the form of *Viaticum*.[73] It is the last sacrament which a person should receive before entering eternal life. If one is unable to receive the Eucharist under the Sacred Species of Bread, one may receive the Eucharist under the Sacred Species of Wine.[74] Canon 191 has already listed, in order of obligation, who is responsible to bring Viaticum to a person in real danger of death, beginning with priests who are entrusted with the pastoral care for souls.[75]

Canon 923 has a limited ecumenical tone. Thus, one can participate in the Eucharistic Sacrifice and receive the Eucharist in any of the Catholic rites[76] and, under certain conditions, also in those non-Catholic Churches whose Eucharist is recognized as valid by the See of Rome.[77]

---

[68] See *CCC* 1385, 1457, 2042; *Navarre*, 588-589, nn. 915, 196.

[69] It is of interest to note that *CCC* 1388 does not restrict the reception of Holy Communion to two times in a given day. Rather, it states that one can receive Holy Communion each time one participates at Mass. See also W. Woestman, "Daily Eucharist in the Postconciliar Church," *SCa* 23 (1989) 85-100.

[70] C. 918. See also *SC* 55; *CCC* 1388.

[71] See *CCC* 1387, 1389, 2042; *Navarre*, 590, n. 519.

[72] See c. 920.

[73] See *CCC* 1392, 1517, 1524-1525.

[74] See c. 925. See also *Navarre*, 593-594, n. 925.

[75] See *Navarre*, 585-586, n. 911.

[76] This includes the Eastern Catholic rites such as the Byzantine Catholic rite.

[77] See c. 844, 2. See also *CCC* 1398-1401.

8. The Eucharist

The Eucharist — 1

The preceding chapter discussed the Eucharist as a part of the Sacraments of Initiation. The following chapters will discuss the Eucharist in more detail.[1]

Canon 899[2] introduces the notion of the Eucharistic celebration and sets the tone for the disciplinary canons which follow, that is canons 900-933. The latter address issues regarding the minister, participation, rites and ceremonies in the celebration, the time and place of the Eucharist.

Canons 900-911, for the most part, focus on the minister of the celebration of the Eucharist. Canon 900 identifies the priest as the presider at the celebration from the viewpoint that the Eucharist is a Sacrifice and a Sacrament.[3] The canon anticipates what canon 902 will state about the celebration of the Eucharist.[4] The canon emphasizes the doctrinal statement that only a validly ordained priest can celebrate the Eucharist[5] and in so doing he is acting in the name of Christ until the Lord's return.[6] There can be more than one priest celebrating the

---

[1] For a list of suggested readings see chapter entitled, Sacraments of Initiation — 3, nn. 59, 66.

[2] See ibid., n. 58.

[3] C. 900 is based on *LG* 10, 26, 28. See also *CCC* 784, 832, 893, 901, 1141, 1273, 1312, 1535, 1538, 1548, 1552, 1554, 1561, 1564, 1566, 1583, 1675.

[4] C. 902 is based on *SC* 57.

[5] See *CCC* 1348, 1369, 1411, 1577; Pope John Paul II, apostolic letter, *The Dignity of Women*; idem., apostolic letter, *On Reserving Priestly Ordination to Men Alone*.

[6] See *AG* 1; *CCC* 1344, 1404.

same Eucharist.[7] It is expected from each celebrant to make a prayerful preparation and subsequent thanksgiving at each Mass.[8]

Canon 901 is a straightforward canon: the Mass may be applied for anyone. The person may be living or deceased, Catholic or not, sinner or saint.

Canons 904-905 speak about the frequency of the celebration of the Eucharist. Canon 904 makes it clear that the principal function of a priest is the celebration of the Eucharist.[9] On the other hand, canon 905 recommends the daily celebration of the Eucharist and, for pastoral reasons, the priest may celebrate the Eucharist more than once on a given day.[10]

Canon 906[11] indicates that the presence of an altar server is no longer necessary as long as there are some faithful present, even one person. The altar server can be either male or female. The canon also makes provision for the priest to celebrate Mass all alone under certain conditions.

Canons 907[12] and 908[13] make restrictions on the celebration of the Mass to Catholic priests (or bishops), prohibiting deacons and laity from saying especially the Eucharistic Prayer and non-Catholic priests and bishops from concelebrating.

Canon 910[14] speaks about Eucharistic Ministers. While there is the acknowledgment of the need for more clergy, there is also the affirmation of the faithful's right to have accessibility to the Eucharist. The contents of this canon bring out the tension which is inherent in this situation. Canon 910, 1 addresses the ordinary situation for the

---

[7] This is called concelebration.

[8] C. 909. See also *CCC* 1385.

[9] C. 907 is based on *SC* 2, 27; *LG* 3, 28; *AG* 39; and *PO* 2, 5, 13. See also *CCC* 541-542, 669, 763, 766, 771, 960, 1068, 1140-1142, 1175, 1181, 1324, 1364, 1392, 1405, 1464, 1466, 1517, 1548, 1554, 1562-1564, 1566, 1582.

[10] Due to the shortage of priests in many parts of the world, including the United States, priests usually celebrate more than one Mass on Sundays and Holy Days of Obligation. See *Navarre*, 582-583, n. 905.

[11] C. 906 is based on *SC* 27. See also *CCC* 1140, 1517.

[12] C. 907 is based on *SC* 28. See also *CCC* 1144.

[13] See *Navarre*, 584-585, n. 908.

[14] C. 910 is based on *LG* 29. See also *CCC* 1569-1571, 1582, 1588; *Navarre*, 585, n. 910.

distribution of the Eucharist. In such instances, the ordinary ministers are the bishop, the priest, and the deacon. Canon 910, 2 enumerates the extraordinary minister of the Eucharist by way of exception. Lay persons, male and female, can distribute Holy Communion in the following order: if there is neither a bishop nor a priest nor a deacon nor an installed acolyte,[15] then a lay person may be the extraordinary minister. Thus, an extraordinary minister of the Eucharist should not distribute Communion *instead* of an ordinary minister and/or an acolyte who are participating in the Eucharistic celebration.[16] This is in keeping with the provisions of canon 230, 3 which lists this privilege as one of the liturgical functions of the laity.

The Eucharist — 2

Canons 934 through 944[17] are dedicated to the reservation and veneration of the Eucharist. The canons are rooted in the dogmatic teaching that the Lord is really present, body, blood, soul and divinity, in the Sacred Species of the Eucharist.[18] The contents of the canons are basically straightforward.

Canons 934 through 940 deal with the reservation of the Eucharist. Canon 934[19] states that the Eucharist must be reserved in the diocesan cathedral, every parish in the diocese, and every oratory attached to the canonical residence of members of a community of consecrated life. The Eucharist may also be reserved in the residence of a bishop and, with proper permission, also in other designated places as long as someone is charged with taking care of the place.[20] Canon

---

[15] See c. 230, 2.

[16] See *Navarre*, 1293, n. 910.

[17] These canons are based on *Eucharisticum mysterium*, particularly 49-67.

[18] See *SC* 7; *CCC* 1088, 1373-1381; *Mysterium fidei*, 18, 39, 56, 66; *On the Mystery and Worship of the Holy Eucharist*, 3.

[19] See *Navarre*, 597-600.

[20] For example, Cardinal Roger Mahony of Los Angeles has strongly encouraged every rectory to have a chapel where the Blessed Sacrament is reserved. See Mahony, *Priestly Ministers*, 14 and n. 15.

935 prohibits personal retention of the Eucharist unless this is done for the purpose of taking Holy Communion to the sick or one has a special permission to do so from the bishop. In both instances, such retention is very limited in time. Canon 936 recommends the reservation of the Eucharist in religious houses. Canon 937 insists that the faithful should have access to pray in the presence of the Eucharist when reserved in a church. This should be made possible for a few hours each day, unless a grave reason dictates that the church should be closed during the day.[21] Canon 938 provides a number of norms on the tabernacle. Although there is no specification or insistence that the tabernacle be placed in the middle of the church, the norm does state that it should occupy a prominent place.[22] Canon 939 states that enough Consecrated Hosts be reserved for the needs of the faithful, and that the Sacrament should be renewed frequently. Furthermore, canon 940 states that there should be a constantly lit sanctuary lamp wherever the Eucharist is reserved.

The Eucharist — 3

Canons 941 through 943 are dedicated to the exposition and veneration of the Eucharist.[23] These canons are a very good example of references to liturgical law found outside the Code of Canon Law for a better and more thorough presentation of the subject matter. Thus, the *Roman Ritual* has a section completely devoted to this topic. It falls under the section entitled, "Holy Communion and Worship of the Eucharist outside Mass."[24]

---

[21] For example, it is reasonable to open a church only for the celebration of Mass and other liturgical services where there is a high crime rate in a neighborhood.

[22] Liturgical law strongly recommends that the Eucharist be reserved in a special chapel. See *General Instructions of the Roman Missal* 276. See also *AG* 128; *CCC* 1183, 1379, 1416.

[23] See *Mysterium fidei* 18, 56, 60-66; *On the Mystery and Worship of the Holy Eucharist* 3; *CCC* 1377-1381, 1418; *Navarre*, 600-601, n. 941-944.

[24] See *Roman Ritual: Holy Communion and Worship of the Eucharist Outside Mass* 82-100.

Canon 941 speaks about the possibility of the exposition and veneration of the Eucharist. The *Roman Ritual* provides more details as background and explains how to properly follow the provisions of this canon. The *Roman Ritual* distinguishes between a lengthy and a brief period of the exposition of the Blessed Sacrament for adoration, as well as adoration celebrated by a religious community. There are certain norms which apply to the three kinds of exposition and adoration: no exposition for any length of time is allowed when Mass is being celebrated in the same place; exposition should be interrupted when Mass is being celebrated in the same sanctuary; exposition for simply giving benediction is not allowed; some faithful should always be present; no matter how long or short the exposition may be, it must always include readings from Scripture, hymns, prayers, and some time set aside for silent prayer.[25]

Canon 942 provides for the solemn exposition and adoration of the Blessed Sacrament. It should take place once a year in churches and oratories where the Eucharist is usually reserved. The exposition need not be continuous, especially when it goes beyond a day.[26]

Canon 943 deals with the minister of the exposition of the Blessed Sacrament and benediction. It basically repeats what is stated in the *Roman Ritual*.[27] The ordinary minister of the exposition of the Blessed Sacrament and benediction is a bishop, a priest, or a deacon. Lay persons properly deputized by the bishop may expose the Blessed Sacrament but may not give benediction.

---

[25] See ibid., 83. See also *Mysterium fidei* 60-66.

[26] See *Roman Ritual: Holy Communion* 63, 86-88.

[27] See ibid., 91.

9. Penance and Reconciliation

Penance and Reconciliation — 1

No human being is perfect. Consequently, no Christian is perfect. All of us commit some kind of sin. The reception of baptism does not guarantee that we will not sin again.[1] Rather, due to human frailty, we usually fall. In order to reestablish the bond of love between humanity and God broken by sin after one's baptism, the Church has been given the sacrament of Penance and Reconciliation.[2]

Canons 959 through 997 are dedicated to the *sacrament of Penance and Reconciliation*.[3] Once again, one has to go outside the Code for a fuller and better understanding of the regulations about the sacrament.[4]

The main thrust of these thirty-nine canons focus on the special relationship between the confessor[5] and the penitent,[6] even though there

---

[1] See *CCC* 1425-1429.

[2] See *CCC* 1420-1498.

[3] Suggested readings: *LG* 8, 11, 22, 26, 40, 48-50; *SC* 26-27; *CD* 30; *PO* 5, 13, 18; *CLSA: Commentary*, 673-701; J. Dallen, "Church Authority and the Sacrament of Reconciliation," *Worship* 58 (1984) 194-214; idem., *"Reconciliatio et Paenitentia*: the Postsynodal Apostolic Exhortation," *Worship* 59 (1985) 98-116; idem., *The Reconciling Community: The Rite of Penance*; R. Gula, *To Walk Together Again: The Sacrament of Reconciliation*; J. Huels, "Preparation for the Sacraments"; Pope John Paul II, apostolic exhortation, *Reconciliation and Penance*; R. Garafalo, "Reconciliation and Celebration: A Pastoral Case for General Absolution," *Worship* 63 (1989) 447-456; International Theological Commission, "Penance and Reconciliation," *Origins* (1984) 513-524; Mahony, *Priestly Ministers*, 17-13; *Navarre*, 608-627; J. Provost, "The Reception of First Penance," *J* 47 (1987) 294-340; *Roman Ritual: Rite of Penance*; Woestman, *Sacraments*.

[4] See *Rite of Penance*.

[5] CC. 965-986. See *Navarre*, 614-624.

[6] CC. 987-991. See *Navarre*, 624-626.

is reference to general absolution[7] and indulgences.[8] It is also important to note that, under normal circumstances, the canons allow priests with regular faculties to hear confessions to do so anywhere in the world.[9] Moreover, *reserved sins* have been dropped since the 1983 Code calls for the external imposition of penalties.[10]

Canon 959[11] is a doctrinal canon which serves as an introduction to the other canons on Penance and a statement about the nature of the sacrament of Penance and Reconciliation. One is reminded that forgiveness comes from God alone[12] and that sin and reconciliation have a direct effect on the entire Church.[13]

The celebration of the sacrament is presented in canons 960 through 964. Canon 960 dictates individual oracular confession of all serious sins as being the *only* ordinary manner of confession.[14] However, the Code also alludes to instances when other reconciliation options might exist.[15] The *Rite of Penance* speaks about the components of individual confession: contrition, sacramental confession, penance, and absolution.[16]

Canons 961-963 deal with general absolution.[17] The Code has a

---

[7] CC. 961-963. See *Navarre*, 610-613, nn. 961, 962, 963.

[8] CC. 992-997.

[9] C. 967, 2-3. In the past, priests had to seek delegation from the proper ecclesiastical authority in order to hear confessions outside their diocese, unless it was an emergency. See *Navarre*, 615-617, n. 967-969.

[10] In the past, the remission of *reserved sins* limited the sacramental power of absolution of the confession. The 1983 Code makes a distinction between remission of *sins* and remission of *penalties*. For example, the remission of the penalty of excommunication of a priest who breaks directly the seal of confession is reserved to the Holy See (c. 1388, 1). See *CCC* 1463, 1467.

[11] See *Navarre*, 608-609, n. 959.

[12] See *CCC* 1466.

[13] See *CCC* 1461-1462, 1466.

[14] See *SC* 72; *Navarre*, 609-610, n. 960.

[15] See c. 961. See also *Navarre*, 610-612, n. 961.

[16] See *Rite of Penance* 3-7.

[17] General Absolution is the *Third Rite* presented in the *Rite of Penance* 31-32. See *CCC* 1483; *Navarre*, 610-613, nn. 961, 962, 963. Suggested readings: R. Garafalo, "Reconciliation and Celebration: A Pastoral Case for General Absolution," *Worship* 63 (1989) 447-456; R. Malone, "General Absolution and Pastoral Practice," *Chicago Studies* (1985) 47-58; L. Orsy, "General Absolution: New Law, Old Tradition, Some Questions," *Theological Studies* 45 (1984) 676-689.

clearly restrictive approach toward general absolution for fear of abuses and a decline in oracular confession. Canon 961 presents the general conditions under which general absolution may be *validly* imparted. The diocesan bishop, considering the pastoral needs of the situation and in harmony with the criteria set by the conference of bishops, is the one to give permission for general absolution. In case of danger of death, no permission is needed since the priest has to decide on the spot what he should do and will have no time to contact the diocesan bishop.

Canons 962-963 address the required disposition of the penitent to *validly* receive general absolution. The sorrowful penitent must resolve that he or she intends to personally confess serious sins in due time[18] and is to do so before the reception of another general absolution,[19] which is not the same as the provision of canon 989 which prescribes, as minimum, the annual confession of serious sins.

Canon 964 provides for the place where confessions may be heard. It should be either a confessional or another designated place,[20] affirming the right to anonymity of the penitent.

Penance and Reconciliation — 2

Canons 965-986 are dedicated to norms regarding the confessor and matters which are closely related to his ministry. The introductory canon 965 clearly states that only one who is ordained a priest is the valid minister of the sacrament of Penance and Reconciliation.[21]

---

[18] C. 962. See also *Rite of Penance* 6 and 33; *Navarre*, 612-613, n. 962.

[19] C. 963. See *Navarre*, 613, n. 963.

[20] The 1983 Code leaves it to the conference of bishops to define what a suitable place for confession might be. For example, the conference of bishops in the United States recommends a chapel or a room designated for the celebration of sacramental reconciliation. It is up to the *penitent* and not to the confessor to decide whether to confess face to face or anonymously.

[21] See *LG* 26; *PO* 5, 13; *CCC* 1461-1467; *Navarre*, 614-615, nn. 965-966. By definition, a bishop is already an ordained priest. Hence, without mentioning the bishop as the minister of this sacrament, the canon also includes him as such. The bishop has been considered as the principal minister of reconciliation in a diocese since ancient times.

Canon 966 makes two statements: the power to sacramentally absolve sins is rooted in priestly ordination and the power to exercise it validly comes either from the law itself[22] or from the office one holds[23] or from the competent ecclesiastical authority.[24] Thus, every priest, unless there is danger of death, needs some kind of *faculties* to hear confessions.[25] When there is danger of death any priest, regardless of whether he is active or inactive in the ministry, may grant absolution.[26] Every priest in charge of caring for souls has the obligation to hear confessions.[27] On the other hand, every Catholic has a right to have an individual confession.[28]

The Code is very clear in stating that only qualified priests should be given faculties to hear confessions.[29] The faculties to hear confessions should be given in writing[30] and can be either for a specified or unspecified period of time.[31] When a priest is given faculties to hear confessions in his own diocese, he can also hear confessions in any other part of the world except when the local ordinary of that place prohibits him from doing so.[32] It should be noted that canon 977 invalidates the absolution of a priest who attempts to absolve an accomplice in sexual matters, except when there is danger of death.[33] There

---

[22] C. 967, c. 976 and c. 977. See *CCC* 1462, 1463.

[23] C. 968. See *CCC* 1462.

[24] C. 969. See *CCC* 1462.

[25] CC. 967-969. See *Navarre*, 615-617, n. 967-969.

[26] C. 976 and c. 977. These two canons deal with special cases when, due to danger of death, a priest may absolve the penitent. This faculty is granted by the law itself. See also *CCC* 1463.

[27] C. 986. See *CCC* 1464.

[28] See *Navarre*, 624-624, n. 986.

[29] C. 970.

[30] C. 973.

[31] C. 972. The diocesan bishop issues a decree to the priest which lists his faculties in that diocese. The faculty to hear confessions is specified in the decree. See also *CCC* 1462.

[32] C. 974. See *Navarre*, 618-619, n. 974.

[33] It should be recalled that c. 982 demands a public retraction of the false denunciation of an innocent confessor. Reparation of damage is also demanded. See *CCC* 2487.

is no exception to breaking the confessional seal[34] or to using confessional knowledge to the detriment of a penitent.[35]

Canons 978-981 describe and direct the confessor how he is to exercise his ministry as reconciliator. Keeping before his eyes the teaching of the magisterium, he is to serve as judge and healer for the penitent.[36] The confessor is to be prudent when asking a penitent any questions.[37] He is to bestow absolution on the properly disposed penitent.[38] Canon 981 states that a prudent penance should be imposed on the penitent.[39]

Canons 987-991 address the penitent who seeks sacramental absolution. The penitent must have a basic disposition of sorrow, renounce sin, and intend to avoid sin.[40] Catholics are bound to confess in number and in kind, at least once a year,[41] all grave sins committed since their last confession after baptism, and are encouraged to confess venial sins as well. This is to be done after a careful examination of conscience.[42] The right of the penitent to choose a confessor is upheld.[43]

---

[34] C. 983. It should be noted that c. 1388, 1 attaches automatic excommunication to the priest who breaks directly the seal of confession. The lifting of this penalty is reserved to the Apostolic See. See *CCC* 1467, 2490, 2511.

[35] C. 984.

[36] C. 978.

[37] C. 979.

[38] C. 980. See also c. 213 and c. 843, 1, which deal with a well-disposed person's right to the sacraments. C. 987 describes who is a well-disposed penitent. See also *CCC* 1450-1460.

[39] See *CCC* 1459-1460.

[40] C. 987. See *Rite of Penance* 6-7; *CCC* 1450-1453; *Navarre*, 624-625, nn. 987-988.

[41] C. 989. This norm is parallel to the *Easter Duty* which is stated in c. 920. See *CCC* 1457, 2042.

[42] C. 988. See *Rite of Penance* 7 and 34; *CCC* 1454-1458.

[43] C. 991.

10. Anointing of the Sick

Anointing of the Sick — 1

On the eve of Vatican II, the Sacrament of the Anointing of the Sick was perceived to be that of Extreme Unction. It was the anointing of one who was on the verge of dying. This mentality and practice was inherited from the Middle Ages.

The *sacrament of the anointing of the sick* has undergone some changes as a result of Vatican Council II and post-conciliar teachings. For example, the *Constitution on the Sacred Liturgy*[1] and the *Dogmatic Constitution on the Church*[2] of Vatican II, and especially the Instruction *Eucharisticum mysterium*[3] issued by the Sacred Congregation of Rites on May 25, 1967, attempted to recover the older Church tradition where anointing was bestowed on a person who could have been in danger of death or seriously impaired due to old age.[4]

There was also a change in the title of the sacrament from *extreme unction* to the *anointing of the sick*. Since only a person who is alive is capable of receiving a sacrament, no dead person may be

---

[1] See *SC* 73-75.
[2] See *LG* 11.
[3] See *Eucharisticum mysterium* 18.
[4] Suggested readings: *CLSA: Commentary*, 702-711; T. Green, "The Revision of Sacramental Law: Perspectives on the Sacraments other than Marriage," *SCa* 11 (1977) 261-269; C. Gusmer, "Liturgical Traditions of Christian Illness: Rites of the Sick," *Worship* 46 (1972) 528-543; idem., *And You Visited Me: Sacramental Ministry to the Sick and the Dying*; *Navarre*, 628-632; Pope Paul VI, apostolic constitution, *Sacram unctionem infirmorum*; *Rite of Anointing and Pastoral Care of the Sick*; Woestman, *Sacraments*; J. Ziegler, "Who Can Anoint the Sick?" *Worship* 61 (1987) 25-44; idem., *Let Them Anoint the Sick*; *CCC* 1499-1523.

anointed.[5] Moreover, Viaticum and not anointing is presented as the sacrament for the dying.[6]

Canons 998 to 1007 are devoted to the sacrament of the anointing of the sick. They follow a clear-cut outline. After an introductory canon,[7] the remaining nine canons are treated in three separate groupings: the celebration of the sacrament of the anointing of the sick,[8] the minister of anointing,[9] and those to be anointed.[10] The full meaning of these canons cannot be understood unless one refers to the liturgical laws found outside the 1983 Code, that is in the *Rite of Anointing*.

Anointing of the Sick — 2

Canon 998 supplies the definition of the anointing of the sick. It immediately places the sacrament within the realm of faith. In so doing, the 1983 Code is faithful to the teachings of Vatican II.[11]

Canon 999 specifies who can bless the oil to be used for the sacrament. It should be the oil blessed by the diocesan bishop, or one equivalent to him,[12] during the annual Mass of the Chrism.[13] In case of necessity, the priest who is administering the sacrament can bless the oil.[14] Canon 1000 states that the minister should anoint with his own hands, using the required sacramental form.[15] A single anointing

---

[5] See c. 1005. See also *Rite of Anointing and Pastoral Care of the Sick* 15, 35.

[6] See chapter entitled, Sacraments of Initiation — 3. See also *CCC* 1524.

[7] C. 998. The canon is rooted in *LG* 11. See also *Navarre*, 628, n. 998.

[8] CC. 999-1002. See *Navarre*, 628-630, nn. 999, 1000, 1001, 1002.

[9] C. 1003. See *CCC* 1516; *Navarre*, 630, n. 1003.

[10] CC. 1004-1007. See *SC* 73; *CCC* 1514; *Navarre*, 631-632.

[11] See *SC* 73; *LG* 11; and *PO* 5. See also *Rite of Anointing* 5 and 6; *CCC* 1512-1514.

[12] See c. 368 and c. 381, 2. See also *Rite of Anointing* 21; *CCC* 1519, 1530.

[13] See *Rite of Anointing* 22.

[14] See ibid., 21b. This kind of blessing is by way of exception and is not meant to be the norm.

[15] *Rite of Anointing* 23, 24. The prescribed formula for anointing is presented in the *Rite of Anointing* 25. See also c. 847, 1; *SC* 75; *CCC* 1513.

is sufficient and it does not have to be on a person's forehead.[16] Canon 1001 charges those with the pastoral care of the sick, those who treat the sick, and family members to see to it that a sick person receives the sacrament.[17] The canon presents the celebration within the context of a community of believers.

Canon 1002 speaks about the communal dimension of the sacrament in that a number of persons may be anointed during the same celebration. It should be kept in mind that sick persons, through their illness, become a praying community as they witness in faith to one another. When there is a large number of persons to be anointed, a number of priests may be the ministers of the sacrament.[18]

Canon 1003 addresses the minister of anointing.[19] He must be in priestly orders.[20] Furthermore, every priest is allowed to carry the blessed oils with him so that they are always accessible whenever the administration of the sacrament is needed.[21]

Canons 1004-1007 deal with those who are to receive the sacrament. Canon 1004 states that any believer who is seriously ill and has reached the age of reason[22] or is seriously impaired due to old age may receive the sacrament.[23] The repetition of the sacrament may be done either when the person has a relapse or the illness reaches a more severe crisis.[24] Only a person who desires[25] to receive the sacrament may receive it.[26] Therefore, a publicly obstinate sinner who clearly is not repentant might not be receptive to receive the sacrament.[27] If the sac-

---

[16] See *Rite of Anointing* 21; *Navarre*, 629, n. 1000.

[17] See *Rite of Anointing* 13, 43. See also *SC* 73; *Navarre*, 629, n. 1001.

[18] See *Rite of Anointing* 17, 19, 83. See also *CCC* 1517-1519; *Navarre*, 629-630, n. 1002.

[19] See *Rite of Anointing* 16-18. See also *Navarre*, 630-631, n. 1003.

[20] See *Rite of Anointing* 16.

[21] See *CCC* 1516.

[22] C. 11 specifies that usually a person reaches the age of reason at seven.

[23] See *Navarre*, 631, n. 1004.

[24] See *Rite of Anointing* 8-12. See also *SC* 73; *CCC* 1514-1515.

[25] The desire may be explicitly expressed or implicitly desired.

[26] C. 1006. See also *Rite of Anointing* 14.

[27] C. 1007. See *CCC* 1517.

rament is to take effect, a basic intention to receive it is required. In any case, this should be presumed of every baptized Catholic, unless proven otherwise.

Finally, this is one of the sacraments which has ecumenical implications. Under certain conditions, a non-Catholic Christian can receive the sacrament of the anointing of the sick from a Catholic priest.[28]

---

[28] C. 844, 3-4. See *CCC* 1399, 1401.

11. Christian Burial

Christian Burial — 1

All of the sacraments, particularly the Sacraments of Christian Initiation, are aimed at the passage of the Christian from an earthly journey to eternal life. This is brought about through death.[1] For the faithful Christian, his or her day of death marks the end of sacramental life and the beginning of the celebration of the eternal banquet in the Kingdom of God. The Church, through which the Christian was given sacramental life, liturgically celebrates his or her passing,[2] reminding those who grieve and the entire community of the Paschal character of Christian death.[3]

The 1983 Code has ten canons dedicated to Christian burial.[4] Canon 1176 provides the notion and purpose for a Christian funeral. The opening statement of canon 1176, however, immediately refers one to liturgical law *outside* the 1983 Code.[5] One must refer to the *Order of Christian Funerals* in order to know how the rite of Christian Burial should be celebrated. The Code affirms the right of *every* Catholic to a Christian funeral. The atmosphere in which the liturgical funeral service is to take place is full of faith, hope, love, and re-

---

[1] See *EN* 48. See also *CCC* 1525, 1680.

[2] See *LG* 48; *SC* 81-82. See also *CCC* 1010-1014, 1020, 1680-1690, 2299.

[3] Suggested readings: F. McManus, "The Reformed Funeral Rite," *American Ecclesiastical Review* 116 (1972) 45-59, 124-139; *Navarre*, 737-741; R. Rutherford, *The Death of a Christian*; R. Sparkes and R. Rutherford, "The Order of Christian Funerals: A Study in Bereavement and Lament," *Worship* 60 (1986) 499-510; *Order of Christian Funerals*, especially 1, 10, 41, 57, and "Prayer of Commendation."

[4] CC. 1176-1185.

[5] C. 1176, 1-2. See *Navarre*, 737-738, n. 1176.

spect.[6] Thus, the Church community, especially the bereaved, pray for the faithful departed in faith, honoring with respect and charity the body which had been consecrated at baptism, and reaffirm their hope in the resurrection.[7] Furthermore, the competent conference of bishops can determine added liturgical rites for burial.[8] Although the Code does not address the issue of autopsies and organ donations, the former may be carried out for legal or scientific purposes, while the latter can be deemed as meritorious.[9] However, the Church *prefers* that bodies be buried. The church of burial should keep a record of those who were buried from that place.[10]

It has become quite common in recent years that the body of a deceased loved one is cremated. Often this is done for financial reasons. Cremation is allowed as long as it is not carried out as some affirmation against the Christian teaching of the resurrection of the body.[11] The cremens[12] can be either buried or disposed of in a dignified manner, such as their dispersion at sea while prayers are recited. When cremation takes place, funeral rites can be celebrated at the place of cremation as long as necessary precautions are taken to ensure the avoidance of scandal or indifferentism.

Christian Burial — 2

The celebration of funeral rites is discussed in canons 1177-1182. Although one's parish church, where one had worshipped and celebrated the sacraments so frequently, is the normal place from where one should be buried, funeral rites may take place in any other church for a good reason.[13]

---

[6] See *SC* 81-82. See also *CCC* 1687, 2300.

[7] See c. 1176, 2. See also *CCC* 2300.

[8] C. 838, 3.

[9] See *CCC* 2301.

[10] See c. 1182. See also *Navarre*, 740, n. 1182.

[11] See c. 1176, 3; *CCC* 2301.

[12] The ashes of the cremated body of a person.

[13] See c. 1177. See also *Navarre*, 738-739, n. 1177-1179.

The *Order of Christian Funerals* provides three stages of the funeral rites. One should take place at home or the funeral home, one at the church, and one at the cemetery. The *Rite* also encourages that celebrations according to family wishes, local customs, and popular piety should be taken into account when planning a funeral liturgy. Thus, the entire rite of burial calls for careful preparation and sensitivity to those who rarely practice the faith and/or are not Catholics and/or are not Christians. The celebration should follow a basic pattern, namely, the greeting in faith to the community, the liturgy of the Word, the Eucharist, and the final farewell.[14]

Canon 1178 states that the usual celebration of the funeral rites for a bishop should be in his cathedral. Canon 1179 addresses the issue of burial rites for those in vows. In many countries parish churches have their own cemeteries where parishioners can be buried. This is usually no longer allowed in the United States. Canon 1180 provides a person with the liberty to choose his or her burial place.[15] If there were no arrangement at the time of death, a member of the family or a friend makes the decision.

The sensitivity of the Code in upholding equal rights for the deceased, be they rich or poor, is reflected in canon 1181.[16] The Code assures a Christian burial for those who cannot pay for it, just as canon 848 prohibits the denial of the sacraments to persons who cannot make an offering.

Canons 1183-1185 deal with the issue of who may or may not receive a Christian burial.[17] Canon 1183, 1 affirms the right of a catechumen to receive a Christian burial as if the person was already a member of the Church.[18] Canon 1183, 2 states that the local ordinary can permit a Christian burial to a non-baptized child when it is evi-

---

[14] See *Order of Christian Funerals* 1, 10, 41-43, 57. See also *CCC* 1684-1690.

[15] See *Navarre*, 739-740, n. 1180.

[16] C. 1181 is faithful to the directive of *SC* 32. See also *Navarre*, 740, n. 1181.

[17] See *Navarre*, 740-741, nn. 1183, 1184.

[18] See c. 206, 2. It states that catechumens, under certain conditions, have certain prerogatives proper to Christians. C. 1183, 1 is an example when the directive of c. 206, 2 is enacted.

dent that the parents intended to baptize their child. The reason why permission is needed is to reinforce the Church's consistent teaching on infant baptism and to encourage the baptism of a child as soon as possible after birth. It should be remembered that the Code is for the entire Latin Rite, which includes many third world countries where infant mortality is very high, and canon 1183, 3 permits the Catholic burial of a baptized non-Catholic. This is understandable especially when a non-Catholic Christian has been attending Catholic services with the Catholic spouse and family.

Finally, there is the issue of denying Catholic burial to a deceased person. The Code is very clear and precise when denial can take place. The legislation for this instance is found in canon 1184. The law must be followed *literally* in this case for it deals with a Catholic's right to Christian burial.[19] Thus, denial of a Catholic burial can be *only* when it is *very* clear that a person dies as a non-repentant sinner. If there was the *least sign* of repentance, the person should not be denied a Catholic burial, though it is reasonable to assume that the celebration of the burial should be low-keyed lest scandal is given. The *unrepentant* persons who can be denied a Catholic burial are those who have publicly and officially left the Church or chose cremation in contempt of the Church's teachings. The other instance is when the Christian burial of a well-known and public sinner can create a scandal. It is always wise and advisable to seek the advice of the local ordinary when there is a hint of the possibility that a deceased person might be denied Christian burial.

---

[19] C. 18 states that a law which restricts a person's rights must be interpreted strictly.

12. Marriage Impediments

Impediments to Marriage — 1

Canon 1058 states that every person has a natural right to marry. This right includes the free choice of a marriage partner. Since this right is rooted in natural law, it may be restricted only for grave and just reasons. The restriction must be strictly interpreted so that whenever there is a doubt, one's natural right to marry must be upheld.

A marriage can be invalid due to the presence of certain *impediments* or obstructions to a valid union. In other words, one or both of the partners is incapable of entering a valid marriage because of some impediment. An impediment may be due to either a circumstance or a condition which has such a direct bearing on marriage that the law forbids such a marriage. An impediment rooted in a circumstance which is directly related to the person ceases when the circumstance is no longer present. An impediment rooted in a condition in the person might or might not cease in a person. The current law contains only *diriment impediments*.[1]

Church lawyers and Church legal scholars have always distinguished between impediments which are based on *divine law* and impediments rooted in *Church law*.[2] Those impediments which are rooted in divine law are based on marriage as a natural institution. Such impediments affect *all* human beings, baptized or not. On the other

---

[1] C. 1073 defines a diriment impediment, that is an impediment whose presence renders invalid the marital consent between the spouses. CC. 1083-1092 are dedicated to impediments. See *Navarre*, "Diriment Impediments in General," 667-669.

[2] See J. O'Rourke, "The Scriptural Background of the Marriage Impediments," *J* 20 (1960) 29-41.

hand, those impediments rooted in Church law are based on the sacramental nature of marriage and its relation to the Catholic community.[3] The Holy See *alone* is competent to interpret and state which impediments are based on divine law. Furthermore, the Holy See is the *only authority* which has the power to state what are impediments rooted in Church law and to establish new ones.[4]

There are basically two kinds of impediments: absolute and relative. The terms are practically self-explanatory. *Absolute impediments* affect a marriage with all persons, whether baptized or not. *Relative impediments* affect marriages only with certain persons. Some impediments are *perpetual* since the situation which causes them is always present, while others are *temporary* since their cause may disappear in time or the person is *dispensed* by a competent Church authority. The latter may dispense only certain types of impediments.[5]

Impediments to Marriage — 2

Canon 1083 deals with the diriment impediment of *insufficient age.* This is an interesting impediment because it has two kinds of applications: one deals with Catholics and the other deals with non-baptized persons. The impediment ceases by the passage of time.

The canon states that Catholic men who have not completed their sixteenth birthday and Catholic women who have not completed their fourteenth birthday may not contract a valid marriage. On the other hand, non-baptized persons are not bound by this impediment but are bound by the civil laws regulating the minimum age for a civilly valid marriage. Thus, the impediment for Catholics is based on Church law, while the impediment for the non-baptized is based on civil law.[6] This

---

[3] Impediments rooted in Church law affect only baptized Catholics who have not left the Catholic Church through a formal act by the time of exchanging marital consent. This understanding is based on c. 11.

[4] C. 1075. See *Navarre*, 669-670, n. 1075.

[5] C. 1078. See *Navarre*, 671-672, n. 1078.

[6] A marriage between two non-baptized persons which is considered invalid by civil law is also considered invalid by canon law. This is one of those very few instances where canon law adopts (*canonizes*) civil law.

impediment for Catholics is rooted in a balanced approach toward a person's natural right to marry. On the one hand there is the minimum age to contract marriage validly, on the other hand earlier canons about marriage strongly discourage the marriage between two very young persons.[7] The Code allows each conference of bishops to raise the minimum age for marriage, but such an act has to do with the *liceity* and not the validity of marriage.[8] At present, many conferences of bishops around the world have established guidelines which deal with marriage preparation and readiness, including the requirements of minimum age.

Canon 1084 deals with the impediment of *physical impotence*.[9] This impediment arises from the incapacity of a man or a woman to have normal sexual intercourse. When the impediment is present, that marriage is automatically invalid. Since this impediment deals with the very essence of marriage, it is rooted in divine law. No power on earth has the power to dispense from it.

The issue of what precisely constitutes the presence of this impediment has been a matter of dispute. Due to the fact that this impediment may involve physical and psychic issues, the contribution of research by experts in the medical and behavioral sciences is most valuable to determine its presence. Furthermore, the impediment must be *antecedent* and *perpetual*. This means that it must have been present since the time prior to the marriage and incurable by natural human means. The impediment must be present always. Thus, if a person becomes impotent subsequent to the marriage ceremony, it does not render that marriage invalid. The condition can be *absolute*, that is a person is incapable of having normal sexual intercourse with all persons, or *relative*, that is a person is incapable of having normal sexual intercourse with one or some but not all persons. While the presence of physical impotence invalidates a marriage, sterility does not invalidate a marriage. Sexual potency deals with a person's capacity to en-

---

[7] See c. 1071, 1, 6° and c. 1072. See *Navarre*, 666-667, n. 1071.

[8] C. 1083, 2. The Holy See alone may establish impediments which deal with the invalidity of a marriage (c. 1075). See *Navarre*, 669-670, n. 1075; 675, n. 1083.

[9] See *Navarre*, 675-676, n. 1084.

gage in normal sexual intercourse. On the other hand, sterility deals with a person's capacity to have children. If sterility were an invalidating factor in a marriage, then women beyond child-bearing age would be prohibited from marrying validly. But this is not the case.

Marriage Impediments — 3

Canon 1085 deals with the impediment of a *valid prior marriage bond* at the time of a subsequent marriage. It is important to note that the prior marriage bond must be a valid one. There may be instances when there has been a prior marriage which, for some reason, was invalid.[10] The valid bond must also be in existence at the time of the person's subsequent marriage. Thus, a widow or a widower may have been in a prior valid marital bond but is now free to marry because the other party is deceased.

The *marriage bond* is a reality which goes beyond the spouses. Once established through the valid exchange of the marriage vows, it continues to exist independently of the couple's will to continue or to terminate their marital union. Once a valid marital consent is exchanged between man and wife, there arises a juridical obligation of mutual fidelity between the spouses until death.[11] It is by its very nature exclusive and, therefore, it does not allow one to have more than one spouse at a time.

This valid marriage bond can either be *natural* or *sacramental*. It is a natural bond when there is the valid exchange of marital consent between two persons, one or both of whom are non-baptized.[12] It is a sacramental bond when there is the valid exchange of marital consent between two baptized persons, be they Catholics or not.

---

[10] For example, one or both parties were invalidly married to another person due to defect or absence of the canonical form.

[11] Church law, independent of civil law, has its own procedures for arriving at the presumption of the death of a spouse in the absence of proof of death (c. 1707). If, in fact, the spouse is still alive, the other spouse's second marriage is invalid. See *Navarre*, "The Process in the Case of the Presumed Death of a Spouse," 1053-1054.

[12] A valid marital bond can be dissolved. See chapters entitled Marriage Dissolution.

A valid sacramental marital bond which has been consummated through the sexual act ceases *only* with the death of one of the spouses. A sacramental but *non-consummated* bond can be *dissolved* by the Holy Father.[13] A valid *natural* marital bond ceases with the death of one of the spouses or it can also be *dissolved* by the Holy Father.[14] If a former marriage, which had been presumed to be valid, was eventually adjudicated as null, the person may enter a subsequent valid union during the lifetime of his or her former marriage partner. The reason for this is that the prior union was never a valid marital bond and, therefore, the impediment of a valid marriage bond is absent. The fact that a person is no longer held bound to a prior bond does not release that person from natural and moral obligations toward the children and/or former spouse of that union.

The following are some straightforward examples of the impediment of a valid prior marriage bond:

(a) Jane married James in a church or chapel or a civil ceremony. Both are non-Catholic Christians. This is the first marriage for both. The couple divorced. While Jane is still alive, James marries Anne, also a non-Catholic Christian. James' second marriage is null and void due to a presumed valid sacramental prior marriage bond.

(b) Jane, a non-Catholic Christian, married James, an unbaptized person, in a church or chapel or a civil ceremony. This is the first marriage for both. The couple divorced. While Jane is still alive, James marries Anne, a non-Catholic Christian. James' second marriage is null and void due to a presumed valid natural prior marriage bond.

(c) Jane married James in a church or chapel or a civil ceremony. Both are unbaptized. This is the first marriage for both. The couple divorced. While Jane is still alive, James marries Anne, a non-Catholic Christian. James' second marriage is null and void due to a presumed valid natural prior marriage bond.

---

[13] C. 1142. The fact that such a bond is *dissolved* indicates that the bond is valid.

[14] C. 1143. See *Navarre*, 720, n. 1143.

(d) Jane married James in a church or chapel or a civil ceremony. Both are unbaptized. This is the first marriage for both. The couple divorced. While Jane is still alive, James marries Anne, also an unbaptized person. James' second marriage is null and void due to a presumed valid natural prior marriage bond.

(e) Jane married James in a church or chapel or a civil ceremony. Both are non-Catholic Christians. This is the first marriage for both. The couple divorced. While Jane is still alive, James marries Anne, a non-Catholic Christian. Then Anne divorces James and marries Tom, also a non-Catholic Christian, in a church or chapel or a civil ceremony, while James is still alive. This is Tom's first marriage and Jane's second marriage. This marriage is presumed a valid sacramental marriage since James' marriage to Anne is null and void due to a presumed valid sacramental prior marriage bond.

(f) Jane married James in a church or chapel or a civil ceremony. Both are unbaptized. This is the first marriage for both. The couple divorced. While Jane is still alive, James marries Anne, also an unbaptized person. Then Anne divorces James and marries Tom, also an unbaptized person, in a church or chapel or a civil ceremony, while James is still alive. This is Tom's first marriage and Anne's second marriage. This marriage is presumed a valid natural marriage since James' marriage to Anne is null and void due to a presumed valid natural prior marriage bond for Jane.

Marriage Impediments — 4

Canon 1086 deals with the impediment of *disparity of cult*.[15] A sacramental marriage entails that both parties are baptized. A marriage between a Catholic and a non-baptized person is not a sacrament but a natural bond.[16] The Catholic Church has regulated the relationship

---

[15] See *Navarre*, 677-679, n. 1086.

[16] The marrying couple are the ministers of marriage. However, in order to have a sacramental marriage *both* parties must have first received the sacrament of baptism.

between such persons as an impediment *only* for Catholics. It is not an impediment for a non-Catholic Christian or those Catholics who left the Church by a formal act[17] and marry an unbaptized person.[18]

A *dispensation from disparity of cult* is required of a Catholic to marry validly a non-baptized person. This dispensation is subject to the same canonical conditions in the case of permission for a mixed marriage.[19] Canon 1125 dictates the conditions for the dispensation: the declaration of the Catholic party that he or she removes all danger from falling away from the Catholic faith and will raise the children of that union as baptized Catholics; the unbaptized party is made aware of the obligations of the Catholic party; both parties are instructed in and accept the essential ends and properties of marriage.[20]

A competent Church authority may grant a dispensation from disparity of cult so that a Catholic may validly marry a non-baptized person.

Canon 1087 deals with the impediment of *sacred orders*.[21] This impediment is rooted in Church law and every bishop, priest, and deacon is bound by it for all have the obligation of celibacy.[22] A dispensation from this impediment is *never* granted to a bishop. The Holy See *alone* can grant a dispensation from this impediment to priests.[23] The Holy See may also grant this dispensation to a deacon. In case of danger of death, however, the local ordinary may grant a dispensation to deacons but not to priests.[24] Married men who have been or-

---

[17] A person who has departed from the Catholic faith by a formal act is not in the same situation as a Catholic who does not practice the faith. The latter is still bound to the impediment when it comes to marrying a non-baptized person.

[18] Included among the non-baptized are members of certain Christian denominations who do not baptize or whose form of baptism is considered invalid by the Catholic Church, e.g. Jehovah's Witnesses.

[19] A mixed marriage is a marriage between a Catholic and a validly baptized non-Catholic.

[20] See *Navarre*, 712-713, n. 1125.

[21] See *Navarre*, 679-680, n. 1087.

[22] C. 277, 1. The Code for the Catholic Eastern Churches has its own regulations on clerical celibacy and marriage.

[23] C. 1078, 2, 1°. See *Navarre*, 670-671, n. 1078.

[24] C. 1079, 1. See *Navarre*, 671-673, n. 1079.

dained permanent deacons may not marry validly after ordination should they become widowers or have their marriage declared null. On the other hand, single men who wish to become permanent deacons are bound to perpetual celibacy if they are not married by the time of their diaconate ordination.[25]

Canon 1088 deals with the impediment of a *public perpetual vow of chastity*.[26] Those men and women who made a public vow of perpetual chastity, which is one of the three evangelical counsels in a religious Community, are bound by this impediment, which invalidates an attempted marriage. A public vow is one taken by a member of a religious institute of either pontifical or diocesan right.[27] The phrase *public vow* is very important since the impediment is attached to only this type of vow and not to the other kinds of commitment to the same evangelical counsel which are allowed in other types of institutes of consecrated life as stated in canon 573, 2. The vow must also be *perpetual* and not temporary. A person who has taken a public perpetual vow of chastity may be dispensed from this vow so that he or she may enter a valid marriage.

Marriage Impediments — 5

The next two canons on impediments are rare, if they ever occur in the United States. There are very strict penalties in the civil code should such abhorrent acts take place. Canon 1089 deals with the impediment of *abduction of a woman* for the purpose of marriage.[28] The impediment ceases when the woman is free to make her choice to marry. But there always remains the lingering doubt about how much the woman has overcome her trauma by the time she marries either her kidnapper or his accomplice. Canon 1090 deals with the impediment of *crime*.

---

[25] C. 1037.

[26] See *Navarre*, 680, n. 1088.

[27] See all the chapters dedicated to Consecrated Life.

[28] See *Navarre*, 680-681, n. 1089.

The first degree of crime is when a spouse murders the other spouse for the purpose of becoming free to marry someone in the future. The second degree of crime is when the spouse and his or her accomplice murder the innocent spouse so that the guilty parties can marry. This impediment, whether the crime is uncovered or not, never ceases.[29]

Canon 1091 is a complicated canon. It deals with the impediment of *consanguinity*. The basis for this impediment is that of *true blood relationship* between two individuals, irrespective of the marital status of their common ancestor.[30] There is the direct line and the collateral line in this relationship. The *direct line* is based on the biological descent from one person to another. The impediment is always present between a person and his or her direct descendants. For instance, a person may never marry his or her child, grandchild, great grandchild, and so on.[31] Such a marriage is automatically invalid. The *collateral line* is rooted in blood relatives. The impediment of consanguinity exists between brother and sister,[32] between uncle and niece, between aunt and nephew, and between first cousins. The best way to establish whether there is the impediment of consanguinity between blood relatives is to count the number of persons between the man and the woman, leaving out their common ancestor. If the number is four or less, then the impediment stands. If the number of persons is five or more, then there is no impediment.[33] The following diagram might explain better how to pin down the impediment of consanguinity on the collateral line:

---

[29] See *Navarre*, 682, n. 1090.

[30] See *Navarre*, 682-683, nn. 1091-1094.

[31] Marriage between such individuals is prohibited by divine law. See *Navarre*, 683, n. 1091.

[32] Marriage between persons related to one another on the second degree of the collateral line, that is brother and sister or a half-brother and a half-sister, is prohibited by divine law.

[33] C. 108 states how consanguinity is calculated.

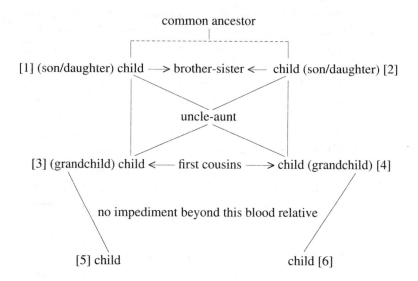

The prohibition of a marriage between persons who are in the second degree on the collateral line applies to every person, Catholic or not. But, the impediment for a marriage between people in the third and fourth degree on the collateral line applies *only* to Catholics for the prohibition is based on Church law. The Church, however, can grant a *dispensation* for those who belong to the last two degrees. Special attention should be given to civil law since some of the States may prohibit such unions. Hence, it is important to check with the legislation of the State where the proposed marriage is going to take place. If such a prohibition exists in that particular State, the marriage may not take place in that civil jurisdiction even if a church dispensation has been procured.

Marriage Impediments — 6

Canon 1092 deals with the impediment of *affinity*. The impediment is present between a spouse and all of his or her in-laws in the *direct line.*[34] The impediment includes the direct descendants of one's spouse through another marriage, that is stepchildren and so on. It remains even after the death of a spouse. Canon 109 defines affinity as that relationship with arises from a *valid* marriage even when the marriage has not been consummated.[35] Since canon 110 terms adopted children as being equivalent to natural children, the impediment applies also to the direct descendants of such a person. The impediment is rooted in Church law and applies to Catholics only. Although Church law prohibits marriage between a spouse and the blood relatives of the other spouse in the direct line, one has to look at the civil code of each State to ascertain whether this is also the case in civil law since some States prohibit marriages only within certain degrees of affinity. Non-Catholics marrying among themselves are bound by the civil code. In the case of a Catholic, that person needs a *dispensation* for the marriage to be validly contracted.

Canon 1093 deals with the impediment of *public propriety*. This impediment arises from the relationship between a man and a woman who are either in an invalid marriage or living together or have a long term sexual relationship, such as a man having a mistress. It should be noted that by the term *invalid* is meant not only those marriages which are considered automatically invalid by the Catholic Church due to some impediment or the absence of abiding by Church law, but also those marriages which have been declared null and void through a canonical trial. The impediment does not arise from a non-sacramental or non-consummated marriage which has been dissolved by the competent Church authority, since these unions are considered valid. This impediment is based on Church discipline and a person may request a *dispensation* to enter a valid union.

---

[34] The *direct line* entails the descendants or ancestors of a spouse, for example, one's mother or daughter or granddaughter. It does *not* apply to the spouse's relations in the *collateral line*, for example, one's brother or uncle or aunt or niece, and so on.

[35] There is no affinity when there has been an invalid marriage on the part of one or both spouses, for example, in a Lack of the Canonical Form marriage case or a marriage which has been declared null and void through a canonical trial.

Finally, there is the impediment of a *legal relationship*, stated in canon 1094. Church law has to depend on the civil code to determine whether such a legal relationship between two persons is present for this relationship arises from the act of civil legal adoption. Once again, one has to study the civil code of each State to determine what procedures and restrictions, if any, a particular State requires for legal adoption and whether that State prohibits or restricts a marriage between such persons. However, canon law, irrespective of civil law, has some prohibitions in regards to marriages between *Catholic persons* who have a legal relationship. Church law prohibits marriages between a legally adopted person and his or her legally adoptive parents, as well as between legally adopted siblings. Church law does not prohibit marriages between a person and the members of a family with whom he or she has lived without being legally adopted. Church law also prohibits the marriage between a person and the adopted children of his or her spouse by another marriage unless a *dispensation* from the competent Church authority has been procured. The impediment ceases when a civil legal act terminates the legal adoptive relationship.

13. Marriage Tribunals

Tribunals — Introduction

Matthew 18:15-18 presents to the Church the basis for the notion of *Church Courts* or *Tribunals*. The Lord states that a certain procedure should be followed to resolve an issue. The wrong party should bring to the violator's attention the harm done. If the latter ignores it, reiterate the charge in front of two or three witnesses. If this is ignored, refer the matter to the Church. If this goes unheeded, then the violator should be regarded as an outcast.

St. Paul follows a similar structure. Every case should have a couple of witnesses.[1] In fact, while acknowledging with regret litigation among Christians, he encourages the setting up of some kind of a Christian court.[2] The Church has had in operation some kind of ecclesiastical courts since that time.

Our contemporary Church has a highly developed legal system. The system's model of adjudication is not based on who can win a case, but is aimed at uncovering the truth so that justice may triumph. Thus, all the officers of an ecclesiastical tribunal are charged with the responsibility of finding the truth in the case sitting before them. An *ecclesiastical trial* consists of a discovery, hearing, argumentation, and settlement by an ecclesiastical court or forum of a controversy in an issue or allegation over which the Church enjoys competence or jurisdiction.

There are one hundred canons in the 1983 Code which deal with

---

[1] See 2 Corinthians 13:1; 1 Timothy 5:19.

[2] See 1 Corinthians 6:16.

ecclesiastical trials in general.[3] An ecclesiastical trial basically consists of five elements: the material object, the formal object, the active subject, the passive subject, and the form of the adjudication process.

The *material object* of a trial deals with matters which, generally speaking, can be addressed by a tribunal.[4] The *formal object* in a
trial is the precise claim which is being made by either or both parties
in a trial.[5] Cases are adjudicated by an ecclesiastical judge or collegiate tribunal. The latter form the *active subject* in a trial.[6] The Church
affirms its area of competence over spiritual[7] and spiritually connected
matters,[8] and cases involving the breaking of Church law.[9] The *passive subject* in a trial is the petitioner and the respondent.[10] They form
the parties to the case which is being adjudicated. Finally, the *form* of
adjudication deals with the procedures which are followed in the course
of a trial.[11]

As is the case with the secular legal system, the Church has different kinds of courts. One type of Church court is called the *ordinary
tribunal*. Its purpose is to prosecute or vindicate rights or declare legal facts through a *contentious* trial. Another purpose of such a court
is to investigate crimes with the view of imposing or declaring a penalty. In this case, it is a *penal* trial.[12] Another type of Church court is
an *administrative tribunal*. Its purpose is to settle a dispute which has

---

[3] The canons are 1400 through 1500.

[4] C. 1400. See *Navarre*, 869-870, n. 1400.

[5] C. 1491. See *Navarre*, 929, n. 1491. The claim is treated in cc. 1491-1500.

[6] C. 1401. See *Navarre*, 870, n. 1401.

[7] For example, marriage cases (c. 1671). The Roman Pontiff has reserved to the Roman
Rota the adjudication of marriage cases which involve persons who occupy the highest
civil position in a country, such as a sovereign or a governor in the United States and
his or her children. The rationale behind this law is to remove possible pressure on the
local judge from the interested powerful civil authority (c. 1405, 1, 1°).

[8] For example, the rights of parish priests.

[9] For example, when a priest abuses his responsibility as a pastor.

[10] C. 1476. See *Navarre*, 920-921, n. 1476. The petitioner and the respondent, as well as
the procurators and advocates who represent them, are discussed in cc. 1476-1490.

[11] C. 1402.

[12] See c. 1400, 1.

arisen from an administrative decision or decree of either a bishop or a superior. If a matter cannot be settled informally, then it can be settled by an administrative tribunal or hierarchical resource.[13]

Tribunal Officials — 1

Church tribunals, like civil tribunals, have officials. Some of the tribunal officials are involved throughout an entire case, while others are involved at different stages in a case. This chapter will present the role of tribunal officials involved in a marriage case on a regular basis.

The diocesan tribunal is the tribunal of first instance.[14] According to canon 1419, 1 the diocesan bishop is the judge in this kind of tribunal in all of its marriage cases, except those enumerated in the Code as belonging to other tribunals.[15] Though the diocesan bishop has judicial power[16] and can exercise it personally, he usually exercises it through others.[17] It is his duty to establish a functional tribunal in his diocese, with a *judicial vicar* in charge.[18]

Canon 1420, among other canons in the Code, presents the role and qualifications of the judicial vicar. The judicial vicar[19] and the diocesan bishop constitute one tribunal. He must be a cleric[20] of unimpaired reputation, with a licentiate or doctorate in canon law, and be at least thirty years of age. His jurisdiction is ordinary, vicarious,

---

[13] In this case, one goes to the superior of one's superior, and so forth. See c. 1400, 2 and c. 1445, 2.

[14] See chapter entitled, Tribunals — 4.

[15] For example, c. 1400, 2 speaks about cases which are heard by an administrative tribunal. C. 1404 states that no tribunal may judge the Holy Father. The other cases which the Code explicitly states do not belong to the diocesan tribunal are listed in c. 1405, c. 1419, 2 and c. 1427, 1-2.

[16] C. 391, 1.

[17] C. 391, 2 states that the diocesan bishop can exercise his judicial powers through the judicial vicar (c. 1420) and judges (c. 1421) duly appointed to such offices.

[18] C. 1420. See *Navarre*, 881-883, n. 1420.

[19] This ecclesiastical office is also known by the titles of *officialis* or chief judge. See Wrenn, *Procedures*, 13-14.

[20] C. 274, 1. An ordained person, including a deacon, can be a judicial vicar.

and judicial. His consent is required when another tribunal seeks to adjudicate a marriage case based on canon 1673, 3° and 4°.[21] It is his duty to assign judges to hear a marriage case in the order the cases have been received by the tribunal.[22] He possesses the authority to issue a decree by which he substitutes judges, for a serious reason, during the process of a case.[23] Moreover, the judicial vicar is responsible to send the proper notifications[24] once a marriage has been declared null and void. He is also responsible to adjudicate or designate a judge to adjudicate documentary cases.[25]

Although the judicial vicar is a vicar, his role is quite different than that of the other vicars in a diocese.[26] His jurisdiction rests over matters which are judicial and not over those in the executive or administrative spheres. As in the case with other vicars, the Code lists him as an *ex officio* member of a diocesan synod when it is convened.[27] He is not, however, included in the episcopal council.[28] The judicial vicar is appointed for a definite term.[29] He does not lose his office when

---

[21] C. 1673, 3° states that when the respondent does not live in the diocese of the petitioner's domicile but resides within the same conference of bishops, the tribunal where the petitioner has domicile can be competent to hear the case as long as the respondent's judicial vicar gives his consent, after hearing from the respondent. C. 1673, 4° states that the tribunal of the place where *in fact* there are most proofs may competently hear the case after procuring the consent of the respondent's judicial vicar who grants it once he had discovered if the respondent has any objections. See chapter entitled, Tribunals — 4.

[22] C. 1425, 3. This is effective as long as the diocesan bishop has not designed some other system to assign marriage cases to the judges.

[23] C. 1425, 5.

[24] C. 1685 states that once the decision of marriage nullity has been published, the judicial vicar is responsible to notify the ordinary of the place of the marriage contract as well as the churches where the marriage and the Catholic baptism of the parties occurred. He is also to alert them to any restrictions which the decree of nullity contains. See chapter entitled, Marriage Formal Trial — 8, n. 109.

[25] C. 1686. See *Navarre*, 1041, n. 1686 and chapters entitled, Lack of Canonical Form, Defect of Canonical Form.

[26] See chapters dedicated to the Vicar General and the Episcopal Vicar as well as c. 418, 2, 1°; c. 463, 1, 2°; c. 472; c. 473, 4; cc. 476-481; c. 833, 5°.

[27] C. 463, 1, 3°.

[28] See chapter entitled, Code and Diocesan Consultation — 6.

[29] C. 1422.

the diocese becomes vacant, though he needs to be confirmed in it once the new diocesan bishop takes possession of his diocese.[30]

Tribunal Officials — 2

Canon 1420, 3[31] states that the judicial vicar may have assistants. The latter are known as *adjutant judicial vicars* or *vice officiales*. Their qualifications, term of office, and status when the see is vacant, are identical to those of the judicial vicar.[32]

Canon 1421 states that it is the duty of the diocesan bishop to appoint *judges* to serve on the tribunal. Thus, apart from the judicial and adjutant judicial vicars, there are also judges. The norm is that these judges should be clerics.[33] The Code, however, also states that judges can be lay persons, male and female, whether or not they are members of institutes of consecrated life. Two conditions must be met in order to have non-ordained persons serve as judges: the competent episcopal conference must have voted to allow the appointment of such persons in the dioceses within the conference,[34] and only one lay judge can serve as a member of a collegiate tribunal.[35] In other words, when a marriage case involves one judge, he must be a cleric[36] and never a lay person, but when there is a collegiate tribunal, one of the judges can be a lay person. The qualifications of a judge are slightly different than those required for the judicial vicar and his adjutants in that the latter must be clerics. The rest of the qualifications[37] are identical for these ecclesiastical offices except that there is no minimum age requirement for a judge.[38]

---

[30] C. 1420, 5.

[31] See *Navarre*, 881-883, n. 1420.

[32] See chapter entitled, Tribunal Officials — 1.

[33] C. 1421, 1. See *Navarre*, 883, n. 1421.

[34] C. 1425, 4

[35] C. 1421, 2. A collegiate tribunal is composed of at least three judges.

[36] A *deacon* can be a sole judge because he is a cleric.

[37] C. 1421, 3.

[38] C. 1421, 3.

Canon 1428 states that a judge may appoint an *auditor* to carry out the instruction of a case.[39] The auditor can be a cleric or a lay person approved by the bishop.[40] He or she is not required to have a degree in canon law, but must be outstanding in character, prudent and learned.[41] It is the duty of the auditor to collect the evidence in an assigned case in accordance with the judge's mandate and present them to him. The auditor, unless specifically directed by the judge to do otherwise, has the discretion to decide in what manner and what proofs are to be collected.[42] This approach gives a lot of operational latitude and responsibility to an auditor.

Tribunal Officials — 3

Canon 1432 speaks about the *defender of the bond*. The defender, appointed by the diocesan bishop, can be a cleric or a lay person of unimpaired reputation, with a degree in canon law, prudent and with a zeal for justice.[43]

Canon 1436, 2[44] states that every diocese must have a defender of the bond and a particular defender may be appointed either permanently or on an *ad hoc* basis. There must be, however, a defender of the bond in every marriage case, whether the petition is for a declaration of nullity or dissolution. Canon 1433[45] rules that when the defender is not consulted before the sentence is rendered, the entire procedure is rendered *invalid* by the law itself. In other words, the Code calls for

---

[39] The title *auditor* goes back to the beginning of the Roman Rota when the Pope judged cases but appointed others to hear (audit) the witnesses and collect and prepare the evidence in the case.

[40] C. 1428, 1-2. See *Navarre*, 888-889.

[41] C. 1428, 2.

[42] C. 1428, 3.

[43] C. 1435. Suggested readings: J. Burke, "The Defender of the Bond in the New Code," *J* 45 (1985) 210-229; *Navarre*, 893, n. 1435; Pope Pius XII, "The Defender of the Bond and the Advocate," in L. Wrenn, *Annulments*, 4th ed. rev., 133-135.

[44] See *Navarre*, 893, n. 1436.

[45] See *Navarre*, 892, n. 1433.

the *active* involvement by the defender. He or she can propose anything which can reasonably uphold the validity of a marriage.[46] It is also his or her responsibility to ensure that all the proper canonical procedures have been followed. He or she can also appeal the decision of the judge to a higher court.

The defender may not serve in the capacity of judge in the same case, no matter what instance the case is at. He or she can propose questions to be posed to the petitioner and/or respondent in a marriage case. He or she can examine the witnesses in the case. He or she has a right to be present when the parties and witnesses are giving testimony and while experts are submitting their comments and evaluation.[47]

The *notary* is another tribunal official. The appointment is made by the diocesan bishop.[48] A notary can be a cleric or a lay person, of good character and reputation.[49] He or she must be Catholic.[50] Canon 1437 states that the notary should be present during each procedure at a marriage trial. The acts of the marriage case are considered null if they are not notarized.

It is the responsibility of the notary to commit to writing a petition that has been presented through an oral request,[51] and verify the presence of the parties if they are present at the proceedings.[52] He or she is to certify when the acts of the case are read to the petitioner and the respondent.

Tribunals — 1

There are various *grades* and *kinds* of tribunals or Church courts.[53] A *grade* deals with the hierarchical level of the tribunal. There are four

---

[46] C. 1432. See *Navarre*, n. 1432.

[47] C. 1678, 1. See *Navarre*, 1035-1036, n. 1678.

[48] C. 483.

[49] Ibid.

[50] C. 149.

[51] C. 1503, 2. See *Navarre*, 936, n.1503.

[52] C. 1507, 3. See *Navarre*, 939-940, n. 1507.

[53] See *Navarre*, 878-879.

grades of tribunals. The first grade is that of the diocesan tribunal or the interdiocesan tribunal for an ecclesiastical province.[54] The second grade is the metropolitan tribunal.[55] The third grade is the regional tribunal.[56] The fourth grade is the tribunals of the Apostolic See.[57] The grade of a tribunal does not necessarily coincide with the instance or level of adjudicating a case. For example, a metropolitan tribunal may be the tribunal of first instance in a case.

There are also four *kinds* or *types* of tribunals. One kind of tribunal may have one judge or a collegiate of three or five judges.[58] Another kind of tribunal may be diocesan or interdiocesan[59] or religious.[60] Another kind of tribunal may be ordinary or administrative.[61] Still another kind of tribunal may be matrimonial or of general jurisdiction.

There is also the *grade of judgment* in the tribunal system. This grade refers to the *instance* in the case and not to the hierarchical level of the tribunal. For example, a marriage case is usually submitted to the diocesan tribunal which is first instance. The decision is either reviewed or appealed to the metropolitan tribunal, which is second instance. The same decision may be further appealed to the Roman Rota, which serves as third instance in the same marriage case.[62] All marriage cases are adjudicated in the order in which they were presented and put on a docket.[63] All tribunals follow the rules of appeal as stated in canon 1438.[64]

---

[54] An ecclesiastical province is a territorial grouping of neighboring dioceses, one of which has been designated by the Apostolic See as an archdiocese (c. 431).

[55] A ecclesiastical metropolis is an archdiocese (c. 435).

[56] An ecclesiastical region is comprised of a number of ecclesiastical provinces. The Holy See alone can erect an ecclesiastical region (c. 433, 1).

[57] See chapter entitled, Tribunals — 2, n. 70.

[58] See cc. 1424-1426. See *Navarre*, 884-887, nn. 1424, 1425, 1426.

[59] See c. 1423. See *Navarre*, 884, n. 1423.

[60] See c. 1427. See *Navarre*, 887-888, n. 1427.

[61] See c. 1400, 2 and c. 1445, 2.

[62] See chapter entitled, Tribunals — 2, n. 70.

[63] C. 1458.

[64] See *Navarre*, 895-896, n. 1438.

A tribunal's constitution is rather straightforward. Canon 1424[65] states that when there is one judge, he may use two assessors as consultors. The assessors may be either clerics or lay persons. Canon 1425, 1 states that marriage cases[66] should have at least three judges since such cases are contentious. Canon 1425, 4, however, states that if such a collegiate tribunal cannot be established, the pertinent episcopal conference can approve a norm where a single *clerical* judge can adjudicate a marriage case in first instance. Furthermore, he should use an assessor and an auditor whenever possible. Finally, the court of second instance must have a collegiate tribunal to rule on the same case.[67]

A tribunal cannot adjudicate a petition when it is not competent to do so because it does not enjoy the required jurisdiction over the case in question. Furthermore, unlike civil jurisprudence, Church tribunals do not have a precedence setting system. Decisions rendered by prominent tribunal judges, such as those on the *Roman Rota*, are perceived as scholarly interpretations of Church, positive and natural laws. Though an ecclesiastical judge is not bound to follow them, wise judges always do so.

Tribunals — 2

The code distinguishes between *absolute* and *relative* incompetence. This is dictated by the competent forum. Canons 1404-1406 list the competence of the *extraordinary forum*. The acts and decisions in the cases listed in these three canons are considered null when carried out by a tribunal which does not enjoy competence over them.[68] Moreover, the court officials participating in the process may be liable to

---

[65] See *Navarre*, 885, n. 1424.

[66] The exception to having three judges is stated in c. 1686 and c. 1688, that is documentary cases. See chapters entitled, Lack of Canonical Form and Defect of Canonical Form.

[67] C. 1441 and c. 1682, 2. See *Navarre*, 897-898, n. 1441; 1038, n. 1682.

[68] See c. 1620, 10. See *Navarre*, 1002-1003, n. 1620.

incur Church sanctions or penalties. Thus, all tribunals in the Church are *absolutely incompetent* to adjudicate the Holy Father. He is judicially immune.[69]

Canon 1405 lists those cases which are reserved to the Apostolic See or which the Apostolic See declares reserved to itself or to its delegated tribunal. Other tribunals are absolutely incompetent to adjudicate such cases. There are also cases which are reserved to the Roman Rota,[70] such as the *third instance* in marriage cases.[71] Canon 1406 states that there are no exceptions to the cases listed in the prior canon. In summary, unless a tribunal falls within the category of canon 1405, its acts and decisions are absolutely incompetent.[72]

Canons 1407-1416 deal with the *ordinary forum*. These canons legislate not only on marriage cases but on other cases as well, such as contracts and obligations ensuing from such contracts. The latter kind of cases are rarely, if ever, adjudicated at tribunals in the United States.

Canon 1407[73] lays down the general principles to be followed by the competent ordinary forum. Thus, no one can be cited by a court of first instance unless a competent judge does so. The forum of the respondent always takes precedence over the forum of the petitioner.[74] If a person is cited by a judge who does not enjoy jurisdiction in the ordinary forum, then the judge is relatively incompetent. *Relative incompetence* is based on canons 1408-1414 in regards to trials in general, and canon 1673 for marriage cases. Relative incompetence ren-

---

[69] C. 1404. See *Navarre*, 872, n. 1404.

[70] The *Roman Rota* is one of the three tribunals of the Roman Curia. The other two tribunals are the *Apostolic Penitentiary* and the *Supreme Tribunal of the Apostolic Signatura*. The Roman Rota is the principal appellate court of the Roman Curia. The Roman Rota has competence to hear appeals of marriage cases in second and third instance (cc. 1443-1444). See Broderick, "Apostolic Signatura," 47-48; idem., "Penitentiary, Sacred Apostolic," 468; idem., "Rota, Sacred Roman," 530.

[71] The exception to this is the country of Spain which, due to an ancient privilege granted by the Holy See, has been specifically designated to have its own *Rota*. This means that Spain has its own tribunal of third instance.

[72] See *Navarre*, 873, n. 1406.

[73] See *Navarre*, 874, n. 1407.

[74] See c. 1407, 3 and c. 1673, 20.

ders the legal process irregular but not invalid.[75] It occurs when a judge acts illicitly because there is a territorial defect,[76] that is the place of contract[77] or the respondent's domicile[78] or quasi-domicile do not fall within the jurisdiction of that court.

Canon 1417 states that every member of the faithful has a right to bring his or her case to the Apostolic See.[79] In practice, however, it is better to begin a case at the local diocesan or interdiocesan tribunal since every affirmative decision on a marriage petition is sent to the Court of Appeals.[80]

Tribunals — 3

Church courts or tribunals are not limited to marriage cases. However, in the United States, marriage nullity cases are the primary and, in many cases, the sole purpose of having a tribunal in a diocese. Thus, the chapters which deal with tribunals will be principally limited to *marriage tribunals*.[81]

---

[75] See c. 1620, 10.

[76] For the validity of a decision in a marriage nullity case, see chapter entitled, Tribunals — 4, particularly n. 93.

[77] See c. 1411, 1.

[78] C. 102 states that domicile is acquired when a resident, already living within the territorial boundaries of a diocese, intends to live there permanently or has been already living there for five years. Quasi-domicile is established by the same conditions except that the time is three months. C. 105 states that domicile and quasi-domicile are lost by departing from the place with no intention to return.

[79] See *Navarre*, 879, n. 1417.

[80] See chapter entitled, Tribunal of Second Instance.

[81] The term *marriage tribunal* is a species or kind of tribunal which falls under the genus *Tribunal*. The canonical literature on marriage tribunals and marriage cases is vast. The following are some suggested readings: J. Alesandro, ed., *Marriage Studies*, vol. IV; J. Burke, "The Defender of the Bond in the New Code," *J* 45 (1985) 210-229; F. Daneels, "The Forum of Most of the Proofs," *J* 50 (1990) 289-309; idem., "The Right to Defense," *SCa* 27 (1993) 77-98; T. Doyle, ed., *Marriage Studies*, vols. I-III; I. Gramont and L. Wauk, "Capacity and Incapacity to Contract Marriage," *SCa* 22 (1988) 147-168; Z. Grocholewski, "Theological Aspects of the Judicial Activity of the Church," *J* 46 (1986) 552-567; J. Hosie, *With Open Arms*; A. McGrath, "Conformity of Sentences in Marriage Nullity Cases," *SCa* 27 (1993) 5-22; idem., "At the Service of Truth: Psychological Sciences and Their Relation to the Canon Law on Nullity of

The Code considers every marriage case brought to one of its tribunals as being contentious. It is the presumption of the law that a marriage entered into by two persons who are free to marry is *valid*.[82] Thus, a marriage contracted between two baptized Christians is a sacrament. A marriage contracted between a baptized Christian and a non-baptized person or between two non-baptized persons is not a sacrament but a natural bond. However, *all* of these marriages are presumed *valid*.[83]

When a spouse petitions for an annulment, what is being sought is a canonical declaration on the status of the parties: were they truly married or not? The ultimate aim of the tribunal, then, is to discover the truth regarding the marital status of the parties involved.

The spouse who approaches the tribunal to initiate the process is called the *petitioner*.[84] He or she is alleging that there is proof that the marriage in question is invalid. One should keep in mind that it is neither the Church nor its courts that are making such an allegation.[85] On the contrary, the Church upholds the presumption of the validity of a marriage and gives it protection until it is proven through a canonical process that the presumption of the validity of that particular marriage has been overturned. Once this is done there ensues a declaration by the tribunal that the marriage in question is *null and void from its inception*. The burden of proof rests on the petitioner. The

---

Marriage," *SCa* 27 (1993) 379-400; A. Mendonca, "The Incapacity to Contract Marriage: Canon 1095," *SCa* 19 (1985) 259-325; idem., "The Theological and Juridical Aspects of Marriage," *SCa* 22 (1988) 265-304; J. O'Rourke, "The Competent Forum of Marriage Cases," *J* 54 (1994) 234-236; L. Orsy, *Marriage in Canon Law*; Pope Pius XII, "The Defender of the Bond and the Advocate" in Wrenn, *Annulments*, 133-135; idem., "Moral Certitude," in Wrenn, *Procedures*, 121-124; J. Provost, "The Requirement of Canonical Law Degrees for Court Officials," *J* 43 (1984) 422-429; idem., "Remarks Concerning Proofs and Presumptions," *J* 43 (1983) 237-245; F. Wallace, "Lack of Witnesses," *J* 49 (1989) 280-285; W. Woestman, "Respecting the Petitioner's Rights to Dissolution Procedures," *J* 50 (1990) 1: 342-349; L. Wrenn, "In Search of a Balanced Procedural Law for Marriage Nullity Cases," *J* 46 (1986) 602-623.

[82] See c. 1060. See also *CCC* 1601-1666.

[83] See chapter entitled, Marriage Cases — Introduction.

[84] The other party is called the *respondent*.

[85] The only exception is when the *promoter of justice*, in rare and exceptional cases, can also challenge the validity of a marriage (c. 1674, 20). See *Navarre*, 1032, n. 1674.

decisions of Church courts in the United States have no civil effects since these fall under the competence of civil courts.[86]

While the Catholic faith is not the only Christian faith, Christianity is not the only religion in the world. The Code affirms the Catholic Church's proper right to adjudicate marriages between *baptized* persons.[87] This right to adjudicate marriage cases is in regards to the validity or dissolution of a specific marriage between Christians. It should be noted that the claim is not only over marriages between baptized Catholics, but over all those between baptized Christians. In practice, however, the right to adjudicate a marriage case between two baptized non-Catholics is never exercised unless one of the former spouses wishes to marry a Catholic.

The Catholic Church asserts that any non-baptized spouse can seek from it a declaration of nullity of marriage. In practice, the Church does rule over such marriages when one of the former spouses wishes to marry a Catholic. This is stated in canon 1476[88] and indicated in canon 1674, 1°.

Tribunals — 4

The 1983 Code provides clear-cut bases on which a tribunal can claim competence over a marriage case. Canon 1673 spells out how a tribunal can claim such competence.

Canon 1673 excludes cases which are reserved to the Apostolic See[89] and of those tribunals which have been specifically designated by the Apostolic Signatura to adjudicate the case.[90] In all the other marriage cases, competence can be claimed by the tribunal of the dio-

---

[86] See c. 1672.

[87] C. 1671.

[88] See *Navarre*, 920, n. 1476.

[89] C. 1405. See also c. 1698 for non-consummated marriage cases. Although the *Petrine Privilege of the Faith* cases are also reserved to the Apostolic See, the restriction is not stated in the 1983 Code. See also chapter entitled, Marriage Dissolution — 3.

[90] C. 1416 and c. 1445, 1, 4°. There can be a number of reasons why the Apostolic Signatura would designate a tribunal which under normal circumstances is not competent to adjudicate a marriage case. For example, this happens when a petitioner or a respondent or the place of contract are in a diocese whose diocesan bishop is related to either party.

cese where the marriage occurred. This is the *place of contract*.[91] Competence can be claimed by the tribunal where the *respondent* has a domicile or quasi-domicile.[92] The next two ways of claiming competence depend on a number of things. Competence may be declared by the tribunal of the petitioner's domicile as long as both parties live within the same episcopal conference and the judicial vicar of the respondent's domicile gives his consent, having already contacted the respondent to inquire if there are any objections.[93] The respondent's consent and/or cooperation is *not* required for the validity of the process.[94] Finally, competence can be claimed by the tribunal of the forum where *in fact* most of the proofs are to be collected once the judicial vicar of the respondent's domicile gives his consent,[95] having already contacted the respondent to inquire if there are any objections. Once again, the respondent's consent and/or cooperation is *not* required. This norm is very important especially when tribunals of different episcopal conferences are involved.[96]

American society is very mobile. There are instances when the whereabouts of the respondent are unknown. In this case the petitioner has to submit to his or her tribunal all the efforts and means which were employed in the attempt to locate the former spouse. Then, the judge or judges in the case decide whether such efforts were sincere and adequate before the process begins.

Tribunal of Second Instance

Canons 1439 to 1441 deal with the *tribunal of second instance*.[97] Every *affirmative decision* in a marriage case must be appealed to the

---

[91] C. 1673, 1° for marriage cases. See also c. 1411 for trials in general.

[92] C. 1673, 2° for marriage cases. See also c. 1407, 3 for trials in general.

[93] C. 1673, 3°.

[94] See n. 93.

[95] C. 1673, 4°. In this case, the consent of the respondent's judicial vicar is required for the validity of the process. See F. Daneels, "The Forum of the Most Proofs," *J* 50 (1990) 289-309; Wrenn, *Procedures*, 10-12.

[96] Puerto Rico, though an American territory, does not belong to the United States Conference of Bishops.

[97] See *Navarre*, 896-898.

competent tribunal of a higher grade, usually that of second instance. If the decision is in the negative, it can be further appealed to a higher tribunal, though it is not mandatory.

Canon 1438 states that the metropolitan or archdiocesan tribunal is the tribunal of second instance for all those marriage cases adjudicated before a suffragan diocesan tribunal of first instance. On the other hand, in those cases which are heard when the metropolitan tribunal is serving as the first instance, the court of second instance is the one stably designated by the Apostolic Signatura.[98]

When several dioceses have a single tribunal of first instance,[99] the pertinent episcopal conference must establish one or more tribunals of second instance with the approval of the Apostolic See *unless* all dioceses are suffragan to the same archdiocese.[100] In this case the metropolitan tribunal serves as court of second instance. In turn, the Apostolic Signatura designates another tribunal to serve as second instance for the archdiocesan tribunal.

When an incompetent tribunal of second instance rules on a marriage case, the decision is absolutely invalid.[101]

The constitution of the tribunals of second instance is identical to that of the tribunal of first instance. The only exception is when, under certain circumstances, a marriage case can be adjudicated by a sole judge on first instance level. The courts of second instance are never allowed to have one judge, but must always have three judges who proceed collegially.[102] A petitioner or respondent can always appeal to the Roman Rota and ask it to serve as the court of second instance.[103]

---

[98] See *Navarre*, 895-896, n. 1438.

[99] This is known as the *interdiocesan* or *regional* tribunal model. See c. 1423.

[100] C. 1439.

[101] C. 1440. See also chapter entitled, Tribunals — 2.

[102] See chapter entitled, Tribunals — 1.

[103] C. 1417 and cc. 1442-1444. See chapter entitled, Tribunals — 2; *Navarre*, 879, n. 1417; 898-899, nn. 1442, 1443, 1444.

14. Marriage Cases

Marriage Cases — Introduction

Tribunals in the United States are usually referred to as *Matrimonial Tribunals*. The reason for calling them such is that they tend to deal mainly with marriage cases. There are a number of procedures used to adjudicate a marriage case. Each procedure depends on whether both parties are not baptized, or one of the parties is a baptized Christian, or both parties are baptized Christians, or one or both parties had a *valid* prior bond which was still in existence when the person contracted a subsequent marriage, or one or both parties were baptized Catholics and bound to follow Church law when he or she marries.

The Church recognizes as a *valid* union a marriage contracted between two non-baptized persons who are free to marry, that is the first marriage for both parties or neither party has a living former spouse at the time of the marriage.[1] This union is called a *natural bond*. The Church also recognizes as a natural bond the marriage between a non-baptized person and a baptized non-Catholic,[2] when both parties are free to marry one another. Furthermore, the Church recognizes as a natural bond the marriage between a non-baptized person and a baptized Catholic.[3] In the two former instances, none of the parties is bound

---

[1] For example, a marriage between two Moslems. See c. 1055 and c. 1134. See also *AA* 11; *GS* 47, 48; *LG* 11, 41; *CCC* 1601-1606, 1639, 1660, 2331; *Navarre*, 659-660, n. 1055; 716, n. 1134-1136.

[2] For example a marriage between a Jew and a baptized Protestant. See c. 1055 and c. 1134. See also *AA* 11; *GS* 47, 48; *LG* 11, 41; *CCC* 1601-1606, 1639, 1660, 2331; *Navarre*, ibid.

[3] For example a Buddhist and a Catholic. See c. 1055 and c. 1134. See also *AA* 11; *GS* 47, 48; *LG* 11, 41; *CCC* 1601-1606, 1633, 1634, 1637, 1639, 1660, 2331; *Navarre*, ibid.

to marry in the Catholic Church. In the latter instance, however, since there is a Catholic partner, the couple is bound to follow the laws of the Catholic Church regarding the *valid* celebration of their marriage. Since each of the three aforementioned marriages is considered a natural bond, each marriage has the possibility of being *dissolved* by the Catholic Church through the *Privilege of the Faith*. There are two aspects of this privilege: the marriage between two non-baptized person can be dissolved through the *Pauline Privilege*, while the marriage between a non-baptized person and a baptized Christian, including a Catholic, can be dissolved through the *Petrine Privilege*. There is no declaration of nullity in any of these cases for the marriage is considered valid. This is why such marriages are dissolved and not declared null.

Another type of marriage which is a *valid bond* and can be *dissolved* is the *ratified non-consummated marriage*. In this instance the Pope uses the vicarious power of his office to bring about the dissolution.[4] Once again, there is no declaration of nullity in such unions because they are considered valid.

The other types of marriage cases involve a *declaration of nullity*. There are different ways in which such a declaration can be procured, depending on the facts of each marriage. There are the *documentary marriage cases*. These cases are called documentary because irrefutable documents are presented by the petitioner where it is absolutely proven that either a diriment impediment, or a lack of canonical form, or a defect in the canonical form was present at the time that the parties exchanged their marital consent.

Canons 1073 through 1094 deal with *diriment impediments*. The presence of a diriment impediment in one or both of the marrying parties *automatically invalidates* their marriage. The impediment must be a fact or a condition or a circumstance whose presence forbids a person to contract marriage with any other person.[5]

---

[4] See chapter entitled, Marriage Dissolution — 1.

[5] C. 1073. See *Navarre*, 667-669.

A *lack of canonical form*[6] applies to a marriage where one of the partners is Catholic. The Catholic party is bound to follow the Church's laws on marriage.[7] If he or she does not follow them, the marriage is *invalid*.

A *defect in canonical form* exists when the proper canonical form of marriage is followed but the minister performing the ceremony does not have proper delegation to witness the marriage,[8] or one or both witnesses are not present at the ceremony,[9] or only one of the parties gives consent.[10]

Finally, there are also marriage cases which require a *formal trial*. These pertain to those *presumed valid* marriages between two Catholics, a validly[11] baptized Christian and a Catholic, or two validly baptized non-Catholics who are free to marry one another. The Church presumes that such a marriage is valid and sacramental until the presumption is overturned. A formal trial may also deal with a marriage between a baptized person, no matter what Christian faith he or she belongs to, and a non-baptized person. In this case, the marriage is presumed valid but not sacramental. Thus, once the marriage fails, one of the parties approaches the Church's tribunal and alleges that he or she has proof to overturn the presumption of the validity of his or her former marriage. A formal trial ensues as a result of the party's petition.

---

[6] C. 1108, 1 and c. 1127, 1. See *LG* 29; *CCC* 1069, 1537, 1621-1631, 2365; *Navarre*, 701-702, n. 1108; 713-715, n. 1127.

[7] The exception to this is when a *dispensation from canonical form* is granted by the proper Church authority. This dispensation is never granted when both parties are Catholic. C. 1108, 1 states that a Catholic is bound to marry in the presence of the Church's official witness (the Church minister) and two witnesses. See also c. 1117 and c. 1127, 2; *CCC* 1633-1636; *Navarre*, 707-709, n. 1117; 713-715, n. 1127.

[8] C. 1111. See *Navarre*, 703-705, n. 1111.

[9] C. 1108, 1. See *Navarre*, 701-702, n. 1108.

[10] See c. 1055; c. 1104, 2; c. 1108, 2. See also *Navarre*, 660-661, n. 1057; 698, n. 1104; 701-702, n. 1108.

[11] There are some baptisms which the Catholic Church does not recognize as valid. For example, the baptism of Jehovah's Witnesses. See *CLSA: Commentary*, 768, n. 79.

Marriage Cases — 1

Any married person, irrespective of being baptized or not, can be a party to a marriage trial. The validity of a marriage can be challenged by either spouse.[12] The spouse who submits the petition for a possible declaration of marriage nullity is called the *petitioner* or *plaintiff*. The other spouse is called the *respondent* or *defendant*. When one of the spouses is insane, the judge appoints a *guardian* or a *curator* to act in that party's name. Thus, it is the guardian rather than the insane spouse who is cited.[13]

A *procurator* is a person appointed by a party to the marriage trial. The petitioner and the respondent can appoint the same or different procurators. The procurator acts by proxy for the party and judicially[14] on the party's behalf. The party, however, always retains the right to respond in person at the trial.[15] Normally, one procurator is allowed for a party in any given case.[16] The procurator is appointed through a signed mandate by the party being represented.[17] The procurator can be a lay person or cleric, male or female, Catholic or non-Catholic, who is at least 18 years of age, and who enjoys a good reputation.[18]

An *advocate* is a person approved by the diocesan bishop to uphold and safeguard the rights of a party in a marriage case by providing arguments in applying the pertinent law to the facts of the case. The petitioner and the respondent can have the same or different advocates at the trial.[19] As in the case with the procurator, the party retains the right to respond in person at the trial.[20] A party can appoint

---

[12] C. 1674. See also c. 1501; *Navarre*, 934, n. 1501; 1032, n. 1674.

[13] C. 1478 and c. 1479. See *Navarre*, 921-922, n. 1478.

[14] C. 1485. See *Navarre*, 926, n. 1485.

[15] C. 1481, 1. See *Navarre*, 923, n. 1481.

[16] C. 1482, 1. See *Navarre*, 924, n. 1482.

[17] C. 1484, 1. See *Navarre*, 925-926, n. 1484.

[18] C. 1483.

[19] Suggested reading: Pope Pius XII, "The Defender of the Bond and the Advocate."

[20] C. 1481, 1. See *Navarre*, 923, n. 1481.

by mandate[21] one or more than one advocate at a marriage trial,[22] though the latter is highly unusual. The advocate can be a lay person or cleric, male or female, Catholic,[23] who is at least 18 years of age, enjoying a good reputation, and who must have either a doctorate or be an expert in canon law.[24] Advocates have a right to be present when the parties, witnesses and experts are being examined.[25] An advocate can never be a judge in the same marriage case at any instance in the same case. He or she can propose questions to be asked by the judge when interrogating a party, witness, and an expert, and also has a right to inspect the acts of the marriage case so that he or she may prepare better for arguing the case on behalf of his or her client.

Marriage Cases — 2

There are further persons involved in a marriage trial. These persons are called *witnesses*. They stand as one of the most important sources which provide proof to the allegations that are being lodged in the trial.

Canons 1547 through 1573 address the issue of witnesses. The Code acknowledges that there can be a variety of witnesses, based on the source of their knowledge. It is the responsibility of the judge to determine how much credibility and weight should be given to the testimony of each witness.[26] Witnesses, having been duly cited,[27] give individual testimony under oath,[28] though one can decline to take an

---

[21] C. 1484, 1. See *Navarre*, 925-926, n. 1484.

[22] C. 1482, 3. See *Navarre*, 924, n. 1482.

[23] The diocesan bishop can make an exception and allow a non-Catholic to act as an advocate in a case (c. 1483).

[24] C. 1483.

[25] C. 1678, 1. See *Navarre*, 1035-1036, n. 1678.

[26] See c. 1608, 3. See also *Navarre*, 995, n. 1608.

[27] C. 1509, c. 1556 and c. 1557. See *Navarre*, 941, n. 1509; 967, n. 1557.

[28] C. 1560, 1. See *Navarre*, 969-970, n. 1560.

oath[29] and instead make a solemn affirmation.[30] The judge can limit the number of witnesses when it is excessive.[31]

The Code restricts the competence of who can be a witness at a marriage trial. Thus, it considers minors under 14 years of age and the feeble-minded as unsuitable witnesses, unless the judge decrees that such persons may testify so as to reinforce the proof of an allegation.[32] Every properly cited witness[33] is bound to tell the truth when giving testimony.[34] Both parties to the case should be informed who the witnesses are.[35] Either party, however, can challenge the inclusion of a witness for a very serious reason.[36] The deposition or testimony of each witness should be signed by the witness, the judge, and a notary.[37] Tape recording of the deposition can be used, provided it is transcribed afterwards.[38] The witness has a right to review his or her own deposition or testimony.[39] The petitioner and the respondent, the judge and the other court officials, those who are assisting the parties in the process of the case, the parties' confessors, and a party's current or prospective spouse are incapable of being witnesses.[40]

Canon 1572 provides the criteria for the judge in evaluating witnesses. The testimony of each witness should be evaluated in terms of the moral integrity of the person,[41] the way through which the witness came across the information being submitted in his or her testi-

---

[29] C. 1532 and c. 1562, 2. See *Navarre*, 954, n. 1532; 970, n. 1562.

[30] C. 1531.

[31] C. 1553. There is no appeal against a judge's decision regarding the limitation of the number of witnesses in a case. See *Navarre*, 966, n. 1553.

[32] C. 1550, 1. See *Navarre*, 964-965, n. 1550. An example is when a minor has witnessed physical abuse inflicted by one of the parties to the case.

[33] C. 1556 states that the witness should be cited by decree.

[34] C. 1548, 1. See *Navarre*, 963, n. 1548.

[35] C. 1554. See *Navarre*, 967, n. 1554.

[36] C. 1555. For example, a respondent can ask the judge to exclude a particular witness because that person, from day one, tried his or her best to destroy the relationship.

[37] C. 1569, 2. See *Navarre*, 973-974, n. 1569.

[38] C. 1567, 1. See *Navarre*, 972, n. 1567.

[39] C. 1569, 1. See *Navarre*, 973-974, n. 1569.

[40] C. 1548, 2, 10 and c. 1550, 2. See *Navarre*, 964-965, n. 1550.

[41] See c. 876. See also *Navarre*, 975-976.

mony, the way the content of the testimony is being presented, and how the individual's testimony stands when compared to the testimony of the other witnesses. The testimony of an eyewitness carries considerable weight since there is personal knowledge based on what the individual saw and/or heard from the couple. The testimony of a witness whose knowledge is based on hearsay carries less weight. The testimony of a witness who, though not an eyewitness, reasonably deduced something from the party's behavior, carries some weight. The testimony of a witness whose testimony is rooted in rumor can have very little weight, if any. The term "corroborative testimony" is very important in the evaluation of a witness.

Marriages Cases — 3

Other sources who can provide proof in a marriage trial are *experts* or *specialists* in the medical or psychiatric or psychological or other behavioral sciences.[42] The purpose of involving an expert in a case is either to establish some fact or to clarify the true nature of an issue. The Code requires that one or more experts must be consulted in marriage cases which involve impotence, psychopathology or severe mental disorder.[43] The judge has the option to either nominate an expert (or experts) to examine and evaluate a party or accept the reports from an expert who has been treating the party or even do both.[44] A judge may exclude the report of an expert for the same reason that a witness may be excluded.[45] When the judge decrees that a party is to be exam-

---

[42] C. 1574. Suggested readings: M. Breitenbeck, "The Use of Psychological Experts in Church Law," *J* 50 (1990) 257-288; J. Hannon, "The Role of Diagnosis in the Annulment Evaluation Process," *J* 49 (1989) 182-190; *Navarre*, 977-981; Wrenn, *Procedures*, 54-58. See also chapter entitled, Marriage Cases — 1, n. 12.

[43] C. 1680. See *Navarre*, 1036-1037, n. 1680.

[44] C. 1575. See *Navarre*, 977, n. 1575.

[45] C. 1576. For example, when the expert is the parent to one of the parties or a prospective spouse to either petitioner or respondent. See also c. 1550 and c. 1555. See *Navarre*, 964-965, n. 1550; 967, n. 1555; 978, n. 1576.

ined and evaluated by an expert, the areas of examination should be specified, the expert should have access to pertinent information in the case, and the expert should be given a specified amount of time to submit his or her report.[46] An expert must indicate the basis of his or her conclusions. Thus, he or she is to state the sources and information, the methodology employed, and the grounds for his or her conclusions.[47] A judge may consult an expert further for more clarification whenever this is necessary.[48]

When more than one expert is employed, the judge should note their points of agreement and disagreement.[49] The judge is also responsible to provide reasons for admitting or rejecting an expert's conclusions when the decision on the case is put to writing.[50]

---

[46] C. 1577 and c. 1581, 2. See *Navarre*, 978-979, n. 1577; 980-981, n. 1581.

[47] C. 1578, 2. See *Navarre*, 979, n. 1578.

[48] C. 1578, 3. See *Navarre*, ibid.

[49] C. 1579, 1. See *Navarre*, 980, n. 1579.

[50] C. 1579, 2. See *Navarre*, ibid.

15. Marriage Trials

Marriage Formal Trial — 1

Canon law perceives marriage nullity cases as *contentious trials*.[1] Canons 1501 through 1525 relate to the introductory phase of such trials. This and the next few chapters will refer principally to those canons pertinent to marriage nullity trials rather than to trials in general.

Every completed formal marriage nullity trial has *five* phases or stages. There is the introductory phase, the probatory phase, the argumentation phase, the decision phase, and the appellate procedural phase. The decision in a marriage nullity trial has *absolutely no civil effects* in the United States.

A petitioner[2] submits to the tribunal a petition[3] for a decree of nullity. This is usually done in writing.[4] In the case of a marriage nul-

---

[1] See chapter entitled, Tribunals — 3. It is suggested that the reader be familiar with the contents of all the chapters on Tribunals, Tribunal Officials, and Marriage Cases for a better understanding of the marriage nullity process. The contents of the chapters are being taken for granted in this and the chapters on marriage nullity trials. Suggested readings: Grocholewski, "Theological Aspects"; Wrenn, "In Search of"; idem., *Procedures* 86-101.

[2] C. 1674, 1°. See also c. 1501. Thus, in the case of a declaration of nullity of a marriage a judge is unable to adjudicate a marriage case without a petition submitted by either one of the (former) spouses or the promoter of justice. See *Navarre*, 935, n. 1501; 1032, n. 1674.

[3] C. 1502 states that a petitioner must present a petition to a competent judge and state the reason for petition, namely, a declaration of nullity of the former marriage is being sought. See *Navarre*, 935, n. 1502. C. 1501 dictates that there can be no trial unless there is a pleading. See *Navarre*, 934-935, n. 1501.

[4] The technical term for a petition is *libellus*. It is an oral petition. However, in the United States, the petition is usually submitted in writing. When there is a *libellus*, it must be put into writing by a notary (c. 1503, 2). See *Navarre*, 936, n. 1503.

lity trial, the petition must specify basic information pertinent to the case: the names of the petitioner and the respondent, their respective baptism status, the place and date of wedding, if a dispensation from canonical form had been granted,[5] the date and place of civil divorce or civil annulment,[6] the canonical grounds on which the case is to be adjudicated, the current domicile or quasi-domicile of both parties. The petition is signed by the petitioner, notarized and dated.[7] Pertinent documentation should also accompany the petition.[8] This is the first step in a marriage nullity trial.

Once the tribunal receives the petition, it is logged and given a *Reference Number* which is comprised of the parties' last names,[9] the current year, and the sequential number in which the case was received by the tribunal.[10] The case is then placed in a docket and when its turn arrives, the judicial vicar appoints to the case a judge or a collegiate tribunal,[11] a defender of the bond, and a notary.[12] Then the judge renders a judicial review of the case. The first issue which is determined is competence.[13] Once the court has declared itself competent to hear the case, the petitioner is asked to appoint an advocate and procura-

---

[5] This applies when a marriage ceremony has taken place between a Catholic and a non-Catholic, celebrated in a place other than a Catholic church with the permission of the local ordinary (c. 1121, 3).

[6] Even if there is a civil annulment of a marriage, the Catholic Church still presumes that the couple is validly married until proven otherwise in Church courts.

[7] C. 1504 states all the elements which should be contained in the *libellus*. See *Navarre*, 936-937, n. 1504.

[8] These documents are the following: a recent baptism certificate of the Catholic party/parties, a copy of the marriage license, and a copy of the decree of civil divorce or civil annulment. There are some tribunals which also request the prenuptial investigation documentation, and still others request a copy of the interlocutory judgment of the civil divorce proceedings.

[9] The names consist of the former husband's last name and the former wife's last name at the time she entered the said marriage.

[10] For example, Smith — Jones, [19]95/001.

[11] The majority of the cases adjudicated in the United States in first instance are done with one judge.

[12] C. 1425, 3 speaks of the constitution of a tribunal. The appointments of a judge or collegiate tribunal, a defender of the bond, and a notary are made by a decree signed by the judicial vicar. See *Navarre*, 885-886, n. 1425.

[13] C. 1673 dictates competence for marriage cases. See *Navarre*, 1031-1032, n. 1673.

tor[14] and, when necessary, the judge appoints a guardian to one of the parties. It is also at this juncture that a petition is either accepted or rejected.[15] The petition may be rejected if the court is incompetent or the petition has no merit.[16] When this is the case, a decree of rejection is issued. It should contain a summary of the reasons for the decision to reject the petition.[17] If the rejection is due to a serious deficiency in the petition, the petitioner is given the opportunity to amend it, or ask for a collegiate tribunal if the case has been entrusted to a sole judge, or have recourse to the appellate court. This must be done within ten days.[18] Once recourse has been initiated, the matter should be determined as soon as possible.

It should be kept in mind that neither the Church nor the tribunal are the ones responsible for questioning the presumption of the validity of a marriage. Rather, the petitioner is the person challenging the validity of the former marriage. Furthermore, although both parties can present proof to overturn the presumption of validity,[19] the *burden of proof* ultimately rests with the petitioner and no one else.[20] One should be aware that a marriage nullity process can be somewhat traumatic for a party to that process.

Marriage Formal Trial — 2

Once the petition for a formal marriage nullity trial is accepted by the competent tribunal, the judge issues a decree of its acceptance.[21] The

---

[14] Each of these appointments is done by a mandate signed by the petitioner (c. 1484). A party to the case can submit his or her choice of such persons who are not on the recommended list supplied by the tribunal. In this case, the judge has to decide whether or not such persons are qualified. If there is no mandate, the actions of these appointees are irremediably null since, in fact, no appointment of such a person has taken place (c. 1620, 6°). The respondent will also appoint his or her advocate and procurator once he or she has been cited. See *Navarre*, 925-926, n. 1484; 1002-1003, n. 1620.

[15] C. 1505, 1 and c. 1677. See *Navarre*, 937-938, n. 1505; 1034, n. 1677.

[16] C. 1505, 2.

[17] C. 1617. See *Navarre*, 1000-1001, n. 1617.

[18] C. 1505, 4.

[19] C. 1516.

[20] C. 1526, 1. See *Navarre*, "Proofs," 949-950.

judge also issues a decree of judicial summons to the respondent, informing the person that the former spouse is petitioning the court for an ecclesiastical declaration of nullity of their marriage.[22] The respondent's citation also includes the date for the joinder of issues. A mandate for the appointment of his or her advocate and procurator[23] is also sent with the citation. Different tribunals have their own approaches to assist the respondent in getting an advocate and a procurator. Usually a list of advocates and procurators is sent along with the citation and the mandate. The respondent might opt to appoint the advocate of the day at the tribunal.[24] It is not uncommon in the United States that along with these documents, there is also a list of questions, pertinent to the case, which the respondent is asked to answer by a set date, normally one month. Canon 1512 states that the trial officially opens with the citation of the respondent and the tribunal acquires exclusive jurisdiction over the entire process in first instance.[25] Both parties are further asked to supply the court with a list of competent witnesses[26] which eventually is made available to both parties.[27] Competent witnesses are subsequently cited to testify.[28]

Canon 1511[29] dictates that the entire trial is null when the respondent is not cited, for this would deny the person the paramount right to defense. This is not the same as when a respondent refuses to cooperate. Canon law dictates that he or she has been duly cited even if the individual refuses to accept the citation or prevents it from be-

---

[21] C. 1507, 1 and c. 1677, 1. See *Navarre*, 939-940, n. 1507; 1034, n. 1677.

[22] C. 1508, 1 and c. 1677, 1. The citation is usually done through the mail. It is preferable that the petitioner informs the former spouse (respondent) of the intention to seek an ecclesiastical declaration of nullity of their marriage. See *Navarre*, 940, n. 1508; 1034, n. 1677.

[23] C. 1484. See *Navarre*, 925-926, n. 1484.

[24] See R. McGuckin, "The Respondent's Rights in a Marriage Nullity Case," *SCa* 18 (1984) 457-482.

[25] See also c. 1517. See *Navarre*, 942, n. 1512; 945-946, n. 1517.

[26] C. 1554.

[27] Ibid.

[28] C. 1556.

[29] See *Navarre*, 941, n. 1511.

ing delivered to him or her or refuses to submit testimony.[30] In this case, the judge issues a decree declaring the respondent either absent or contumacious and the trial proceeds in accordance with the norms of law.[31] There may also be instances when a respondent cannot be located. In this case, the petitioner has to submit to the judge a thorough list of the efforts undertaken to locate the respondent. The judge must decide whether these attempts are adequate and acceptable to the court. If the court is not satisfied with the attempts, further action is taken to locate the respondent.[32] Once it is established that the respondent is unlocatable, an advocate and a procurator are appointed for the respondent.[33] Thus, it is not only the respondent who can appoint his or her own procurator, but the judge can also appoint a procurator for an unlocatable respondent.[34] Whether the respondent cooperates or refuses to do so or is unlocatable, the court always appoints an advocate, at least on a temporary basis, to ensure that his or her rights are upheld and protected.[35]

Once the judge has heard from the respondent, he sets a date for the *joinder of issues*. Both parties are informed of the date.[36] The decree of the joinder of issues is usually very short and presented in the form of a question: *whether the ... (parties' last names) ... marriage has been proven null and void on the grounds of... (canonical grounds are stated)*. The canonical grounds are always based on the statements made by the petitioner and the respondent.[37] Usually, however, the canonical grounds are based on the allegations made by the petitioner

---

[30] C. 1510.

[31] C. 1592, 1. An absent respondent, however, can still exercise the right to appeal the judge's decision at the end of the trial (c. 1593, 2). Notification of all citations must be made in accordance with the provisions of c. 1509 and c. 1510. See *Navarre*, 986, n. 1592; 986-987, n. 1593.

[32] See chapter entitled, Tribunals — 4.

[33] C. 1508, 3.

[34] See chapter entitled, Marriage Cases — 1.

[35] C. 1481, 1. See chapter entitled, Marriage Cases — 1; *Navarre*, 923-924, n. 1481.

[36] Even if the respondent refuses to cooperate or is unlocatable, there is always a date set for the joinder of issues. See c. 1507, 1 and c. 1508, 1. See also *Navarre*, 939-940, nn. 1507, 1508.

[37] C. 1513, 1 and c. 1677, 3. See *Navarre*, 943-944, n. 1513; 1034, n. 1677.

because this individual is the one who is challenging the presumption of the validity of the marriage. The grounds must state on whose part the defect is alleged to have been present. Both parties are then informed of the canonical grounds on which the marriage case is to be adjudicated.[38]

A marriage may be proven null and void on a number of canonical grounds.[39] If a marriage, however, is adjudicated to be null and void on one ground, there is no need to adjudicate it on any other canonical grounds for the simple reason that the marriage is null. Canon 1514 dictates that once the grounds have been determined by decree, they may not be changed unless for a serious reason and at the request of one of the parties, and after the judge consults the other party and evaluates the reasons for such a request. If the grounds are changed, the judge issues a new decree and states the new alleged grounds.

Marriage Formal Trial — 3

The trial in the court of first instance begins with the citation of the respondent.[40] The trial may be suspended or terminated in a number of ways. A marriage trial is *interrupted* when one of the former spouses dies.[41] Since a party's death brings about the termination of a marriage bond it is purposeless for the surviving party to continue that marriage nullity trial.[42] The trial can be *suspended* if a key court official, such as the judge, has been called away for other duties or has died, and so

[38] C. 1513, 3 and c. 1677, 3-4. See *Navarre*, 944, n. 1513; 1034, n. 1677.

[39] The traditional canonical grounds are: impotence (c. 1084); lack of due reason (c. 1095, 1); grave defect of discretion of judgment (c. 1095, 2); incapacity to assume the essential obligations of marriage (c. 1095, 3); ignorance (c. 1096); error of person (c. 1097); fraud (c. 1098); simulation (c. 1101); conditioned consent (c. 1102); force and fear (c. 1103); and defective validation (cc. 1156-1160).

[40] See c. 1512 and c. 1517. See *Navarre*, 942-943, n. 1512; 945-946, n. 1517. See also chapter entitled, Marriage Formal Trial — 2.

[41] C. 1518. See *Navarre*, 946, n. 1518.

[42] See c. 1675, 1. See *Navarre*, 1033, n. 1675.

forth. In essence, this means that the trial is suspended until a proper replacement is made.[43]

When the petitioner and/or the witnesses have been negligent and ignored the directives of the judge[44] and, in fact, not cooperated in the process for six months, the case is *terminated* through abatement.[45] The effect of an abatement is that the trial is terminated. Nonetheless, the depositions and documentation in the case are still preserved. Rather, only the procedural acts of the process are terminated.[46] In practice, however, the judge always warns the petitioner about an impeding abatement. Such notice should make the concerned person more interested in cooperating with the process. Should there arise a time when the petitioner wishes to reopen the petition, he or she will be asked to put in writing the request and send it to the judicial vicar. The letter should include the reasons for seeking such a request and specify the practical ways which will be undertaken by the party if the trial is to be reopened.

A trial may be also terminated through the petitioner's *renunciation* of an instance in the trial.[47] The renunciation must be in writing, accepted by the respondent, and admitted by the judge.[48] The petitioner may submit a renunciation for a number of reasons, the most common being that the evidence needed to overturn the presumption of the validity of the marriage is not available at the time. The renunciation of an instance can take place at any stage of the trial prior to the judge's sentence and has the same effect as that of abatement.[49]

Finally, a trial ends with the definitive sentence of the judge.[50]

---

[43] C. 1519, 1 and c. 1512. See *Navarre*, 942-943, n. 1512; 946-947, n. 1519.

[44] For example, the petitioner refuses the judge's request to undergo a psychological evaluation or none of the witnesses responded to the Court's citations.

[45] CC. 1520-1521. When a case has been suspended in accordance with c. 1519, the suspension time is not computed toward abatement (c. 1520). See *Navarre*, 947, nn. 1520, 1521.

[46] C. 1522. See *Navarre*, 947-948, n. 1522.

[47] C. 1524, 1. See *Navarre*, 948-949, n. 1524.

[48] C. 1524, 3.

[49] C. 1525. See *Navarre*, 949, n. 1525.

[50] C. 1607. See *Navarre*, 994-995, n. 1607.

Marriage Formal Trial — 4

The second phase of a marriage annulment trial is the *probatory phase*. This is the stage where proofs of the allegations are gathered and presented.[51] The phase commences after the joinder of issues has been established.[52] Canons 1526 through 1586 deal with this phase not only for a marriage trial but for all trials.

It is the burden of the petitioner to prove that the presumption of the validity of his or her former marriage is wrong.[53] Thus, unless the presumption of validity is overturned, the marriage continues to be considered valid[54] since the presumption of validity need not be proven. It is taken for granted since marriage enjoys the favor of law.[55]

The Code does not specify what can be admitted to the trial as part of proof. It is the duty of the judge to do so. The Code, however, does state that any legitimate and useful type of proof can be admitted as part of the evidence in the case.[56] The Code also provides for those instances where a party or a witness either refuses or is unable to appear to testify in court before a judge. In this case, in order to procure the testimony of such a person, the judge may either appoint an auditor[57] or ask the individual to submit an affidavit notarized by a notary public or a person who occupies a leadership position in the community.[58]

---

[51] See *Navarre*, "Proofs," 949-950.

[52] C. 1529. See *Navarre*, 952, n. 1529. Suggested readings: P. Reifenberg, "The Revised Code on Proofs and Presumptions," *J* 43 (1983) 237-245; Wrenn, *Procedures*, 33-58.

[53] C. 1526, 1. See *Navarre*, 950-951, n. 1526.

[54] C. 1060 states that once marital consent is exchanged, the said marriage is presumed valid and given the protection of the law. C. 1101, 1 states that once marital consent is exchanged, it is presumed that what has been expressed externally by the couple is a reflection of what they have consented to internally, in other words, they meant what they said. C. 1061, 2 states that once the couple has cohabited, the presumption is that the marriage has been consummated.

[55] C. 1060.

[56] C. 1527, 1. See *Navarre*, 951-952, n. 1527.

[57] See chapter entitled, Tribunal Officials — 2.

[58] C. 1528 and c. 1561. See also c. 1428. See further *Navarre*, "Auditors and Relators," 888-889; 889, n. 1428; 952, n. 1528.

There is a variety of ways through which proof is acquired in marriage nullity cases. Proof is not constituted by the number of items submitted, but by their weight and relevance to the allegations. The judge always has the prerogative to interrogate any person involved in the trial: petitioner,[59] respondent,[60] and witnesses.[61] The judge may also request an expert to establish or clarify certain issues concerning the parties and/or their marriage.[62] Each interrogated party is given the oath[63] or solemnly promises to tell the truth,[64] is bound to keep secret the content of the interrogation,[65] and the other party may not be present during the interrogation.[66] The defender of the bond and the advocates can propose questions to the judge who decides whether or not to include them in the interrogation.[67]

The confessions and declarations of the petitioner and the respondent can form part of the proof for establishing the nullity of a marriage. For example, this is very important in a case involving simulation of marital consent.[68] A *confession* is a statement made against oneself by either the petitioner or the respondent or both regarding the grounds on which the case is being adjudicated. When the confession is made before the judge, it is called a judicial confession. When a confession has been made outside the trial, for instance a spouse had stated to someone that he or she intends or has never intended to have children, it is called an extra-judicial confession. Such a confession is usually made at a time when the validity of the marriage was non-sus-

---

[59] C. 1530. See *Navarre*, 953, n. 1530.

[60] Ibid.

[61] C. 1548, 1. See *Navarre*, 963, n. 1548.

[62] C. 1574 and c. 1578, 3. See *Navarre*, 977, n. 1574; 979, n. 1578.

[63] C. 1532 and c. 1562. See *Navarre*, 954, n. 1532; 970, n. 1562.

[64] C. 1531. See *Navarre*, 953, n. 1531. The commentary speaks about the interpretation of the silent response of a party.

[65] C. 1455, 3. See *Navarre*, 907-908, n. 1455.

[66] C. 1559 and c. 1678, 2. See *Navarre*, 969, n. 1559; 1035-1036, n. 1678.

[67] C. 1533 and c. 1561. See *Navarre*, 954, n. 1533; 970, n. 1561.

[68] Simulation is when one or both parties to the marriage feigned marital consent. Thus, if one truly intends not to have children, not to be faithful, and not to enter into a lifelong marital commitment, the guilty party simulates marriage totally. If one or two of the three elements is excluded, then the simulation is partial (c. 1101).

pect. On the other hand, a *declaration* is a statement made by either or both parties which is not self-accusatory.[69] It is the responsibility of the judge to weigh the credibility of any kind of confession or declaration made by either or both parties.[70] The judge may even refuse to admit a party's confession or declaration for a serious reason.[71] On the other hand, a confession and a declaration never serve as full proof and do not bring a marriage nullity trial to an end for there is much more involved in the process. Furthermore, the statements of one individual do not usually result in full proof.[72]

Marriage Formal Trial — 5

When a respondent and/or competent witness,[73] for some reason, does not wish or is unable to testify before the judge, he or she may submit the testimony through an affidavit.[74] An *affidavit* is a deposition made before an ecclesiastical notary or a notary public under oath or solemn affirmation.[75] In the case of a witness, the deponent is called an *affiant*. The affiant, for a very serious reason, may specifically ask the judge not to publish some parts or the entire contents of the affidavit.[76] The criteria which apply to weighing the credibility of witnesses also apply to the credibility of the affiants.[77]

The Code has twenty-seven canons dedicated to witnesses and

---

[69] C. 1536, 2. See *Navarre*, 955-956, n. 1536.

[70] CC. 1535-1537.

[71] C. 1538. See *Navarre*, 956-957, n. 1538.

[72] C. 1573. See Wallace, "Lack of Witnesses," 280-285.

[73] A competent witness is one who is knowledgeable about the petitioner, and/or the respondent, and/or their marriage and separation. A witness should be cited in accordance with the provisions of c. 1509 and c. 1556.

[74] C. 1528. See *Navarre*, 952, n. 1528.

[75] C. 1562 and 1568. See *Navarre*, 970, n. 1562; 973, n. 1568.

[76] See c. 1546 and c. 1598. See *Navarre*, 962, n. 1546; 989-990, n. 1598.

[77] CC. 1572-1573 for trials in general and c. 1679 speaks specifically about marriage cases. See P. Felici, "Juridical Formalities and Evaluations of Evidence in the Canonical Process," *J* 38 (1978) 153-157. Although this article was written before the 1983 Code, it remains very helpful. See also *Navarre*, 1036, n. 1679.

testimony.[78] A witness is a person who, having been duly cited by the court, gives testimony under oath or solemnly promises to tell the truth before the judge or a person appointed by the judge in a specific marriage nullity trial.[79] Canon 1554 states that the petitioner and the respondent are to be given the names of the witnesses in the trial.[80] A party, for a just reason, may ask the judge to exclude a witness before the person submits any kind of testimony. The decision, however, rests entirely with the judge.[81] He is also able to limit the number of witnesses[82] and can decide to exclude one or more witnesses without being requested to do so by either or both parties.[83] Furthermore, it is the duty of the judge to determine the competence of each witness and to evaluate the testimony of all witnesses.[84] A witness who is unable to testify personally in court may submit an affidavit of his or her deposition. However, the judge has the right to further interview a witness or to ask an affiant to submit further depositions in the process of the trial. Neither party may be present at the deposition of any of the witnesses.[85]

When a marriage nullity petition is being adjudicated on the canonical grounds of impotence or defect of consent due to mental illness, canon 1680 dictates that the services of an expert should be employed.[86] This canon is also applicable to all the grounds stated in canon 1095.[87] There are, however, instances when this is not necessary because the evidence already submitted makes the proof so obvious. In any case, canon 1579, 1 states that it is the duty of the judge

---

[78] CC. 1547-1573.

[79] See chapter entitled, Marriage Cases — 2.

[80] See *Navarre*, 967, n. 1554.

[81] C. 1555. See *Navarre*, 967, n. 1555.

[82] C. 1553.

[83] C. 1555.

[84] See chapter entitled, Marriage Cases — 2.

[85] C. 1559. See *Navarre*, 968, n. 1559.

[86] CC. 1574-81 address the issue and role of the expert in a marriage nullity case. See also *Navarre*, "Experts," 977-981; 1036-1037, n. 1680.

[87] The grounds are lack of due reason (insanity), grave defect of discretion of judgment, and lack of due competence.

to weigh the conclusions of the expert, taking into account the other circumstances of the case.[88]

Marriage Formal Trial — 6

The conclusion of the probatory phase comes with the *publication of the acts*.[89] Canon 1598 concerns the publication of the acts. It is a very important canon since should the judge ignore its provisions, the judicial decision regarding the marriage nullity case is null.

Once all of the proofs have been gathered, the judge must permit the petitioner and the respondent and their respective advocates to inspect those acts which are not yet known to them. The parties are bound to an oath of secrecy when they inspect the acts, that is, they are not allowed to divulge their contents to anyone.[90] The inspection of the acts should take place at the tribunal. If the advocate of one of the parties asks for a copy of the acts, the judge should accede to the request of the advocate. The reasoning behind this canon is to ensure that the right to defense of the petitioner and the respondent remains intact. Thus, even at this stage of the trial, a party can propose additional proof. If there is a need or possibility of additional proof, such proof must be admitted in accordance with the provisions of canon 1600. Once this proof has been procured, the judge publishes the new proof in accordance with the provisions of canon 1598, 1.

Canon 1598 has an inherent tension. On the one hand, each party

---

[88] Read J. Hannon, "The Role of Diagnosis in the Annulment Evaluation Process," *J* 49 (1989) 182-190; R.W. Guiry, "Canonical and Psychological Reflections on the Vetitum in Today's Tribunal," *J* 49 (1989) 191-209; Wrenn, *Proceedings*, 54-58. Refer also to the bibliography stated in chapter entitled, Tribunals — 3, n. 81. See also *Navarre*, 980, n. 1579.

[89] Suggested readings: E. Dillon, "Confidentiality of Testimony — An Implementation of Canon 1598," *J* 45 (1985) 289-296; J. Johnson, "Publish and Be Damned: The Dilemma of Implementing the Canons on Publishing the Acts and the Sentence," *J* 49 (1989) 210-240; L. Orsy, "The Interpretation of Laws: New Variations of an Old Theme," *SCa* 15 (1983) 107-110; J. G. Proctor, "Procedural Changes in the 1983 Code: The Experiences of the Ecclesiastical Provinces of California," *J* 44 (1984) 468-485; Wrenn, *Procedures*, 59-62.

[90] C. 1455, 1 and 3, and c. 1546. See *Navarre* 907-908, n. 1455; 962, n. 1546.

should know what is being alleged. On the other hand, there is the confidentiality aspect for those who are witnesses since a witness might be more forthcoming with information and insight if confidentiality of testimony is assured. This situation calls for a delicate balance. The canon, however, does not give a carte blanche to the parties to examine *every* act in their marriage nullity case. On the other hand, all of the acts must be made available to both the defender of the bond and the advocates of the parties to ensure that the right of defense is upheld. For example, lest the expert run the risk of being sued in civil court because of what had been stated in the report, the judge may issue a decree of exemption for that report. The judge may issue a similar decree for a witness' testimony for a similar reason. On the other hand, the canon empowers the judge to protect the confidentiality of the expert and the witnesses, under certain serious conditions.[91] The judge, however, cannot exempt from publication all of the evidence submitted in a given case. This would be perceived as a serious violation of canon 1598 and could well incur the penalty of nullity of the sentence.[92] In the case when a respondent was unwilling to testify and tried to impede the process of justice, the judge, having issued a decree of absence for the party,[93] is not bound to allow such a person the right to inspect the acts at this stage of the trial.

Once the parties declare that they have nothing to add or the time to produce additional proof has expired or the judge is confident that the case has been sufficiently instructed, the judge issues a decree, indicating that the probative phase of the trial has been completed.[94]

---

[91] See *Navarre*, 989-990, n. 1598.

[92] In the instance where some of the acts are exempt from publication to the petitioner and the respondent, their advocates and the defender of the bond are bound with the provisions of c. 1455, 3 which binds these persons by an oath of secrecy concerning the matter contained in the decree of exemption from publication. If any of these persons allege that the exempted acts violate the right of defense of either or both parties to the case, they can challenge the decree by lodging a complaint of nullity of the sentence (c. 1621) or propose an incidental case (cc. 1587-1588).

[93] C. 1592. See *Navarre*, 986, n. 1592.

[94] C. 1599. See *Navarre*, 990, n. 1599.

Marriage Formal Trial — 7

The third phase in a marriage nullity trial is the *argumentation phase*.[95] It is at this stage of the trial that the discussion of the marriage case begins. In practice, however, there has been an ongoing dialogue between the judge, the parties, their advocates, and the defender of the bond since the acceptance of the petition. For example, the joinder of issues usually follows a discussion between the judge, the advocates and the defender of the bond about what is being alleged by the petitioner as the canonical grounds for having the said marriage declared null and void. When the judge formally interrogates the parties and their witnesses, there is also a dialogue going on since some of the judge's questions could have resulted from the testimony submitted by any of the aforementioned persons. However, the formal discussion of the case does not begin until the probative phase of the trial has been concluded.

Canon 1601 dictates that the judge sets a reasonable time for the advocates and the defender of the bond to present their briefs. Although canon 1602, 1 allows for an oral discussion of the case, in practice the advocates and the defender of the bond always submit written briefs. The advocates of the parties can revise and expand their briefs if this becomes necessary.[96] The defender of the bond should also be given a further opportunity[97] to present his or her animadversions.[98] The law also requires that whatever presentations and argumentation have been made on the oral level[99] must be committed to writing and notarized.[100] Then they should be entered as part of the acts since the judge is to

---

[95] CC. 1601-1606.

[96] C. 1603, 2.

[97] C. 1603, 3.

[98] Animadversions are reasons which the defender of the bond presents to the judge, arguing for the validity of the said union as well as verifying whether the proper procedures have been followed.

[99] C. 1602 and c. 1604, 1.

[100] C. 1604, 1 and c. 1605.

render his decision based only on what appears in the acts and from the proofs of the case.[101]

Marriage Formal Trial — 8

Once the advocates of the parties and the defender of the bond have submitted their briefs, the trial moves to the fourth phase: the *decision*. The judge, the advocates and the defender of the bond are all concerned with the uncovering of the truth. The uncovering of truth is aimed at supplying the answer to the doubt which had been formulated in the joinder of issues, namely whether the said marriage is null and void on the alleged canonical grounds. The judge is now faced with the evidence gathered from the testimonies of the parties, their witnesses and, when applicable, the evaluation of the expert. The judge also has in his possession the briefs of the advocates of both parties and that of the defender of the bond. The judge is now responsible to state and apply the pertinent law to the facts which stand in front of him. Once he has evaluated the testimony in the case, the arguments of the advocates, and the brief of the defender of the bond, he renders his decision.[102] The decision is reached through *moral certitude*,[103] that is the judge is certain of his decision but there is always the possibility that the opposite might be true.[104] Thus, moral certitude is not equivalent to absolute certitude. If the judge fails to reach moral certitude, then he must let stand the presumption of the validity of the marriage in question.[105]

---

[101] C. 1608, 2.

[102] C. 1608, 2-3. See L. Wrenn, "Outline of a Sentence," in *Decisions*, 2nd rev. ed., 194-195; idem., *Procedures*, 66-69.

[103] C. 1608, 1. See *Navarre*, 995-996, n. 1608.

[104] The classical statement on moral certitude is found in Pope Pius XII's allocution to the officials of the Roman Rota on October 1, 1942. The English text may be read in Wrenn's *Procedures*, 121-124. See also A. Caron, "The Concept of Moral Certitude in Canonical Decisions," *J* 19 (1959) 12-28; V. Peter, "The Judge Must Judge Justly," *J* 164-178.

[105] C. 1608, 4.

Canons 1608 through 1616 are dedicated to the elements which constitute the definitive sentence and its publication. A definitive sentence is a legitimate judicial pronouncement by a judge in which, in the case of a marriage nullity trial, the question of whether a specific marriage was valid or not is settled.

The judge reaches moral certitude from the acts and proofs set in front of him. He evaluates the proofs according to his conscience.[106] If the trial involves a collegiate tribunal, then each judge must submit his or her written conclusions with his or her reasoning in law as applicable to the facts presented during the trial. These conclusions are kept secret[107] until the president of the collegiate tribunal invokes the Divine Name.[108] Once the conclusions are revealed, the judges may discuss among themselves the *dispositive*[109] aspect of the sentence. At this time a judge, having heard the reasoning and application of the law to the facts, can retract his or her decision or insist that his or her dissenting opinion be included in the final version of the written sentence. The collegiate tribunal may also decide to further instruct the case.[110] Once the collegiate tribunal renders its decision,[111] the judge[112] assigned to write the definitive sentence writes its draft and submits it for the approval of the other two judges.[113] There is no discussion of a decision if there is only a sole judge in the trial, and he himself writes the definitive sentence.[114]

Canon 1612 provides an outline of what should appear in a definitive sentence. After the invocation of the Divine Name, certain persons are identified by name, that is the Pope, the diocesan bishop,

---

[106] C. 1608, 1-3.

[107] C. 1609, 2. See *Navarre*, 996, n. 1609.

[108] C. 1609, 3.

[109] The dispositive aspect of the sentence is the actual decision or judgment of the case, that is "in the affirmative" or "in the negative."

[110] C. 1609, 4.

[111] The decision of the majority of the judges carries the day.

[112] The technical term for this judge is *ponens*.

[113] C. 1610, 2. See *Navarre*, 997, n. 1610.

[114] C. 1610, 1.

the judge,[115] the defender of the bond, the advocates, the petitioner, and the respondent. The basis for the court's competence must be stated, as must the canonical grounds on which the petition is being adjudicated. Then follows the *expositive* part of the definitive sentence: the facts of the case, the law pertinent to those facts, and the argument, that is the application of the law to the facts. Then comes the *dispositive* part of the definitive sentence. If there is a restriction imposed on either or both parties, it is stated at this time.[116] The place and the date are stated. Then follows the notarized signature of the judge or the collegiate tribunal.

Canons 1614 and 1615 regulate the notarized publication of the definitive sentence by the judge's signed decree to the parties and their procurators.[117] Once again the place and date are stated. Finally, in accordance with the provisions of canon 1437, the notary attests to the authenticity of the substantive and procedural acts of the case. The petitioner and the respondent are given fifteen days to appeal the definitive decision.

Marriage Formal Trial — 9

The fifth, and usually final, phase in the declaration of the nullity of a marriage is the *appellate procedural phase*. Canon 1682[118] provides special norms for the appellate process in marriage nullity cases. The court of second instance can either be the *ordinary* Court of Appeals

---

[115] When there is a collegiate tribunal, the names of the three judges appear at this point. When there is a sole judge, the provisions of c. 1425, 4 are to be stated in the Sentence.

[116] A tribunal may impose a restriction or prohibition (*vetitum*) or a warning (*monitum*) on either or both parties in accordance with c. 1684. A restriction limits or sets conditions to the party's right to remarry. However, the restriction is for the liceity and not the validity of a party's future marriage (c. 1077, 2). Read J. Hopka, "The *Vetitum* and *Monitum* in Matrimonial Nullity Proceedings," *SCa* (1985) 357-399; J. Lucas, "The Prohibition Imposed by a Tribunal: Law, Practice, Future Development," *J* 45 (1985) 588-617; Wrenn, *Procedures*, 83-84. See also *Navarre*, 1039, n. 1684.

[117] See *Navarre*, 999-1000, nn. 1614, 1615.

[118] See *Navarre*, 1038, n. 1682.

for that tribunal, that is the designated tribunal of second instance, or the *extraordinary* Court of Appeals, the Roman Rota.[119] When there is an appeal to the latter, the court of first instance usually helps the person to submit the appeal. Every *Affirmative Decision* of the court of first instance is *automatically* appealed within twenty working days of the publication of the sentence.[120]

The kind of court of second instance depends on what kind of a tribunal paradigm is being followed in a diocese or region. Thus, it could be a metropolitan court,[121] or a designated diocesan court,[122] or an interdiocesan court.[123] Canon 1632, 1 states that unless there is a specific appeal to the Roman Rota, the Decision of the court of first instance is appealed to the ordinary court of second instance.

The court of second instance can do a number of things. It can confirm or ratify the Affirmative Decision of the first instance.[124] It can reopen an Affirmative Decision to a new examination which can involve the gathering of new evidence which leads to another Affirmative Decision or decides "in the negative."[125] The court of second instance can also determine if the procedures followed in the first instance were correct. Should there be any irregularities, the same court should determine whether there should be a complaint of nullity of sentence that is remediable[126] or irremediable by virtue of the provisions of canon 1620.[127] When the court of second instance cannot confirm or ratify the first instance's Decision on the original canonical

---

[119] C. 1444, 1, 1° affirms that either party to a marriage nullity case can appeal the Decision of First Instance to the Roman Rota. See chapter entitled, Tribunal of Second Instance.

[120] C. 1682, 1.

[121] C. 1438, 1°.

[122] C. 1438, 2°.

[123] C. 1439, 2.

[124] C. 1682, 2.

[125] Ibid.

[126] C. 1622. In the case of remediable nullity, the Decision remains intact and the error or errors suffered at first instance are corrected. See *Navarre*, 1003-1004, n. 1622.

[127] A Complaint of Nullity of Sentence can be lodged by either or both parties to the case, or either of their advocates, or the defender of the bond (c. 1626, 1). See *Navarre*, 1005-1006, n. 1626.

grounds it should determine whether there are any other grounds on which the case may be heard. Furthermore, second instance may ask first instance to hear the case on new grounds or may hear the case itself on new grounds; thereby the court itself becomes that of first instance for the new grounds.[128] The court of second instance may also review an initial Negative Decision in first instance, reopen the case, and decide "in the affirmative"[129] or "in the negative"[130] on the same grounds. Since nullity decisions deal with the status of a person in the Church, that is whether one is single or married, the issue is never definitive for the decision on each instance is always arrived at through moral certitude, which is not absolute.[131]

Marriage Formal Trial — 10

The court of second instance must always have a collegiate tribunal. The only time when a single judge is allowed is in the court of first instance and under certain conditions.[132] The court of second instance has before it the same juridic facts as the court of first instance. The collegiate tribunal always proceeds as a collegial body.[133] It is the sole responsibility of the collegiate tribunal to determine whether to ratify the first instance Affirmative Decision or reopen the case. The collegiate tribunal, however, must hear the observations of the defender of the bond and, if there are any, those of the parties and/or their advocates to the case.[134] The collegiate tribunal pronounces its determination by a decree.[135]

---

[128] C. 1683. See *Navarre*, 1039, n. 1683.

[129] When there are two discordant Decisions, the validity of the marriage is upheld. In this case, the next appeal is to the Roman Rota as third instance.

[130] Usually an appeal is not permitted to the Roman Rota when there have been two concordat Affirmative or Negative Decisions *unless* there are new and solid proofs or arguments that call for such an appeal. This is known as a *new presentation* of the case (c. 1644, 1). See *Navarre*, 1015-1016, n. 1644.

[131] C. 1643. See *Navarre*, 1015, n. 1643.

[132] C. 1425, 4. See chapter entitled, Tribunals — 1.

[133] C. 1426, 1. See *Navarre*, 886-887, n. 1426.

[134] C. 1682, 2. See *Navarre*, 1038, n. 1682.

[135] See chapter entitled, Tribunal of Second Instance.

When the court of first instance has rendered an Affirmative Decision, the collegiate tribunal of the court of second instance may *confirm* or *ratify* the Decision of the court of first instance. Before rendering its decision, the collegiate tribunal must first hear the observations made by the defender of the bond in the given case and any observations which the parties and/or their advocates might have submitted.[136] The court of second instance must adjudicate the marriage case on the same grounds on which it was adjudicated in first instance. However, there may be instances when, using the same juridic facts of the first instance, the court of second instance decrees in the affirmative on a slightly different ground. In this case, since the same juridic facts were used, the two sentences are deemed as equivalently concordant.[137] Once there are two concordat Affirmative Decisions, the parties are free to remarry,[138] even if there is a new presentation of the case at the Roman Rota.[139]

When the court of first instance had rendered a Negative Decision, the Code does not require an automatic appeal because a Negative Decision, in fact, upholds the presumption of the marriage's validity. Such a Decision must be formally appealed in order to involve the court of a higher grade. The appeal can be made by either party.[140] The appeal can be made to either the ordinary forum of second instance or to the Roman Rota, the extraordinary forum. When the appeal is made directly to the Roman Rota, the latter becomes the court of second instance. The Roman Rota, however, may decline to accept the appeal. In this case, the case is sent to the ordinary court of second instance which then proceeds to adjudicate the case. If there is a discordance between the two Decisions, the case then goes to the Roman Rota which serves as the court of third instance.

The court of second instance informs the court of first instance

---

[136] C. 1682, 2.

[137] See J. Cuneo, "Toward Understanding Conformity of Two Sentences of Nullity," *J* 46 (1986) 568-601.

[138] C. 1684, 1. See *Navarre*, 1039, n. 1684.

[139] An appeal to the court of third instance does not suspend the execution of a definitive sentence of marriage nullity (c. 1644). See also chapter entitled, Marriage Formal Trial — 9, n. 129.

of its Decision, whether it is "in the affirmative" or "in the negative." Then the court of first instance informs the parties of the Decision of the court of second instance. If both courts have decided "in the affirmative," the court of first instance issues a *Declaration of Nullity* of the said marriage.[141] The parties are free to marry *unless* there is a restriction or prohibition.[142] It is the responsibility of the Judicial Vicar of first instance to notify the proper persons and places of the nullity of a marriage. Thus, notification, accompanied with any restrictions imposed on one or both parties, is sent to the church of baptism of the Catholic party/parties and the Catholic church where the marriage is registered so that the records indicate the nullity of the said marriage and any restriction imposed on a party.[143]

---

[140] C. 1634. See *Navarre*, 1009-1010, n. 1634.

[141] C. 1684, 1.

[142] See chapter entitled, Marriage Formal Trial — 8, n. 116.

[143] C. 1685. See chapter entitled, Tribunal Officials — 1 and *Navarre*, 1040, n. 1685.

Marriage Formal Trial — 11

The following is a basic outline of the procedures involved in a formal trial for a declaration of nullity of a marriage:

COURT OF FIRST INSTANCE

a. Introductory Phase:

1. Petitioner submits petition (*libellus*) to a tribunal

2. Petition at tribunal
- petition is logged
- petition is given a reference number
- petition is put into a docket

3. Judicial vicar assigns judge (or collegiate tribunal), defender of the bond, and notary

tribunal competent on
- place of contract or respondent's quasi/domicile
- petitioner's quasi/domicile or place of most proofs:
- seek respondent's judicial vicar's consent (if consent is denied: transfer petition)

4. Judge determines competence

if tribunal is not competent
- petition rejected (transfer of petition)
- petition rejected: no grounds alleged: petition amended

5. Judge's action
- petition amended
- judge issues decree of acceptance of petition and sets date for joinder of issues
- respondent is cited for joinder of issues (trial officially opens)
- advocates and procurators (if necessary also guardian) are appointed by mandate

6. Joinder of issues is made by judge: doubt is formulated on testimony submitted — grounds are determined

7. Petitioner and respondent informed of grounds and cited to testify and submit list of witnesses within a set time limit

b. Probatory Phase:

1. Petitioner and respondent testify. Both parties are asked to submit all documents pertinent to the case

2. Witnesses/affiants are cited to testify within a time limit

3. Judge determines if there is a need for experts — if so, each expert is given time limit to submit report/evaluation

4. Judge evaluates credibility of witnesses and expert/s report

5. Judge determines if evidence is sufficiently present

6. Publication of the Acts of the case: judge permits petitioner, respondent, their advocates to inspect acts

7. Conclusion of the case: petitioner, respondent, their advocates affirm proofs are complete; judge decrees conclusion of case

c. Argumentation Phase:

1. Brief submitted by petitioner's advocate, within a set time limit, arguing for nullity

2. Brief submitted by respondent's advocate, within a set time limit — could argue for validity

3. Brief submitted by defender of the bond, within time limit — raises reasonable arguments for validity; raises procedural objections if a party's rights were not fully protected and upheld

d. Decision Phase:

1. Judge decides if moral certitude has been reached from acts and proofs, having also received briefs of advocates and defender of the bond

2. Judge writes sentence
   - facts
   - law
   - application of law to facts
   - pronouncement of decision ("in the affirmative/negative")
   - restrictions on petitioner and/or respondent (*vetitum* or *monitum*)

3. Publication of the sentence to parties and their procurators — fifteen days to appeal decision

COURT OF SECOND INSTANCE

e. Appellate Procedural Phase:

1. When sentence is "in the affirmative" — automatic appeal*: sentence, appeal, acts of case forwarded

2. When sentence is "in the negative" — either party can appeal. If so, follow above (#1)

3. Court of Appeals to — determine if procedures were followed
    ratify/confirm affirmative decision (by decree)
    gather new evidence
    (or) reopen case to reach another affirmative decision or a negative decision
    (or) if it cannot ratify affirmative, it determines if case be heard on new grounds
    (or) review initial negative decision and decide to overturn it

4. Court of second instance informs court of first instance of its decision

5. If both sentences are concordant "in the affirmative" — court of first instance issues Decree of Nullity (and restrictions)

6. If the two sentences are discordant — can appeal to the Roman Rota (court of third instance)

7. If Rota rules "in the affirmative" and upholds an affirmative of a lower court — marriage is declared null

8. If Rota rules "in the negative" and a lower court has already ruled the same — validity is upheld

*A party may appeal to the Roman Rota as the court of second instance in the case.

Note that a petitioner may renounce the case at any stage of the process. A petitioner should also be very careful of how a petition is abated through negligence for six months.

16. Marriage Dissolution

Marriage Dissolution — Introduction

There is a fundamental difference between a marriage which has been declared null and a marriage which is dissolved. The former states that while a marriage was presumed to be valid, it was adjudicated by Church courts that the presumption was erroneous for it was never a valid marriage; on the other hand, the latter upholds the validity of a marriage which is now being dissolved under specified conditions. A *sacramental* or *ratified* marriage is a valid union which takes place between a Catholic and another baptized Christian, Catholic or not. It is also considered a valid marriage when two baptized persons, both of whom belong to a non-Catholic Christian faith, marry. A sacramental marriage becomes *absolutely indissoluble* when the union is consummated by the spouses through sexual intercourse performed in a human manner.[1] Canon 1141 dictates that no power on earth is capable of dissolving such a sacramental and consummated union. Even if the marriage is dissolved or annulled by a civil procedure, the bond perdures because only death dissolves such a union. The basis for this teaching is rooted in the Gospels.[2]

---

[1] The conciliar document *Gaudium et spes* 49 states what is meant by sexual intercourse performed *in a human manner*. The exchange of marital consent which is subsequently followed by rape is definitely not considered a consummated marriage by Catholic theologians and canonists.

[2] Matthew 5:52; 19:9; Mark 10:9, 11-12; and Luke 16:18. Suggested readings: D. Crossan, "Divorce and Remarriage in the New Testament," *The Bond of Marriage*, 1-40; T. Doyle, "Select Bibliography on the Sacrament of Marriage," *Marriage Studies* I, 83-85; J. Fitzmeyer, "The Matthean Divorce Texts and Some New Palestinian Evidence," *Theological Studies* 37 (1976) 176-226; W. Harrington, "The New Testament and Divorce," *Irish Theological Quarterly* 39 (1972) 178-187; W. Kasper, *Theology of Marriage*; T. Mackin, "Ephesians 5:21-23 and Radical Indissolubility," *Marriage Studies* III, 1-45; idem., *Marriage in the Catholic Church: What is Marriage?*

The Church acknowledges that there are degrees of stability in a marriage. These are based on the relationship between baptism and the marital consent of the spouses. Thus, the consummated marriage between a baptized and a non-baptized person, and the marriage between two non-baptized persons, though they may be valid, are not indissoluble because they are not sacramental. The valid but non-consummated marriage between two baptized persons can also be dissolved since it is not indissoluble. The rationale for this is that although the Gospels establish the indissolubility of marriage, it is left to the competent Church authority to determine the degree of stability in a valid marriage. This competent Church authority is vested in the Roman Pontiff and those he delegates to act in his name in such petitions. When it is the case of a valid union between two non-baptized persons, the converting party can exercise his or her right to dissolve the union and the competent Church authority verifies the existence of the right.

Marriage Dissolution — 1

Canon 1142 addresses one kind of marriage which can be dissolved by the Roman Pontiff. It deals with the dissolution of a *ratified but non-consummated* marriage. This canon recognizes that there has been a *valid bond* between the spouses and that the Roman Pontiff, by the vicarious power of his office, dissolves the bond. There are a number of instances in which this dissolution may take place. The canon requires that at least one of the spouses is a validly baptized Christian.[3] Thus, the Roman Pontiff can dissolve a valid non-consummated marriage (1) between two baptized Catholics, (2) between a baptized Catholic and a baptized non-Catholic, (3) between a baptized Catholic and a non-baptized person, (4) between two baptized non-Catho-

---

[3] If there has been sexual intercourse before marital consent was exchanged between the couple and there was no sexual intercourse between the couple after the exchange of their marriage vows, or if sexual intercourse has taken place in the form of rape, the marriage is still considered *not* consummated.

lics, (5) between a baptized non-Catholic and a non-baptized person. This canon does not include the dissolution of a valid marriage between two non-baptized persons.

The canon states that both or either party may request the dissolution of the said marriage. It goes on to state that one of the parties may seek such a dissolution even if the other party is unwilling to let this happen. The latter situation can lead to a lot of sensitive interpersonal and pastoral issues which require the patient assistance of a very empathic Church minister or Church-recommended expert. Moreover, the seeking of the dissolution also requires that it is being sought for a *just cause* and not simply because the marriage has never been consummated. Such a just cause should be based on the assumption that a greater pastoral good to at least one of the parties will result from the dissolution of the said marriage.

The process of obtaining a dissolution for ratified but non-consummated marriage is presented in canons 1697 through 1706.[4] These canons are rather straightforward in their approach. Canon 1697 states that only the spouses, either or both, have the right to seek the dissolution of their ratified but non-consummated marriage. Canon 1698 states that the Apostolic See alone has the right to decide the merits of the dispensation[5] and the Roman Pontiff alone has the power to grant it.[6] Canon 1699 states that the diocesan bishop of the domicile or quasi-domicile of the petitioner is the competent person to accept the petition and he or his duly appointed representative should undertake the preparation of the petition. There might be an instance where the diocesan bishop, due to some serious difficulty with the case, may consult the Holy See. Furthermore, if the diocesan bishop rejects the pe-

---

[4] C. 1681 reminds the diocesan bishop that if in the course of a nullity trial a very probable doubt arises in regards to the non-consummation of the marriage in question, the canonical process should be suspended and the proper procedures for a dispensation from a non-consummated marriage should be sought from the Apostolic See. If the latter cannot be procured, then the petition for a declaration of nullity should be resumed. See *Navarre*, 1037-1038, n. 1681; "The Process for the Dispensation from a Ratified and Non-Consummated Marriage," 1046.

[5] While c. 1698 speaks of a *dispensation*, c. 1142 speaks of a *dissolution* of a ratified and non-consummated marriage.

[6] See *Navarre*, 1047, n. 1698.

tition, the petitioner can make recourse to the Holy See.[7] Canon 1700 directs the diocesan bishop to commit the instruction of such cases to a specific tribunal or priest instructor.[8] Canon 1701 states that the defender of the bond must always intervene in such cases and that the petitioner or respondent can seek canonical advice from a competent person.[9] Canon 1702 states that the rules for collecting proofs are the same as those applicable in an ordinary marriage trial.[10] C. 1703 states that there is no publication of the acts, though, for some serious reason, the judge instructor in the case may decide to show some of the testimony to either or both parties.[11] Canon 1704 states that the bishop must submit his opinion[12] on the truth of the petition concerning the fact of non-consummation and the just cause and merit for the dissolution of the marriage at that time.[13] Canon 1705 directs the bishop to send the acts of the case, his opinion, and the observations of the defender of the bond to the Apostolic See. The latter may ask for further instruction and information about the case.[14] Finally, canon 1706 states that once the Apostolic See has sent the document of the dispensation to the bishop,[15] the latter is responsible to notify both parties, the place of contract and the parish of baptism of the dispensation.[16]

Marriage Dissolution — 2

A marriage where at least one of the spouses is not baptized is a valid natural bond. It is not a sacramental union. A *valid and non-sacra-*

---

[7] See *Navarre*, 1047-1048, n. 1699.

[8] See *Navarre*, 1048-1049, n. 1700.

[9] See *Navarre*, 1049, n. 1701.

[10] See chapters entitled, Marriage Cases, 2-3, and Marriage Formal Trial, 4-5. See also *Navarre*, 1049-1050, n. 1702.

[11] See *Navarre*, 1050-1051, n. 1703.

[12] The technical term for the bishop's opinion is called *votum*.

[13] See *Navarre*, 1051-1052, n. 1704.

[14] See *Navarre*, 1052, n. 1705.

[15] The document is called a *rescript*. See *Navarre*, 1053, n. 1706.

[16] These notifications, for obvious reasons, are sent to the pertinent places of the Catholic party or parties only.

mental consummated marriage bond can be dissolved through the invocation of the *Privilege in Favor of the Faith*. This Privilege encompasses two kinds of marital unions, each with its own set of requirements and conditions. The first kind is called the *Pauline Privilege*, while the second kind is referred to as the *Petrine Privilege*. This chapter is dedicated to the Pauline Privilege. The next chapter will deal with the Petrine Privilege.

The Pauline Privilege is based on the Catholic Church's interpretation of a passage in Paul's First Letter to the Corinthians.[17] The Apostle advised converts to depart from their marriage if their non-baptized spouse refuses to continue marital life in peace. The Catholic Church has interpreted this advice to mean that the convert is not obliged to continue in a marriage with a troublesome non-baptized spouse, once the non-baptized party departs, and is free to marry another person. Canon 1143 states that a true marriage bond between two non-baptized persons can be dissolved by the invocation of the (Pauline) Privilege in Favor of the Faith by a spouse who has become baptized and upon entering a new valid marital union.[18] The Pauline Privilege is invoked for the dissolution of a natural bond between two persons who were not baptized at the time of their exchange of marital consent and at least one of them remained non-baptized throughout the union. The invocation of the Pauline Privilege imposes on the petitioner the requirements to be fully instructed so as to receive baptism; that the non-baptized party has no intention to live with the Christian spouse;[19] that the petitioner marries a specified person who is free to marry in the Catholic Church; and the condition that the petitioner and the prospective spouse are not the cause of the breakup of the first union. The petitioner's conversion to Catholicism is not required. What is required is that the petitioner becomes a baptized Christian. It is the second marriage which dissolves the first marital union. If the petitioner or the prospective spouse is the cause of the breakup of the first

---

[17] See 1 Corinthians 7:12-15.

[18] See *Navarre*, 720, n. 1143.

[19] The fact that there had been a civil divorce or a civil annulment of the said union and the non-baptized party has remarried clearly indicates that there is no hope of reconciliation between the petitioner and the respondent.

union, the Pauline Privilege may not be invoked. Furthermore, if the petitioner desires to receive baptism in the Catholic faith rather than any other Christian faith, a full course of instruction in the Catholic faith prior to baptism is always necessary. The petitioner should not be baptized until the bishop or his representative authorizes the petitioner's baptism.

The Pauline Privilege can be applied to a number of situations. It can be applied to bring about a marriage between a Catholic and a prospective spouse who is converting to the Catholic faith and who was formerly non-baptized and married to another non-baptized person. It can be applied in the case when a Catholic seeks to marry a prospective spouse who is converting to Christianity (not Catholicism) and who was formerly non-baptized and married to another non-baptized person. It can also be invoked in the case of a convert to Catholicism who was formerly non-baptized and married to a non-baptized person and now seeks to marry a baptized or non-baptized person, provided that the proper permission for a mixed marriage or dispensation from disparity of cult is procured.[20]

Canon 1144 dictates that before the petitioner enters a second marriage, his or her non-baptized spouse must be asked if he or she wishes to receive baptism and is willing to live peacefully in marriage with the baptized spouse.[21] The answers to these questions should be procured after the petitioner has received baptism, though, for some serious reason, they can be procured before the person's baptism or be omitted because the other party's disposition is clearly antagonistic to Christianity.[22]

The process for applying for a Pauline Privilege is rather straightforward. The diocesan bishop is asked by the petitioner to issue a decree of dissolution after it has been affirmed by the judge instructor that the conditions necessary for the dissolution of the marriage in question are present and the defender of the bond has raised no reasonable objections.

---

[20] See cc. 1124-1129 and c. 1147.

[21] This interview is technically called an *interpellation*.

[22] CC. 1145-1146.

The way to prove the non-baptism of both parties is straightforward. Each party is to procure the testimony of his and her parents or two other competent witnesses who have known each person from birth and affirm that the party has never been baptized in any Christian church whose baptism is recognized as valid by the Catholic Church. Each party is also asked to submit a list, if any, of every Christian church he and she attended, specifying his and her time span of attendance. The tribunal will check with each church to affirm that although the party attended that church, the said party was never baptized in that church. Each party is asked to state whether his or her siblings have been baptized and at what age. The fact that each sibling has not been baptized during childhood and young adulthood reinforces the argument that the party was never baptized. There is also an inquiry into whether any of the children of the couple have been baptized Christian, where and when. It has to be proven that the converting party and the prospective spouse are not the cause of the break-up of the union, and that the non-baptized party refuses to reconcile with the petitioner. Moreover, the petitioner has to be recommended by his or her parish priest, who must also verify that the converting party has received a complete course of instruction in the Catholic faith. The Instructor or Delegate must also be provided with the name, baptism and marital status of the prospective spouse, and the latter's freedom to marry in the Catholic Church. The following documents are to be submitted regarding the union in question: marriage certificate, final decree of divorce or decree of civil annulment, and when applicable, the baptism certificate of each of the children from the union.

Marriage Dissolution — 3

A valid and non-sacramental consummated marriage bond can be dissolved through the invocation of the *Petrine Privilege*, which is the second kind of the Privilege of the Faith.[23] Although this Privilege is

---

[23] See L. Wrenn, "Petrine Privilege Instruction and Norms," *Annulments*, 4th rev. ed., 136-140.

not mentioned in the Code, its invocation must follow a canonical procedure. It is the Holy Father, through his apostolic power, who directly dissolves the first natural bond of marriage at the moment he grants the dispensation.

The Petrine Privilege can be applied to a number of unions. It can be applied to dissolve a valid marriage between two non-baptized persons, one of whom cannot prove his or her non-baptized status. It can be applied to dissolve a valid marriage between a non-baptized person and a baptized non-Catholic Christian. It can be applied to dissolve a valid marriage between a non-baptized person and a baptized Catholic which took place with a dispensation from disparity of cult. Furthermore, unlike the case with the Pauline Privilege which requires the petitioner's conversion to a Christian faith, the Petrine Privilege does not necessarily require the reception of baptism by a non-baptized party.[24]

There are three absolute conditions which must be fulfilled for the exercise of the Petrine Privilege: one of the spouses must have remained non-baptized until the couple separated permanently; there was no sexual intercourse between the parties after the baptism of the non-baptized party;[25] the petitioner who wishes to remain non-baptized or who receives a non-Catholic Christian baptism must allow the prospective Catholic spouse to practice the Catholic faith and to baptize and educate the children of their union in the Catholic faith.

Apart from these absolute conditions, there are further requirements which must be met for the invocation of the Petrine Privilege. Thus, it has to be established that there is no hope for the petitioner and the former spouse to reestablish marital life between them. This is clearly established in the case when either party has already entered a second marriage or when the respondent affirms his or her refusal to cohabit with the petitioner. Secondly, the granting of the dispensation would not provoke any scandal or notoriety. This is especially clear

---

[24] The only time when conversion to the Catholic faith is required is when the non-baptized petitioner is marrying a non-baptized prospective spouse.

[25] Since the Petrine Privilege deals with only one non-baptized party, when the latter becomes baptized, there are now two Christians in that union.

when the parties are not known in the area where they are living. Thirdly, neither the petitioner nor the prospective spouse was the cause of the breakup of the marriage between the petitioner and the respondent. This is clearly proven when the petitioner and the prospective spouse met some time after the former separated permanently from his or her spouse. There may also be the case where the couple's marriage failed for reasons which were beyond their control.[26] Fourthly, the respondent does not offer any reasonable objections to the former spouse's prospective marriage. Finally, the dispensation is not granted if there is no prospective spouse and/or if that person is not free to marry in the Catholic Church. The dispensation is more readily granted if it is clear that there is a serious doubt about the validity of the union in question.[27]

The regulations also spell out more instances when the dispensation is not granted. The dispensation will not be granted to either a Catholic or a non-baptized person who was married in the Catholic Church with a dispensation from disparity of cult and now wishes to marry another party with another dispensation from disparity of cult.[28] The dispensation will not be granted if it is the second petition which is being requested, having already obtained a dissolution from the first valid natural bond.

The procedure to procure the Petrine Privilege is rather straightforward. The judge instructor ascertains that the conditions necessary for the granting of the dispensation are all present and the defender of the bond has raised no reasonable objections.

The discovery of the non-baptism of one of the parties follows the same procedure as that applied in the Pauline Privilege. The discovery of the baptism status of the children from the union also follows the same method of the Pauline Privilege. The parish priest has

---

[26] For example the couple married when they both were very young and very immature and never learned from their mistakes or the couple married because the woman was pregnant and they wanted to give a name to their child.

[27] For example the respondent was insane since the time prior to the union.

[28] In this case, the request (dissolution of marriage) will be granted if the marriage is to take place between a baptized Catholic and one who will convert to Christianity, though not necessarily to the Catholic faith.

to recommend the petitioner and the prospective spouse and ascertain that, if there is going to be a conversion to Catholicism, the person has received a complete course of instructions in the Catholic faith. If the petitioner (or the prospective spouse) is not converting, the priest must ascertain that the non-converting party has been adequately instructed in the Catholic faith and will not impede the children born of the union to be raised as Catholics. The case is then submitted to the diocesan bishop for his recommendation to grant the dispensation. The case is then sent in its entirety to the Congregation for the Doctrine of the Faith which, in turn, evaluates the merits of the petition. The Congregation can either ask for further information or recommend that the dispensation be granted.[29] The decree of dispensation is issued by the Congregation and forwarded to the appropriate local Church authority who, in turn, notifies the petitioner.

---

[29] If the subsequent marriage is between a Catholic and a baptized non-Catholic, the Congregation issues the permission for a mixed marriage. If the subsequent marriage is between a Catholic and a non-baptized person, the Congregation issues the dispensation from disparity of cult.

17. Marriage Documentary Cases and Summary Trials

Lack of Form — 1

The Latin Rite of the Roman Catholic Church perceives the spouses as the ministers of the sacrament of marriage. Since the celebrated Council of Trent,[1] the Church has demanded that Roman Catholics of the Latin Rite must follow the prescribed *canonical form* when the spouses exchange their marital consent in order to have a valid marriage.[2] The Tridentine rule required that when one of the prospective spouses was Catholic, the marriage had to take place before the proper pastor of either Catholic party or another priest delegated by him. The presence of at least two witnesses at the marriage ceremony was also required for validity. This legislation was originally intended to apply to the entire Latin Church, but it became binding only in those dioceses where it was promulgated. Consequently, until the early part of this century, Catholics marrying in those dioceses where the legislation had not been promulgated, were not bound by the canonical form of marriage for the validity of their union. The impracticality of this

---

[1] The celebrated Council of Trent was opened by Pope Paul III in 1545 to reform the Roman Church, following the upheaval of the Protestant Reformation. The Council was interrupted a number of times. It was finally brought to a conclusion by Pope Pius IV after its twenty-fifth session in December 1563. Its work was so thorough that it took another 300 years or so to convene the next Council (Vatican I). See Broderick, "Trent, Council of," 583.

[2] C. 1055, 2: the validity and the sacramentality of a marriage cannot be separated when both parties are baptized since in such instances a valid marriage is simultaneously sacramental.

legislation led to a lot of confusion. Hence, Pope Pius X, in 1909, decreed that the requirement of canonical form for the validity of marriage applied to all Catholics baptized in the Latin Rite. There was also some modification as to who can officiate at such weddings. When Church law for the Latin Rite was finally codified in the 1917 Code of Canon Law, the requirement of canonical form for the validity of the marriage of a Latin Rite Catholic was upheld with the proviso that only those Roman Catholics who were either raised in the Latin Rite Church or joined it as adults were bound to the canonical form.[3] This provision proved to be problematic as well since it was difficult to determine what was meant by "Catholic upbringing." Finally, in 1948, Pope Pius XII, in an attempt to clarify this issue, decreed that all baptized Catholics in the Latin Rite are bound by the canonical form of marriage for the validity of the union.[4] Canon 1108, 1 of the 1983 Code of Canon Law retains the requirement of canonical form for the validity of a marriage, though it provides for a proper dispensation from this requirement under certain conditions. The dispensation is called *Dispensation from the Canonical Form of Marriage*.[5]

In summary, then, current Church law requires for validity that a marriage where at least one of the parties is Catholic must take place in the presence of at least three persons: the official minister of the Church[6] and two witnesses.[7]

---

[3] C. 1099 of the 1917 Code.

[4] This regulation became effective on January 1, 1949.

[5] See chapter entitled, Lack of Form — 2.

[6] The official minister can be a bishop or priest or deacon or, under certain circumstances, a designated lay person. The special circumstances are stated in c. 1112, 1; c. 1116; c. 1127, 2 and 3.

[7] The witnesses may be of the same or either sex, capable of understanding what is taking place, and do not have to be Catholic. Baptism is not a prerequisite for a person to act as a witness in a Catholic marriage ceremony.

Lack of Form — 2

The absence of the canonical form of marriage without a dispensa-tion renders that marriage of a Catholic party *invalid*. Church law has a documentary procedure to affirm the invalidity of such a marriage.[8] There are a number of facts which must be established to petition for a declaration of nullity of marriage based on *Lack of Canonical Form*.[9] It must be first established that at least one of the spouses was *Roman Catholic at the time of the marriage*. If the said marriage took place before January 1, 1949, the Catholic party must prove that he or she was given a Catholic upbringing. Usually this is established by sub-mitting a certificate of First Holy Communion or Confirmation or some record which indicates attendance at a Catholic school or Confrater-nity of Christian Doctrine or shows that the party is the child of two Catholic parents. Such documents point to circumstantial evidence that the Catholic party was bound to the canonical form of marriage when he or she got married. If the marriage took place between January 1, 1949 and before November 27, 1983, all that is required is a recent copy[10] of his or her baptismal certificate. If the marriage took place on or after November 27, 1983, it must be established that the Catho-lic party never left the Catholic Church by a formal act before the marriage took place. Canon 1117 of the 1983 Code states that a per-son who abandoned the Catholic faith by a formal act is not bound to the canonical form of marriage for the validity of that union. The ab-sence of practicing the Catholic faith does not automatically mean that the person left the Catholic Church in a formal fashion. There are, however, a number of ways through which one can abandon the Catho-lic faith through a formal act. The following are some examples: a public renunciation of one's membership in the Catholic Church; a public formal affirmation of atheism; an explicit act of enrollment in another Christian or non-Christian faith; baptism in another Christian

---

[8] C. 1686. See *Navarre*, 1041, n. 1686.

[9] See *Navarre*, "The Documentary Process," 1040-1041.

[10] A recent copy of a Church document means that the document in question was issued within six months of the petition.

faith. The act of making contributions to another denomination does not of itself mean that the Catholic donor has left formally the Catholic Church and joined that particular denomination.

Secondly, it must be established that the said marriage was never *validated* or *sanated* in the Catholic Church. This means that the civil union was never subsequently either celebrated according to the laws of the Catholic Church[11] or that there was an intervention by a competent ecclesiastical authority which rendered valid the originally invalid marital consent.[12] The best way to establish this fact is to have the deposition of the other party which verifies that the marriage took place outside the Catholic Church and was never validated in the Catholic Church. The affidavit of two competent witnesses affirming such a fact strengthens the proof. If the other party cannot be located, the affidavit of two competent witnesses is required.

Thirdly, if the marriage took place on or after January 1, 1971, it must be established that the Catholic party never requested or was never granted a dispensation to have the marriage celebrated in the religion of the non-Catholic spouse.[13] The dispensation is called "Dispensation from the Canonical Form of Marriage."

These proofs must accompany the petitioner's petition for a declaration of nullity of marriage due to lack of canonical form. Copies of the marriage certificate and the final decree of civil divorce or civil annulment must accompany the copy of the Catholic party's baptism. A party does not qualify to this kind of declaration of marriage nullity if both parties were not Catholics at the time they married and one of

---

[11] This celebration is usually called "convalidation," that is, the spouses renewed their marital consent in accordance with the required canonical form for marriage (c. 1156). Thus, this is a new marriage, for it requires a new marital consent (c. 1160). See *Navarre*, "Simple Validation," 727-729; 727, n. 1156.

[12] This is called "radical sanation," that is, the competent ecclesiastical authority decreed as valid the marital consent which was initially invalid for some reason, for instance, the non-Catholic party refused to marry the Catholic party in accordance with Church law (c. 1161). In this case, there is no renewal of marital consent and the marriage is healed in its roots. See *Navarre*, "Retroactive Validation," 729-730; 730, n. 1161.

[13] C. 1127, 2. A dispensation from canonical form is never granted to two Catholic partners. See *CLSA: Commentary*, 804-806.

them became a Catholic subsequent to the exchange of their marriage vows.

After the aforementioned documentation and proofs are assembled, they should be forwarded to the bishop's office, along with the person's petition, so that a determination may be made on the validity or invalidity of the said marriage. Once it is determined that at least one of the parties was bound to the canonical form and that this regulation had been ignored, the proper Church authority issues a document affirming that the said marriage was invalid due to the absence of the canonical form of marriage.

The following are some straightforward examples of lack of canonical form cases:

(a) Jane, a Catholic, marries James, also a Catholic, in a non-Catholic church or chapel or in a civil ceremony. The marriage is null and void for the couple is bound with the canonical form of marriage and a dispensation from the canonical form of marriage is never granted to a couple who are both Catholics.

(b) Jane, a Catholic, marries James, a non-Catholic Christian, in a non-Catholic church or chapel or in a civil ceremony without the required dispensation from the canonical form of marriage. The marriage is null and void because Jane is bound to the canonical form of marriage.

(c) Jane, a Catholic, marries James, a non-baptized person, in a non-Catholic church or chapel or in a civil ceremony without the required dispensation from the canonical form of marriage. The marriage is null and void because Jane is bound to the canonical form of marriage.

(d) Jane, a Catholic, marries James, a non-Catholic Christian, in a non-Catholic church or chapel or in a civil ceremony with the required dispensation from the canonical form of marriage. The marriage is valid.

(e) Jane, a Catholic, marries James, a non-baptized person, in a non-Catholic church or chapel or in a civil ceremony with the required dispensation from the canonical form of marriage. The marriage is valid.

(f) Jane, a non-Catholic Christian, marries James, also a non-Catholic Christian, in a non-Catholic church or chapel or in a civil ceremony. The marriage is valid since neither is bound to observe the Catholic canonical form of marriage.

(g) Jane, a non-Catholic Christian, marries James, a non-baptized person, in a non-Catholic church or chapel or in a civil ceremony. The marriage is valid because neither is bound to observe the Catholic canonical form of marriage.

(h) Jane, a non-baptized person, marries James, also a non-baptized person, in a non-Catholic church or chapel or in a civil ceremony. The marriage is valid because neither is bound to observe the Catholic canonical form of marriage.

(i) Jane, a Catholic, marries James, a member of one of the Oriental Orthodox Churches, according to the rites of his Church. The marriage is valid but illicit and cannot be declared invalid due to lack of canonical form since the Catholic Church upholds the validity of such unions.

(j) Jane, a Catholic, marries James, a member of one of the Oriental Orthodox Churches, in a ceremony not according to the rites of either the Catholic or Orthodox Churches. The marriage is invalid since both parties are bound to observe the canonical form of marriage of either Church.

Defect of Canonical Form — 1

There are instances when a couple have followed the Catholic Church's regulation by marrying according to the Church's requirement of canonical form but the marriage is *invalid* due to a *defect in canonical form*. There are a number of reasons why this may happen.

The official witness to a marriage is normally an ordained cleric, that is a bishop or a priest or a deacon. However, the cleric must have the authority to act in the capacity of the official witness, otherwise the marriage is invalid. The authority is invested in him either through the office he occupies or through delegation.[14] Thus, the diocesan bishop has the authority to be the official witness at a marriage which takes place within his diocese. The local ordinary and those equivalent to him in law[15] may be the official witness to a marriage within the territory of their jurisdiction. The pastor of a parish and those equivalent to him in law[16] may witness a marriage within their parish. All of the aforementioned clerics have this *faculty* because of the Church office they hold. The jurisdiction to be the official witness at a marriage is also based on territory or parish boundaries. When a cleric, be he a bishop or local ordinary or a priest[17] or deacon,[18] has been asked to be the official witness at a marriage outside his jurisdiction, that cleric must seek *delegation* from the one who has the power to delegate the individual.[19]

The diocesan bishop may grant the *faculty* to certain priests or all of the priests and deacons of his diocese to be the official witness at a marriage within his diocese. The local ordinary or those equivalent to him in law may grant such a faculty to the priests and deacons within his jurisdictional territory. The pastor of a parish may grant this faculty to the priests and deacons who are assigned to his parish.[20] When the official witness lacks the faculty to act in that capacity at the marriage ceremony, the marriage is invalid on the canonical grounds of lack of delegation.[21]

---

[14] C. 1108, 1. C. 131, 1 states that this authority, called a *faculty*, is either attached to the office one has or is delegated by the one who has such an office.

[15] C. 134, 1 states who is a local ordinary.

[16] C. 543 states what comprises a *team ministry* in a parish.

[17] A pastor, an associate pastor, or a religious priest.

[18] A diocesan or a religious deacon.

[19] C. 137 provides the rules which must be followed to acquire proper delegation to a cleric to validly witness a marriage.

[20] See c. 1111.

[21] C. 1108, 1.

Defect of Canonical Form — 2

Canon 1108, 2 states that the Church's official witness at a marriage is not only present but plays an active role in the ceremony. The official witness is bound to ask for and receive the marital consent of the parties. He does so *in the name of the Church*.[22] Although the official witness does not administer the sacrament of marriage, for it is the marrying couple who are the ministers of this sacrament, the former must freely receive the marital consent of the parties. In the current rite of marriage, the official witness asks the couple three questions[23] and then invites them to express their marital consent. When the official witness asks for and receives the marital consent of the parties under constraint or fear, the marriage is *invalid* due to defect of form.[24]

The official witness must also seek and receive the consent of *both* the bride and the groom.[25] If the consent is sought and received from only one party, the marriage is invalid due to defect of form in the expression of consent. There might be some instances when more than one priest or deacon is present at the marriage ceremony. If the official witness asks the consent of one party and then another priest or deacon or a non-Catholic minister[26] asks for the consent of the other party, that marriage is also invalid for the same reason because only *one* person can be the official witness at a marriage ceremony.[27] The same regulation applies to those marriages celebrated in a non-Catholic

---

[22] *Rite of Marriage* 23.

[23] The three questions which the couple are asked are about their free choice to marry one another, their lifelong fidelity to one another, and their openness to become parents and fulfill the obligations which accompany parenthood. If the marrying couple is past childbearing years, the third question is omitted. *Rite of Marriage* 24.

[24] It might be unheard of in the United States that a Church official witness might be forced to officiate at a wedding. However, it might happen in some other part of the world though it is usually rare.

[25] C. 1108, 1. See also c. 1104; c. 1057, 1; and *Navarre*, 660-661, n. 1057; 698, n. 1104; 701-702, n. 1108.

[26] It is not unusual that a non-Catholic minister is present at a wedding ceremony when one of the parties is non-Catholic.

[27] C. 1108, 2. See *Navarre*, 701-702, n. 1108.

ceremony with a dispensation from the canonical form of marriage, except for the fact that the official minister at such a marriage is not Catholic.

Finally, there must be at least *two witnesses* at the marriage ceremony. If there is only one witness or no witnesses, the marriage is *invalid* due to defect of form on the canonical grounds of lack of due witnesses.[28] It is not enough to have two witnesses. They must be capable of understanding what is happening with the marriage ceremony. Those who are incapable of this, even temporarily, may not be witnesses. Thus, infants, the seriously mentally retarded, the insane, and the seriously intoxicated are not considered as capable witnesses at a wedding ceremony. The sex, religious affiliation, and status in life of each witness do not matter since their sole function at the ceremony is to attest that the marriage took place.

---

[28] C. 1108, 1. Usually there is more than the couple, the official witness, and the two witnesses at a marriage ceremony. However, it is customary that two persons are designated as the two witnesses to that ceremony. These are the ones whose names appear in the parish marriage registry, the marriage license, and the marriage certificate. But in fact, all those who are present are witnessing the ceremony and, in effect, are also witnesses to it.

18. Publications

Bishops and Publications — 1

The Second Vatican Council called upon every member of the Christian community at large to use his or her talents in the proclamation of the saving power of the Lord.[1] Although the conciliar document addresses only the laity, the 1983 Code expands its application to clerics and lay people alike, enshrining it as a right and duty of all baptized persons.[2] Hence, it is both an obligation and a right for every Christian to spread the Gospel.[3] Coupled with this is the faithful's right to guidance and instruction in the truth as stated in canon 217. The canon is a summary of the conciliar teaching which upholds the right of every Christian to be educated so as to more consciously grow in the light of faith.[4]

Vatican II gave two meanings to the term *evangelization*. The narrower meaning is the traditional understanding of bringing the Gospel to lands which never heard it before.[5] The broader meaning is that even those countries which are traditionally Christian may be in need of re-evangelization since the Church is missionary by nature.[6] Since canon 211 is situated within the context of the broader under-

---

[1] See *LG* 33.

[2] See c. 211, which is rooted in *LG* 17; *AG* 1, 2, 5, 35-37. See also *Navarre*, 190-191, nn. 208, 211.

[3] See *CLSA: Commentary*, 142.

[4] See *GE* 2. See also *Navarre*, 194, n. 217.

[5] See *AG* 6.

[6] See *AG* 2.

standing,[7] canon 217 should be understood also within this context because education is a means of effective re-evangelization. Education is not only a matter of proclaiming and teaching the Good News through the spoken word, but also of doing so through the *printed word*. Thus, the printed word is one of the effective ways through which members of the People of God can fulfill their universal missionary call.

Theologically and canonically speaking the Pope and the bishops in union with him are the *Official Teachers* in the Catholic Church. Each diocesan bishop occupies the Office of Teacher within his diocese. One of his responsibilities is to initiate and sustain various collaborative processes whereby various charisms can be brought to bear on the realization of the Church's mission. Thus, canon 386, 1[8] speaks of the various facets of the diocesan bishop's teaching office, while 386, 2[9] states that he has the obligation to protect the truth while respecting freedom of inquiry by other responsible members of the believing community. The canon summarizes certain aspects of the conciliar document *Christus Dominus* 12-14, which spoke about the teaching office of a bishop. The Council teaches that each bishop has the obligation to communicate Christian doctrine, to protect the purity of the faith, and to allow the Christian scholar freedom to express his or her opinions with proper *obsequium* for the Church's teaching.[10]

Bishops and Publications — 2

The National Conference of Catholic Bishops of the United States issued a document[11] in 1989 in light of a certain tension which is inher-

---

[7] See *CLSA: Commentary*, 144.

[8] C. 386, 1 is rooted in *LG* 25; and *CD* 13, 14. See also *Navarre*, 305-306, n. 386.

[9] C. 386, 2 is rooted in *LG* 23; *GE* 10; and *GS* 62.

[10] The literal translation of *obsequium* is *assent*. Its meaning is somewhat vague. Consequently, it is the subject of much debate especially among canonists and theologians.

[11] See NCCB, *Doctrinal Responsibilities: An Approach for Promoting Cooperation and Resolving Disputed Issues between Bishops and Theologians*, in *Origins* 19 (1989) 97-107.

ent in the exercise of the Church's official teaching office and the process of theological inquiry and expression made by responsible theologians. On the one hand, bishops have a right to require in the name of the Church that theologians faithfully discharge their own responsibility for the integrity of the Gospel. On the other hand, both bodies should also foster a climate of dialogue and cooperation between the magisterium and theologians so that disputes may be either forestalled or resolved for the good of the faithful.[12] The document called for a constant fraternal dialogue between bishops and theologians since authoritative teaching and theological inquiry are distinct but inseparable and complementary duties. This fraternal ongoing dialogue enhances the respective and diverse service of both parties to the Church and brings about further collaboration between them. At the same time such dialogue deepens their mutual respect and trust in their service to the Gospel.[13]

The Vatican Congregation for the Doctrine of the Faith issued a document[14] about this subject in 1990. One of the issues presented in the document was that of theological dissent. After analyzing the different levels of dissent, the document called for an intimate cooperation between the magisterium and theologians. However, it insisted that dissent should not be carried out in a public fashion and that both bishops and theologians must uphold "unity of truth" and safeguard "unity of charity."[15]

Subsequently, the National Conference of Catholic Bishops of the United States issued another document.[16] The document is imbued with references to the document of the aforementioned Vatican Congregation. The call for fraternal dialogue between bishops and theologians was sounded again, since both teach in different ways. Theo-

---

[12] Ibid., 97.

[13] Ibid., 98.

[14] Congregation for the Doctrine of the Faith, *Ecclesial Vocation of the Theologian*, in *Origins* 20 (1990) 117-123.

[15] See ibid., 118-119.

[16] See USCC, *The Teaching Ministry of the Diocesan Bishop: A Pastoral Reflection*, in *Origins* 21 (1991) 472-492.

logical research and reflection should be done within an atmosphere of fidelity to the magisterium and cooperation between bishops and theologians.[17]

Bishops and Publications — 3

The Congregation for the Doctrine of the Faith issued a document in 1992 entitled, *Instruction on Some Aspects of the Use of the Instruments of Social Communication in Promoting the Doctrine of the Faith.*[18] The document discussed the responsibility of bishops as authentic teachers of the faith and their vigilance to uphold the purity of the faith, especially in publications dealing with faith and morals. The document centered on four different, though interrelated, topics.

The first topic was the bishops' responsibility to foster doctrinal integrity. The Roman Congregation expected bishops to know the norms of the 1983 Code, especially those concerning written works. The document emphasizes that it is the bishops' solemn responsibility to protect the truth.[19]

The second topic was the *approval*[20] or *permission*[21] for various kinds of written works. Bishops were exhorted to be solicitous in their dialogue with writers, promoting the inculturation of the faith in fidelity to the *communio.*[22] The bishops were advised that when controversies arose, they were to resolve them in the spirit of charity and fraternal dialogue.[23] Moreover, in the procedure of granting approval or permission to publish, the bishops were to be mindful of the fact that their relationship with authors should be rooted in respectful dialogue and

---

[17] See ibid., 109.

[18] See Congregation for the Doctrine of the Faith, *Instruction on Some Aspects of the Use of the Instruments of Social Communication in Promoting the Doctrine of the Faith*, in *Acta Apostolicae Sedis* 84 (1991) 381-410.

[19] See ibid., article 3.

[20] The technical term for *approval* is *approbatio*.

[21] The technical term for *permission* is *licentia*.

[22] The notion of *communio* is discussed in the chapter entitled, Code and Laity — 3.

[23] See Congregation for the Doctrine of the Faith, *Instruction on Some Aspects of the Use of the Instruments*, article 3.

communio to ensure that whatever is being published is orthodox.[24] The instruction reiterated what had been stated in the two documents issued by the National Conference of Catholic Bishops of the United States without, however, making any reference to them.

The third topic was the apostolate of the Christian faithful, especially Catholics, in the world of publishing enterprises. Catholic publishers were directed to assume responsibility in this area in that they were to refrain from publishing materials which might prove harmful to their fellow Church members in matters of faith and morals. Rather, they were to publish materials which would safeguard the welfare and deepen the understanding of their readers.[25] Catholic publishing institutes were further encouraged to publish such works after procuring the prescribed ecclesiastical permission.[26]

The fourth topic was the responsibility of religious superiors to supervise the writings of the members of their communities,[27] even though the former are not authentic teachers of faith and morals.[28]

Finally, a basic thrust of the document was to remind all the faithful of their responsibility to uphold the *communio* within the Church.[29] It was within this context that the theologian's and every Catholic author's fidelity to the Church's official teaching on faith and morals were presented as having ecclesial ramifications.

Church and Censorship — Introduction

Canons 822 to 832 of the 1983 Code are contained in *Title IV: Instruments of Social Communication and Specifically Books*. These canons are imbued with history and need to be interpreted within their historical context.

---

[24] See ibid., articles 3 and 12, 3.

[25] See ibid., article 14.

[26] See ibid.

[27] See ibid., article 15, 1.

[28] See ibid., article 16, 1.

[29] See ibid., article 1, 2.

The Church has always promoted learning through publications. At the same time, however, the Church has always insisted on its obligation to safeguard faith and morals. For this reason, soon after the Council of Trent, there was established in 1577 the *Index of Forbidden Books*. This was an official list of books and writings judged by the competent Church authority to be contrary to either faith or morals or reprehensible to the Church. The task of monitoring writings in view of their doctrinal integrity was entrusted to the Congregation of the Holy Office.[30] The *Index* remained in effect until June 14, 1966.[31] By then, the Congregation's name was changed to that of the Congregation for the Doctrine of the Faith. Thus, today the *Index* is no longer a prohibitive listing.

Pope Paul VI, on January 15, 1971, reminded all bishops to be vigilant about publications dealing with faith and morals. Four years later, the Congregation for the Doctrine of the Faith, having procured papal approval, issued an instruction which reorganized the censorship of books entitled, *De Ecclesiae pastorum*.[32] The instruction stated that the norms in the 1917 Code regarding publications were no longer binding,[33] and that bishops were responsible to be vigilant about publications concerning faith and morals.[34] The document then went on to supply a list of the kinds of publications which would need the *imprimatur*[35] from the competent Church authority. The instruction also defined the role of the *censor*, who was restricted to evaluating such writings in the light of the magisterium's teaching, irrespective of the common teaching of prominent theologians.[36] Canons 822 to 832 in the 1983 Code basically repeat the same legislation.[37]

---

[30] The Congregation of the Holy Office was also known as the Inquisition. See Broderick, "Holy Office, Congregation of," 268.

[31] See Broderick, "Index of Forbidden Books," 290.

[32] See Congregation for the Doctrine of the Faith, instruction, *De Ecclesiae pastorum* in *Canon Law Digest* 8:991-996.

[33] See ibid., article 1, 1.

[34] See ibid., article 1, 2.

[35] *Imprimatur* is the Latin term which means *let it be printed*.

[36] See ibid., article 4, 2-3.

[37] See *Navarre*, "The Means of Social Communication and Books in Particular," 532-533.

Church and Censorship — 1

There must be a balance in the relationship between the Christian's fundamental right of inquiry and expression and the Church's right to censorship. Such a balance, however, is very difficult to articulate.

The conciliar pastoral constitution *Gaudium et spes* 62 stated that Christians, particularly theologians, must keep in close contact with the unfolding of contemporary human culture, especially with areas involving the secular sciences. It makes a distinction between the deposit of faith or revealed truths and the way they are formulated, without violating their meaning and significance. Pastoral care should give special attention to psychology and sociology, so that their discoveries and understanding would be interpreted in accordance with Christian morality and doctrine. Such a responsibility calls for lawful freedom of research and expression by the competent Catholic scholar.[38]

Canon 218 draws from this conciliar document and states that those involved in sacred disciplines have freedom of research and expression undertaken within the context of the scholar's respectful submission to the judgment of the Church.[39] On the other hand, canon 223, 1 reminds such scholars that they need to be sensitive to the common good of the Church in the exercise of the aforementioned right.[40] Such theological inquiry is carried out under the leadership of the authentic teachers in the Church. Thus, canon 823, 1 regulates that the bishops, who are the pastors of the Church, have three distinct and separate duties. Bishops have the right and duty of pastoral watchfulness lest believers be misled in matters of faith and morals. Bishops have the right and duty to prior censorship of writings for publications by Catholics in matters of faith and morals. Finally, bishops have the right and duty to reject writings by Catholics and non-Catholics which are harmful to the true faith and good morals.[41] Underlying these rights

---

[38] See *GS* 62.

[39] C. 218 is rooted in *GE* 10 and *GS* 62. See *CLSA: Commentary*, 51; *Navarre*, 194-195, n. 218.

[40] See *CLSA: Commentary*, 158.

[41] C. 832, 1 is rooted in the introduction of *De Ecclesiae pastorum*. See *CLSA: Commentary*, 579-580; *Navarre*, 533-534, n. 823.

and duties is the concept of the integrity of faith and morals to be served by those in episcopal leadership roles.

Church and Censorship — 2

The directives in the 1975 instruction *De Ecclesiae pastorum* 6 of the Congregation for the Doctrine of the Faith brought about one major change in Church policy.[42] The change had to do with the relationship between *permission* to publish and *approval* for publication.

The 1917 Code required that every proposed publication which touched faith and morals must undergo prior censorship and procure permission for publication. This simply stated that the contents of a given work were judged not to be harmful in matters of faith and morals and the publication fell within the range of mainstream Catholic teaching. On the other hand, approval for publication meant that the contents of a given work expressed the official position of the Church regarding the subject matter presented in the publication.

The 1983 Code also contains the terms *permission* and *approval*. The new Code uses the terms equivocally. While *permission* is required by certain kinds of persons who are to publish, such as clerics[43] and religious,[44] *approval* is required for specific categories of publications, such as editions of the Scriptures[45] and liturgical books.[46] The significance of the new legislation, however, goes beyond terminology. Thus, there is a reduction in the type of material which requires prior censorship. Moreover, the phrase *ecclesiastical magisterium* in canon 830, 2 of the 1983 Code is narrower in meaning than the same phrase found in the 1917 Code in that now it involves only the views of the Church's authentic teachers in the strictest sense and leaves out the common teaching of leading theologians.[47] The new legislation implies a higher

---

[42] See chapter entitled Church and Censorship — Introduction, nn. 32-35.

[43] See c. 831, which is rooted in *De Ecclesiae pastorum* 5, 2.

[44] See c. 832, which is rooted in *De Ecclesiae pastorum* 5.

[45] See c. 825, which is rooted in *De Ecclesiae pastorum* 2.

[46] See c. 826. See also *Navarre*, 536, n. 826.

[47] See *Navarre*, 538, n. 830.

level of endorsement by the competent Church authority who grants the *imprimatur,* for the approval goes beyond and is more positive in its approach than the previously intended meaning of *nothing harmful*. Thus, what the *imprimatur* states is that what is being published accurately reflects the official magisterial position on the subject.[48]

Church and Censorship — 3

The 1983 Code lists five categories of publications which require prior submission for the *imprimatur*. They are books of the Sacred Scriptures,[49] liturgical books and books of private prayers,[50] catechisms and catechetical writings,[51] books on Sacred Scriptures, theology, canon law, Church history, and religious or moral discipline used as textbooks in elementary, middle or higher schools,[52] and, finally, books treating religion or morals which are displayed, sold or distributed in churches or oratories.[53] This is a much narrower list than what was required in the 1917 Code.

Canon 1385 of the 1917 Code stated that the following works required the *imprimatur*: books on Scriptures, including annotations and commentaries; books which dealt with Scriptures, theology, Church history, canon law, natural theology, ethics, and religious or moral disciplines of this kind; pamphlets and prayer books, books on devotion, books for C.C.D., books on morals, ascetics, mysticism, and other works aimed at fostering piety; holy cards and the prayers attached to them; and any writings which could involve religion or morality. Canon 1386 required prior censorship for any kind of writing done by clerics and religious, as well as for all Catholics who wrote in periodicals opposed to Catholic religion or morals. Canons 1387 to

---

[48] See J. Coriden, "The End of the *Imprimatur*," in *J* 44 (1984) 351-352.

[49] See c. 825.

[50] See c. 826.

[51] See c. 827, 1.

[52] See c. 827, 2.

[53] See c. 827, 4.

1391 regulated the granting of special permission for works which dealt with beatification and canonization causes, books with collections of indulgences as well as collections of decrees issued by the Roman Congregations, liturgical books, and translations of Scriptures.

Church and Censorship — 4

The person who grants the *imprimatur* is the competent Church authority. The 1983 Code specifies who has the authority to do so. Thus, the Apostolic See or the proper conference of bishops give the *approval* for all books of the Scriptures and their annotations.[54] The conference of bishops grants the *permission* for interfaith translations and their accompanying annotations.[55] The Apostolic See grants *approval* for liturgical books and their translation,[56] as well as for catechisms and catechetical writings to be used in a territory covered by a conference of bishops.[57] The local ordinary[58] grants *approval* for reprints of whole or parts of liturgical books[59] and any prayer books for the faithful,[60] for catechisms and catechetical instructions within his jurisdiction,[61] for textbooks for use in schools below university level, when dealing with the Scriptures, theology, canon law, Church history, or with religious or moral principles.[62] The local ordinary is determined either by the author's domicile,[63] or quasi-domicile,[64] or by the place of publication.[65] The competent Church authority is to approve those books

---

[54] C. 825, 1.

[55] C. 825, 2.

[56] CC. 826, 1 and 838, 2. See *Navarre*, 536, n. 826, and 549-551, n. 838.

[57] C. 775, 2.

[58] C. 134, 1 lists who is a local ordinary.

[59] C. 826, 2.

[60] C. 826, 3.

[61] C. 827, 1.

[62] C. 827, 2.

[63] C. 102, 1.

[64] C. 102, 2.

[65] C. 824, 1 which is based on *De Ecclesiae pastorum* 1.

treating religion or morals which are displayed, sold or distributed in churches or oratories.[66]

There are two kinds of *permission*. One deals with publications and the other deals with authors. The local ordinary is to grant his *permission* for prayer books, other than liturgical ones, for public and private use,[67] and to clergy and religious writers for those kind of publications which usually openly attack Catholic teachings and morals.[68] The competent Church authority is to grant his *permission* prior to the publication of books which are to be exhibited, sold or distributed in churches or oratories,[69] and the collections of decrees or acts issued by that Church authority.[70] Finally, when religious publish writings which deal with issues of religion or morals, they are to seek not only the *approval* or *permission* which is required from the competent Church authority, but also the *permission* of their major superior.[71]

Church and Censorship — 5

A new change introduced by the 1983 Code is the possibility for the conference of bishops to compile a list of censors who are known for their knowledge, sound doctrine and prudence, and put the list at the disposition of the local ordinary. Then the local ordinary would select his censors for specific works.[72] Usually, however, diocesan bishops have a list of their own censors in their diocese and the bishop himself or a local ordinary within that diocese call upon only those persons found on such a list.

A further change in the 1983 Code is that the censor need not necessarily be a cleric as long as he or she meets the above stated quali-

---

[66] C. 827, 4.
[67] C. 826, 3.
[68] C. 831, 1.
[69] C. 827, 4.
[70] C. 828.
[71] C. 832.
[72] C. 830, 1.

fications. Canon 830, 2 states that the criteria which a censor uses in evaluating a manuscript is strict objectivity and consideration only of the Catholic Church's teachings on faith and morals. The censor's sole consideration is restricted to evaluating writings in the light of the magisterium's teaching, irrespective of the common teaching of prominent theologians.[73] The minimum which is required of the censor is the assurance that the writings do not contain anything against the magisterium's teaching on matters of faith or morals. The maximum is that the writings state exactly the magisterial stance on faith or morals. Once the censor has cleared the manuscript by his or her granting of the *nihil obstat*,[74] the way is paved for the local ordinary to give his *imprimatur*.[75]

The procedure to procure the *imprimatur* is straightforward. The manuscript is submitted by either the author or the publisher to the local ordinary, who determines whether the manuscript requires it and if it is within his competence to grant the request. If he is competent, he sends the manuscript to one of his approved censors. The censor, in turn, reviews the manuscript and submits his or her opinion in writing. Subsequently, the local ordinary determines whether he should issue the *imprimatur*. If the decision is in the negative, he contacts the author and explains the reasons. The author has recourse to a higher authority namely, the Congregation for the Doctrine of the Faith, if he or she does not agree with the local ordinary's negative decision.[76] When the decision is in favor of granting the *imprimatur*, it is forwarded in writing to the author or the publisher.

---

[73] See chapter entitled, Church and Censorship — 2.

[74] *Nihil obstat* is the Latin phrase which indicates that *nothing stands in the way*.

[75] The *nihil obstat* and the *imprimatur* are both granted through a decree, in accordance with c. 59, 1.

[76] The regulations for recourse are stated in cc. 1732-1739.

Bibliography

Abbott, W., gen. ed. *The Documents of Vatican II*. London: Geoffrey Chapman, 1966.

Alesandro, J.A. "General Introduction," *CLSA: Commentary*, 1-22. "Title III: The Internal Ordering of Particular Churches," idem., 378-412.

_____., ed. *Marriage Studies*. Washington, D.C.: CLSA, vol. IV, 1990.

Amos, J. "A Legal History of Associations of the Christian Faithful," *Studia Canonica* 21 (1987) 271-297.

Austin, G. *The Rite of Confirmation: Anointing with the Spirit*. New York: Pueblo, 1985.

Azevedo, M. *Vocation for Mission: The Challenge of Religious Life Today*. New York: Paulist Press, 1988.

Baillargeon, P. *The Canonical Rights and Duties of Parents in the Education of their Children*. Ottawa: St. Paul University, 1986.

Balhoff, M. "Age for Confirmation: Canonical Evidence," *The Jurist* 45 (1985) 549-487.

Barrett, R. "Confirmation: A Discipline Revisited," *The Jurist* 52 (1992) 697-714.

Bernardin, Cardinal Joseph. "In Service of One Another," *Origins* 18/11 (1988) 132-138.

Beyer, J. "Religious in the New Code and Their Place in the Local Church," *Studia Canonica* 17 (1983) 171-183.

_____. "Religious Life or Secular Institutes," *Way* 7 (June 1969) 112-132.

Borders, W. "You Are a Royal Priesthood," *Origins* 18/11 (1988) 165, 167-180.

Breitenbeck, M. "The Use of Psychological Experts in Church Law," *The Jurist* 50 (1990) 257-288.

Broderick, R.C., ed. *The Catholic Encyclopedia.* Nashville: Thomas Nelson Inc. Publishers, 1976.
"African Councils," idem., 27.
"Apostolic Signatura," idem., 47-48.
"Archpriest," idem., 51-52.
"Beguines and Beghards," idem., 70.
"Carthage, Councils of," idem., 95.
"Deacon," idem., 153.
"Diocesan Pastoral Council," idem., 163-165.
"Ecumenical Councils," idem., 181.
"Holy Office, Congregation of," idem., 268.
"Index of Forbidden Books," idem., 290.
"Institutes, Secular," idem., 295.
"Ministries," idem., 388-391.
"National Catholic Welfare Conference," idem., 416.
"National Conference of Catholic Bishops," idem., 416-417.
"Nun," idem., 426.
"Parish Council," idem., 451-452.
"Penitentiary, Sacred Apostolic," idem., 468.
"Permanent Deacon," idem., 153-154.
"Priests' Councils," idem., 492-493.
"Religious Life," idem., 520.
"Rite," idem., 527.
"Rota, Sacred Roman," idem., 530.
"Sisters," idem., 555.
"Synods of Baltimore," idem., 63-64.
"Trent, Council of," idem., 583.
"United States Catholic Conference," idem., 590-591.

Brown, R. *Marriage Annulment in the Catholic Church.* 3rd edition. Bury St. Edmunds, 1990.

Buetow, H. *The Catholic School: Its Roots, Identity, and Future.* New York: Crossroad, 1988.

Burke, J. "The Defender of the Bond in the New Code," *The Jurist* 45 (1985) 210-229.

Caparros, E., et al eds. *Code of Canon Law Annotated.* Montreal: Wilson & Lafleur Limited, 1993.

Carlston, R. "The Parish According to the Revised Law," *Studia Canonica* 19 (1985) 5-16.

Caron, A. "The Concept of Moral Certitude in Canonical Decisions," *The Jurist* 19 (1959) 12-28.

Carroll, F. *The Development of Episcopal Conferences*. Sydney: Catholic Press Newspaper (1965) 4-64.

Castillo Lara, Cardinal Rosalio. "Some General Reflections on the Rights and Duties of the Christian Faithful," *Studia Canonica* 20 (1986) 7-32.

Catechism of the Catholic Church. Ireland: Veritas, 1994.

Collins, M. "Order for the Christian Initiation for Children: The Ritual Text," *Catechumenate* 10 (1988) 322-340.

Collins, P. "The Diocesan Synod - An Assembly of the People of God," *The Jurist* 33 (1973) 399-411.

Congregation for Catholic Education. Declaration, "The Religious Dimension of Education in a Catholic School," of April 7, 1988. *Origins* 18/14 (1988) 213, 215-228.

Congregation for the Doctrine of the Faith. Instruction, *De Ecclesiae pastorum* in *Canon Law Digest* 8:991-996.

_____. Instruction, *Ecclesial Vocation of the Theologian*, in *Origins* 20 (1990) 117-123.

_____. *Instruction on Some Aspects of the Use of the Instruments of Social Communication in Promoting the Doctrine of the Faith*, in *Acta Apostolicae Sedis* 84 (1991) 381-410.

Congregation for the Sacraments and Divine Worship. Instruction, *On Certain Norms Concerning Worship of the Eucharistic Mystery*, April 3, 1980.

Congregation of Rites. Instruction, *Eucharisticum mysterium*, May 25, 1967.

Coriden, J.A. "The Teaching Office of the Church," *CLSA: Commentary*, 545-586.

_____. "The End of the *Imprimatur*," *The Jurist* 44 (1984) 351-352.

_____., et al., eds. *The Code of Canon Law: A Text and Commentary*. New York/Mahwah: Paulist Press, 1983.

Crossan, D. "Divorce and Remarriage in the New Testament," in *The

Bond of Marriage, ed. W. Bassett, Notre Dame, IN: University of Notre Dame Press (1968) 1-40.

Cuneo, J. "Toward Understanding Conformity of Two Sentences of Nullity," *The Jurist* 46 (1986) 568-601.

Dallen, J. "Church Authority and the Sacrament of Reconciliation," *Worship* 58 (1984) 194-214.

_____. *"Reconciliatio et Paenitentia*: the Postsynodal Apostolic Exhortation," *Worship* 59 (1985) 98-116.

_____. *The Reconciling Community: The Rite of Penance*. New York: Paulist Press, 1986.

Dalton, W. "Parish Councils or Parish Pastoral Councils," *Studia Canonica* 22 (1988) 169-185.

Daly, D. "Canonical Requirements of Parents in Cases of Infant Baptism According to the 1983 Code," *Studia Canonica* 20 (1986) 409-438.

Daly, R., ed., *Religious Life in the U.S. Church*. New York: Paulist Press, 1984.

Daneels, F. "The Forum of Most of the Proofs," *The Jurist* 50 (1990) 289-309.

_____. "The Right to Defense," *Studia Canonica* 27 (1993) 77-98.

Dillon, E. "Confidentiality of Testimony — An Implementation of Canon 1598," *The Jurist* 45 (1985) 289-296.

Donnelly, F. "The New Diocesan Synod," *The Jurist* 34 (1974) 68-93.

Doogan, H., ed. *Catholic Tribunals: Marriage Annulment and Dissolution*. Newton, 1990.

Dortel-Claudot, M. "The Task of Revising the Constitutions of the Institutes of Consecrated Life as Called for by Vatican II," *Vatican II: Assessment and Perspectives - Twenty-five Years After (1962-1987)*, R. Latourelle, ed., New York/Mahwah: Paulist Press (1989) 90-130.

Doyle, T.P., ed. *Marriage Studies*. Washington: CLSA, vol. I, 1980; vol. II, 1982; vol. III, 1985.

Farrelly, A. "The Diocesan Finance Council: Functions and Duties According to the Code of Canon Law," *Studia Canonica* 23 (1989) 149-166.

Felici, P. "Juridical Formalities and Evaluations of Evidence in the Canonical Process," *The Jurist* 38 (1978) 153-157.

Felknor, L. *The Crisis in Religious Vocations.* Mahwah, NJ: Paulist Press, 1989.

Fitzmeyer, J. "The Matthean Divorce Texts and Some New Palestinian Evidence," *Theological Studies* 37 (1976) 176-226.

Fransen, G. "New Code - New Perspective," *The Jurist* 45 (1985) 370-371.

Garafalo, R.C. "Reconciliation and Celebration: A Pastoral Case for General Absolution," *Worship* 63 (1989) 447-456.

Gauthier, A. "Juridic Persons in the Code of Canon Law," *Studia Canonica* 25 (1991) 77-92.

General Introduction to the Roman Missal

Ghirlanda, G. "Consecrated Life in the Life of the Church," *Consecrated Life* 10 (1986) 190-204.

_____. "Relations Between Religious Institutes and Diocesan Bishops," *Consecrated Life* 14 (1989) 37-71.

Gramont, I., Wauk, L.A. "Capacity and Incapacity to Contract Marriage," *Studia Canonica* 22 (1988) 147-168.

_____. "Moral Certitude and the Collaboration of the Court Expert in Cases of Consensual Incapacity," *Studia Canonica* 20 (1986) 69-84.

Green, T.J. "Section II: Particular Churches and their Groupings (cc. 368-572)," *CLSA: Commentary*, 311-348.

_____. "The Revision of Sacramental Law: Perspectives on the Sacraments other than Marriage," *Studia Canonica* 11 (1977) 261-269.

Grocholewski, Z. "Theological Aspects of the Judicial Activity of the Church," *The Jurist* 46 (1986) 552-567.

Guiry, R.W. "Canonical and Psychological Reflections on the Vetitum in Today's Tribunal," *The Jurist* 49 (1989) 191-209.

Gula, R. *To Walk Together Again: The Sacrament of Reconciliation.* New York: Paulist Press, 1984.

Gusmer, C. "Liturgical Traditions of Christian Illness: Rites of the Sick," *Worship* 46 (1972) 528-543.

_____. *And You Visited Me: Sacramental Ministry to the Sick and the Dying*. New York: Pueblo, 1984.

Hamer, J. "Is Religious Life Still Possible?" *Origins* 15 (1985) 189-191.

Hannon, J. "Diocesan Consultors," *Studia Canonica* 20 (1986) 147-179.

_____. "The Role of Diagnosis in the Annulment Evaluation Process," *The Jurist* 49 (1989) 182-190.

Harrington, W. "The New Testament and Divorce," *Irish Theological Quarterly* 39 (1972) 178-187.

Hayes, M.A. "As Stars for All Eternity: A Reflection on Canons 793-795," *Studia Canonica* 23 (1989) 409-427.

Hermann, D.H.J. "The Code of Canon Law Provisions on Labor Relations," *The Jurist* 44 (1984) 174-176.

Hill, R. "Autonomy of Life," *Review for Religious* 46 (1987) 137-141.

Holland, S.L. "Religious Life," *Chicago Studies* 23 (1984) 77-96.

_____. "The Code and Essential Elements," *The Jurist* 44 (1984) 304-338.

_____. "The New Code and Religious," *The Jurist* 44 (1984) 67-80.

_____. "Title III: Secular Institutes," *CLSA: Commentary*, 525-533.

Hopka, J. "The Vetitum and Monitum in Matrimonial Nullity Proceedings," *Studia Canonica* (1985) 357-399.

Hosie, J. *With Open Arms*. Liguori, MO: Liguori Publications, 1995.

Hubbard, H. "The Collaboration Needed by Bishops and Religious," *Origins* 19 (1989) 332-336.

Huels, J. *Disputed Questions in the Liturgy Today*. Chicago: Liturgy Training Program, 1988.

_____. *One Table, Many Laws*. Collegeville, MN: The Liturgical Press, 1986.

_____. "Parish Life and the New Code," *Concilium* 185 (1986) 64-72.

_____. "Preparation for the Sacraments: Faith, Rights, Law," *Studia Canonica* 28 (1994) 33-58.

_____. "Stipends in the New Code of Canon Law," *Worship* 57 (1983) 513-525.

_____. *The Faithful of Christ: The New Canon Law for the Laity.* Chicago: Franciscan Herald Press, 1983.

_____. "The Interpretation of Liturgical Law," *Worship* 57 (1981) 218-236.

_____. "Title III: The Most Holy Eucharist," *CLSA: Commentary*, 643-672.

Huizing, P. "The Structure of Episcopal Conferences," *The Jurist* 28 (1968) 164-165.

International Theological Commission, "Penance and Reconciliation," *Origins* (1984) 513-524.

Janicki, J.A. "Commentary on Canons 515-572," *CLSA: Commentary*, 414-440.

Jarrell, J. "The Legal and Historical Context of Religious Life for Women," *The Jurist* 45 (1985) 419-434.

Jennings, L. "A Renewed Understanding of the Diocesan Synod," *Studia Canonica* 20 (1987) 319-354.

Johnson, J. "Publish and Be Damned: The Dilemma of Implementing the Canons on Publishing the Acts and the Sentence," *The Jurist* 49 (1989) 210-240.

Kasper, W. *Theology of Marriage.* New York: Abingdon, 1980.

Kavanaugh, A. *Confirmation: Origins and Reform.* New York: Pueblo, 1988.

Kennedy, R. "Shared Responsibility in Ecclesial Decision-Making," *Studia Canonica* 14 (1980) 5-24.

Komonchak, J. "Church and Ministry," *The Jurist* 43 (1983) 273-288.

Kutner, R. *The Development, Structure and Competence of the Episcopal Conference.* Washington, D.C.: Catholic University of America (1972) 3-37.

Linscott, M. "Basic Governance Structures in Religious Institutes," *Review for Religious* 49 (1990) 928-932.

_____. "The Consecrated Lives of Apostolic Religious Today," *Review for Religious* 47 (1988) 3-23.

_____. "The Service of Religious Authority: Reflections on Government in the Revision of Constitutions," *Review for Religious* 42 (1983) 197-217.

Lozano, J. *Life As Parable: Reinterpreting the Religious Life*. New York: Paulist Press, 1986.

Lucas, J. "The Prohibition Imposed by a Tribunal: Law, Practice, Future Development," *The Jurist* 45 (1985) 588-617.

Lynch, J. "Co-Responsibility in the First Five Centuries: Presbyteral Colleges and the Election of Bishops," *The Jurist* 31 (1971) 14-53.

_____. "The Limits of *Communio* in the Pre-Constantinian Church," *The Jurist* 36 (1976) 159-190.

MacDonald, H. "Hermits: The Juridical Implications of Canon 603," *Studia Canonica* 26 (1992) 163-190.

Mackin, T. "Ephesians 5:21-23 and Radical Indissolubility," *Marriage Studies* III, 1-45.

_____. *Marriage in the Catholic Church: What is Marriage?* New York: Paulist Press, 1982.

Mahony, Cardinal Roger. Pastoral Letter, *Priestly Ministers: Signs of Life in Christ*, 2 February 1986. Boston: St. Paul Editions, 1986.

_____. Pastoral Letter, *The Day on Which We Gather*, 31 March 1988. Los Angeles: Office for Liturgy and Worship, 1988.

Malone, R. "General Absolution and Pastoral Practice," *Chicago Studies* (1985) 47-58.

McBrien, R. *Ministry: A Theological, Pastoral Handbook*. San Francisco: Harper and Row, 1987.

McDermott, R. "Consecrated Life and Its Role in the Church and in the World: The *Lineamenta* for the 1994 Synod of Bishops," *The Jurist* 53 (1993) 239-262.

McDonough, E. "Canonical Considerations of Autonomy and Hierarchical Structure," *Review for Religious* 45 (1986) 669-690.

_____. "Exclaustration: Canonical Categories and Current Practice," *The Jurist* 49 (1989) 568-606.

_____. *Religious in the 1983 Code: New Approaches to the New Law*. Chicago: Franciscan Herald Press, 1985.

McGrath, A. "At the Service of Truth: Psychological Sciences and Their Relation to the Canon Law in Nullity of Marriage," *Studia Canonica* 27 (1993) 379-400.

_____. "Conformity of Sentences in Marriage Nullity Cases," *Studia Canonica* 27 (1993) 5-22.

McGuckin, R. "The Respondent's Rights in a Marriage Nullity Case," *Studia Canonica* 18 (1984) 457-482.

McKeown, E. "The National Bishops' Conference: An Analysis of Its Origin," *The Catholic Historical Review* 66 (1980) 565-583.

McManus, F.R. "Introduction to Book IV," *CLSA: Commentary*, 593-597.

_____. "Title IV: The Sacrament of Penance," idem., 673-701.

_____. "The Reformed Funeral Rite," *American Ecclesiastical Review* 116 (1972) 45-59, 124-139.

_____. "The Sacrament of the Anointing of the Sick," *CLSA: Commentary*, 702-711.

_____. *Thirty Years of Liturgical Renewal: Statements of the Bishops' Committee on the Liturgy*. Washington, D.C.: CLSA, 1987.

Mendonca, A. "The Incapacity to Contract Marriage: Canon 1095," *Studia Canonica* 19 (1985) 259-325.

_____. "The Theological and Juridical Aspects of Marriage," *Studia Canonica* 22 (1988) 265-304.

Morrisey, F. "Ordinary and Extraordinary Administration: Canon 1277," *The Jurist* 48 (1988) 709-726.

_____. "The Rights of Parents in the Education of their Children," *Studia Canonica* 23 (1983) 429-444.

Muller, H., "The Relationship between the Episcopal Conference and the Diocesan Bishop," *The Jurist* 48 (1988) 111-129.

NCCB. *Doctrinal Responsibilities: An Approach for Promoting Cooperation and Resolving Disputed Issues between Bishops and Theologians*, in *Origins* 19 (1989) 97-107.

O'Connor, D. "Two Forms of Consecrated Life: Religious and Secular Institutes," *Review for Religious* 45 (1986) 205-219.

_____. *Witness and Service: Questions About Religious Life Today.* New York: Paulist Press, 1990.

Ombres, R. "Dismissal from a Religious Institute," *Clergy Review* 71 (1986) 97-99.

_____. "Separation from a Religious Institute," *Clergy Review* 70 (1985) 414-416.

O'Rourke, J. "The Competent Forum of Marriage Cases," *The Jurist* 54 (1994) 234-236.

_____. "The Scriptural Background of the Marriage Impediments," *The Jurist* 20 (1960) 29-41.

Orsy, L. "General Absolution: New Law, Old Tradition, Some Questions," *Theological Studies* 45 (1984) 676-689.

_____. *Marriage in Canon Law.* Wilmington: Michael Glazier, 1986.

_____. "The Interpretation of Laws: New Variations of an Old Theme," *Studia Canonica* 15 (183) 107-110.

_____. "The Meaning of *Novus Habitus Mentis*: The Search for New Horizons," *The Jurist* 48 (1988) 427-447.

Osborne, K. "Eucharistic Theology Today," *Worship* 63 (1989) 98-125.

_____. *Ministry: Lay Ministry in the Roman Catholic Church, its History and Theology.* Mahwah, NJ: Paulist Press, 1993.

Ottinger, B.M., and Fischer, A.S., eds., *Secular Institutes in the Code: A New Vocation in the Church.* Westminister, MD: Christian Classics, 1988.

Page, R. "Associations of the Faithful in the Church," *The Jurist* 47 (1987) 165-203.

Penna, J. "The Office of Episcopal Vicar," *Proceedings of the Canon Law Society of America* (1990) 107-119.

Peter, V. "The Judge Must Judge Justly," *The Jurist* 164-178.

Pfnausch, E.G., ed., *Code, Community, Ministry.* 2 rev. ed. Washington, D.C.: Catholic University of America, 1992.

Pivonka, L. "The Revised Code of Canon Law: Ecumenical Implications," *The Jurist* 45 (1985) 533-534.

Pope John Paul II. "Code and Council," *The Jurist* 43 (1983) 267-272.

_____. Exhortation, *Familiaris consortio*, November 22, 1981.

_____. Apostolic Constitution, *Pastor Bonus*, June 18, 1988.

_____. Apostolic Letter, *On Reserving Priestly Ordination to Men Alone*, May 22, 1994.

_____. Apostolic Letter, *On the Mystery and Worship of the Holy Eucharist*, February 24, 1980.

_____. Apostolic Exhortation, *Reconciliation and Penance*, December 2, 1984.

_____. Apostolic Constitution, *Sacrae Disciplinae Leges*, January 25, 1983.

_____. Apostolic Letter, *The Dignity of Women*, August 15, 1988.

Pope Paul VI. Apostolic Constitution, *Apostolica Sollicitudo*, September 15, 1965.

_____. Apostolic Constitution, *Ecclesiae sanctae*, August 6, 1966.

_____. Apostolic Letter, *Evangelii nuntiandi*, December 8, 1975.

_____. Encyclical Letter, *Mysterium fidei*, September 3, 1965.

_____. Apostolic Constitution, *Regimini Ecclesiae Universae*, August 15, 1967.

_____. Apostolic Constitution, *Sacram unctionem infirmorum*, November 30, 1972.

Pope Pius XII. "Moral Certitude," in L. Wrenn, *Procedures*, Washington, D.C.: CLSA (1987) 121-124.

_____. Apostolic Constitution, *Provida Mater Ecclesiae*, February 2, 1947.

_____. "The Defender of the Bond and the Advocate," in L. Wrenn, *Annulments*, 4th ed. rev., Washington, D.C.: CLSA (1983) 133-135.

Popko, K. "Contemplating Religious Life's Future," *Origins* 21 (1991) 219-225.

Proctor, J.G. "Procedural Changes in the 1983 Code: The Experiences of the Ecclesiastical Provinces of California," *The Jurist* 44 (1984) 468-485.

Provost, J. "Local Church and Catholicity in the Constitution *Pastor Bonus*," *The Jurist* 52 (1992) 299-334.

_____. "Part II: The Hierarchical Constitution of the Church," *CLSA: Commentary*, 258-305.

_____. "Remarks Concerning Proofs and Presumptions," *The Jurist* 43 (1983) 237-245.

_____. "The Reception of First Penance," *The Jurist* 47 (1987) 294-340.

_____. "The Requirement of Canonical Law Degrees for Court Officials," *The Jurist* 43 (1984) 422-429.

_____. "Title II: Groupings of Particular Churches," *CLSA: Commentary*, 350-376.

_____. "Title II: The Obligations and Rights of the Lay Christian Faithful," idem., 159-170.

Quinlan, M. "Parental Rights and Admission of Children to the Sacraments of Initiation," *Studia Canonica* 25 (1991) 385-401.

Quinn, F.C. "Confirmation Reconsidered: Rite and Meaning," *Worship* 59 (1985) 354-370.

Rademacher, W. *Lay Ministry: A Theological, Spiritual, and Pastoral Handbook*. New York: Crossroad, 1991.

Rahner, K. "On the Relationship between the Pope and the College of Bishops," in *Theological Investigations* 10. New York: Herder and Herder, 1973, 50-70.

_____. "The Hierarchical Structure of the Church, with Special Reference to the Episcopate," in *Commentary on the Documents of Vatican II*. Herbert Vorgrimler, ed. New York: Herder and Herder, 1967, I:186-216.

Ratzinger, J. "Announcements and Prefatory Note of Explanation," *Commentary on the Documents of Vatican II*. Herbert Vorgrimler, ed. New York: Herder and Herder, 1967, I: 297-305.

Rausch, T.P. "The Synod of Bishops: Improving the Synod Process," *The Jurist* 49 (1989) 245-257.

Reese, T., *A Flock of Shepherds: The National Conference of Catholic Bishops*. Kansas City, MO: Sheed and Ward, 1992.

_____. , ed. *Episcopal Conferences: Historical, Canonical, and Theological Studies.* Washington: Georgetown University Press, 1989.

Reifenberg, P. "The Revised Code on Proofs and Presumptions," *The Jurist* 43 (1983) 237-245.

Renken, J. "Pastoral Councils: Pastoral Planning and Dialogue Among the People of God," *The Jurist* 53 (1993) 132-154.

Rite of Anointing and Pastoral Care of the Sick. New York: Pueblo, 1972.

Robertson, J. "Canons 869 and 868 and Baptizing Infants Against the Will of Parents," *The Jurist* 45 (1985) 631-638.

Roman Missal: General Introduction, April 6, 1969.

Roman Ritual:
> *Holy Communion and Worship of the Eucharist outside Mass*
> *Order of Christian Funerals*
> *Rite of Anointing*
> *Rite of Penance*

Ross, D. "The Diocesan Synod: A Comparative Analysis of the 1917 and 1983 Codes of Canon Law," *Monitor Ecclesiasticus* 114 (1989) 560-572.

Rutherford, R. *The Death of a Christian: The Rite of Funerals.* New York: Pueblo, 1980.

Sammon, S. "The Transformation of Religious Life," *Origins* 21 (1991) 187-191.

Schotte, J. "The Synod of Bishops: A Permanent Yet Adaptable Church Institution," *Studia Canonica* 26 (1992) 289-306.

Seasoltz, R.K. "The Sacred Liturgy: Development and Directives," *The Jurist* 43 (1983) 1-28.

Sparkes R., and Rutherford R. "The Order of Christian Funerals: A Study in Bereavement and Lament," *Worship* 60 (1986) 499-510.

_____. *The Rites of the Catholic Church.* 2 vols. New York: Pueblo, 1976-1979.

Turner, P. *Confirmation: The Baby in Solomon's Court.* Mahwah, NJ: Paulist Press, 1993.

USCC. *Christian Initiation of Adults: A Commentary.* Washington, D.C.: USCC Publications Office, 1985.

_____. *Eucharistic Celebration.* Washington, D.C.: USCC Publications Office, 1978.

_____. *Holy Communion: Commentary on the Instruction "Immensae Caritatis."* Washington, D.C.: USCC Publications Office, 1973.

_____. *The Body of Christ.* Washington, D.C.: USCC Publications Office, 1977.

_____. *The Teaching Ministry of the Diocesan Bishop: A Pastoral Reflection,* in *Origins* 21 (1991) 472-492.

_____. *United in Service: Reflections on the Presbyteral Council.* Washington, D.C.: USCC Publications Office, 1992.

Verbrugghe, A. "The Figure of the Episcopal Vicar for Religious in the New Code of Canon Law," *The New Code of Canon Law.* Ottawa: St. Paul University, 1986, 2: 705-742.

Wallace, F.T. "Lack of Witnesses," *The Jurist* 49 (1989) 280-285.

Woestman, W. "Daily Eucharist in the Postconciliar Church," *Studia Canonica* 23 (1989) 85-100.

_____. "Respecting the Petitioner's Rights to Dissolution Procedures," *The Jurist* 50 (1990) 1: 342-349.

_____. *Sacraments: Initiation, Penance, Anointing of the Sick: Commentary on Canons 840-1007.* Ottawa: St. Paul University, 1992.

Wrenn, L. "In Search of a Balanced Procedural Law for Marriage Nullity Cases," *The Jurist* 46 (1986) 602-623.

_____. "Outline of a Sentence," *Annulments,* 2nd ed. rev. Washington, D.C.: CLSA, 1983, 194-196.

_____. "1973 Norms for Petrine Privilege Cases," *Procedures.* Washington, D.C.: CLSA, 1987, 108-113.

Ziegler, J. "Who Can Anoint the Sick?" *Worship* 61 (1987) 25-44.

_____. *Let Them Anoint the Sick.* Collegeville, MN: Liturgical Press, 1987.